Context of a
Late Neandertal

Context of a Late Neandertal

Implications of Multidisciplinary Research for the Transition to Upper Paleolithic Adaptations at Saint-Césaire, Charente-Maritime, France

Edited by François Lévêque, Anna Mary Backer, and Michel Guilbaud
Articles translated from the French by Anna Mary Backer

Monographs in World Archaeology No. 16

PREHISTORY PRESS 1993
Madison, Wisconsin

© 1993 by the Editors.
All Rights Reserved
Manufactured in the U.S.A.

Prehistory Press
2515 Frazier Avenue
Madison, WI 53713
Order directly from the Publisher

James A. Knight, Publisher and Editor
Francis S. Stanton, Design and Layout

ISBN 1-881094-05-7
ISSN 1055-2316

Library of Congress Cataloging-in-Publication Data
  Context of a late Neandertal: implications of multidisciplinary research for the transition to Upper Paleolithic adaptations at Saint-Césaire, Charente-Maritime, France / edited by François Lévêque, Anna Mary Backer, and Michel Guilbaud.
   p.   cm. -- (Monographs in world archaeology; no. 16)
  "Papers presented at the Fifty-Sixth Annual Meeting of the Society for American Archaeology in New Orleans in April 1991" -- Acknowledgements.
  Includes bibliographical references.
  ISBN 1-881094-05-7 (PB): $25.00
  1. Saint-Césaire Rockshelter (France)--Congresses.
  2. Chatelperrionian culture--France--Poitou-Charentes--Congresses.
  3. Neanderthals--France--Poitou-Charentes--Congresses. 4. Animal remains (Archaeology)--France--Poitou-Charentes--Congresses. 5. Palynology--France--Poitou-Charentes--Congresses. 6. Poitou-Charentes (France)--Antiquities--Congresses. I. Lévêque, François, 1935- . II. Backer, Anna Mary, 1956- . III. Guilbaud, M. (Michel) IV. Title: Context of a late Neanderthal. V. Series.
  GN772.2.C43C66 1993
    936.4--dc20   93-14145
                                                                    CIP

Acknowledgments

This volume consists of papers presented at the Fifty-Sixth Annual Meeting of the Society for American Archaeology in New Orleans in April 1991. The editors and contributors wish to thank the Society for giving us the opportunity to present our results to the American archaeological community. Professors Randall White of New York University and Olga Soffer of Southern Illinois University graciously agreed to be discussants at the symposium, and they supplied useful comments that were taken into account in paper revision. We also wish to thank the French Foreign Office; the Centre National de Recherche Scientifique-CEA; the Centre National de Préhistoire, Périgueux; and the Regional Council for Poitou-Charentes for funding, which enabled our multidisciplinary research team to travel from France to New Orleans and participate in these meetings. The editors wish to thank the contributors for their cooperation in submitting their revised papers promptly. Professor Lawrence G. Straus made some useful suggestions. June-el Piper was very helpful in her assistance with technical editing, typing, and stylistic editing of text translated from the French. The translator takes responsibility for any mistranslations.

List of Contributors

Anna M. Backer
Department of Anthropology
University of New Mexico
Albuquerque, NM 87131

Michel Guilbaud
Department of Anthropology
University of New Mexico
Albuquerque, NM 87131

J-L. Joron
Groupe des Sciences de la Terre
Laboratoire Pierre Süe, CEN, Saclay
91191 Gif-sur-Yvette, France

Françoise Lavaud-Girard
16, route de Ligugé
86280 Saint-Benoît, France

Arlette Leroi-Gourhan
U.A. 275 du CNRS
Paris, France

Chantal Leroyer
Centre National de Préhistoire
38, rue du 2ème R.I.
24000 Périgueux, France

François Lévêque
Direction des Antiquités Historiques
et Préhistoriques
Hôtel de Rochefort
102 Grand Rue
86000 Poitiers, France

Norbert Mercier
Centre des Faibles Radioactivités
Laboratoire mixte CNRS-CEA
Domaine du CNRS
Avenue de la Terrasse
91198 Gif-sur-Yvette Cedex, France

Jean-Claude Miskovsky
Laboratoire d'Hydrologie et Géochimie Isotopique
Département des Sciences de la Terre
Université Paris Sud
91405 Orsay Cedex

Marylène Patou-Mathis
Institut de Paléontologie Humaine
1, rue René Panhard
75013 Paris, France

J-L. Reyss
Centre des Faibles Radioactivités
Laboratoire mixte CNRS-CEA
Avenue de la Terrasse
91198 Gif-sur-Yvette Cedex, France

Lawrence Guy Straus
Department of Anthropology
University of New Mexico
Albuquerque, NM 87131

Hélène Valladas
Centre des Faibles Radioactivités
Laboratoire mixte CNRS-CEA
Domaine du CNRS
Avenue de la Terrasse
91198 Gif-sur-Yvette Cedex, France

Bernard Vandermeersch
Laboratoire d'Anthropologie
Université de Bordeaux I
Avenue des Facultés
33405 Talence, France

Contents

Tables and Figures ix

Preface xi
    Lawrence G. Straus

1. Introduction to Saint-Césaire 1
    François Lévêque

2. The Sediments and Stratigraphy of Saint-Césaire:
    Contributions to the Paleoclimatology of the Site 7
    Jean-Claude Miskovsky and François Lévêque

3. Thermoluminescence Dating of the Prehistoric Site of
    La Roche à Pierrot, Saint-Césaire 15
    N. Mercier, H. Valladas, J-L. Joron, and J-L. Reyss

4. The Castelperronian Industry of Saint-Césaire: The Upper Level 23
    François Lévêque

5. Debitage from the Upper Castelperronian Level at Saint-Césaire:
    Methodological Approach and Implications for the Transition from
    Middle to Upper Paleolithic 37
    Michel Guilbaud

6. Pollen Analysis at Saint-Césaire 59
    Chantal Leroyer and Arlette Leroi-Gourhan

7. Macrofauna from Castelperronian Levels at Saint-Césaire 71
    Françoise Lavaud-Girard

8. A Taphonomic and Paleoethnographic Study of the Fauna
    Associated with the Neandertal of Saint-Césaire 79
    Marylène Patou-Mathis

9. Spatial Distributions at La Roche à Pierrot, Saint-Césaire:
    Changing Uses of a Rockshelter 103
    Anna M. Backer

Appendix 129
    Bernard Vandermeersch

Tables

3.1.	Thermoluminescence results and radioactivity data for the flints from Saint-Césaire	18
7.1.	Chronostratigraphic succession of faunal complexes from other levels at Saint-Césaire	75
7.2.	Chronostratigraphic succession of faunal complexes from La Grande Roche de Quinçay	76
8.1.	Faunal Remains from Level EJOP Superior of Saint-Césaire	82
8.2.	Distribution of Bone Splinters at Saint-Césaire by Square and Size Class	86
8.3.	Meat Weight Estimation for Herbivores from Level EJOP Superior at Saint-Césaire	95
8.4.	Bones with Cutmarks from Butchering, Level EJOP Superior, Saint-Césaire	96
9.1.	Artifact Inventory, EJOP Superior	111

Figures

1.1.	The village of Saint-Césaire	4
1.2.	Locations of archaeological deposits in the Poitou-Charentes region	5
2.1.	Stratigraphy of Saint-Césaire	10
2.2.	Stratigraphic profile	11
2.3.	The two Castelperronian levels	12
3.1.	The TL ages of burned flint from Saint-Césaire	19
4.1.	Sidescrapers	29
4.2.	Points and endscrapers	30
4.3.	Backed points	31
4.4.	Backed blades	32
4.5.	Foliates	33
5.1.	Model of reduction process in EJOP superior	40
5.2.	Model sequence illustrating the concept of reduction field	41
5.3.	Three elementary reduction sequences	43
5.4.	The reduction center of level EJOP superior	44
5.5.	Quantitative estimate of the dominant themes 1 to 7 in level EJOP superior	45
5.6.	Three examples of conceptual associations on cores of level EJOP superior	46-47
5.7.	Quadripolar orientation	50
5.8.	Three different Castelperronian orientations in reference to the quadripole	51
6.1.	Localization of sample columns at the site of Saint-Césaire	62
6.2.	Complete diagram of the first pollen sequence obtained at Saint-Césaire	63
6.3.	Simplified diagram of results obtained from pollen samples	64
6.4.	Simplified diagram of the first pollen sequence at Saint-Césaire	65
6.5.	Simplified diagram of the second pollen sequence at Saint-Césaire	67
6.6.	Simplified diagram of the third pollen sequence of Saint-Césaire	68
8.1.	Age histograms for cervids, bovines, and equids from level superior, Saint-Césaire	83
8.2.	Comparison of age curves for cervids, bovines, and equids from level EJOP superior	84
8.3.	Preservation of different anatomical elements of reindeer, bovines, and equids from level EJOP superior	85
8.4.	Large mammals from level EJOP superior, Saint-Césaire, by MNI	87
8.5.	Ecological diagram (by MNI) of fauna from level EJOP superior, Saint-Césaire	88
8.6.	Preservation of bovine remains	89
8.7.	Preservation of horse remains	90
8.8.	Preservation of reindeer remains	91
8.9.	Period of antler shedding for reindeer present in level EJOP superior, Saint-Césaire	92
8.10.	Preservation of shed reindeer antler	93
8.11.	Distribution of shed reindeer antler	94
8.12.	Distribution of burned bone fragments	97

Figures continued

8.13.	Distribution of identified bone	98
8.14.	Distribution of all bones from level EJOP superior, Saint-Césaire	99
9.1.	Excavated area, EJOP superior	106
9.2.	Distribution of unretouched flakes greater than 2 cm in maximum length	108
9.3.	Distribution of unretouched flakes less than or equal to 2 cm in maximum length	109
9.4.	Distribution of cores	112
9.5a.	Distribution of tools: steep retouch, backed blades and backed points	113
9.5b.	Distribution of tools: sidescrapers and points	114
9.5c.	Distribution of tools: endscrapers and becs	115
9.5d.	Distribution of tools: denticulates, foliates and burins	116
9.6.	Distribution of "naturally" modified pieces	117
9.7.	Whole, large flakes	118
9.8.	Small-flake surplus	119
9.9.	Distribution of whole flakes	120
9.10.	Distribution of faunal remains	122
9.11.	Distribution of bovine remains	123
9.12.	Distribution of reindeer remains	124
9.14.	Distribution of reindeer antler	125
A.1.	Neandertal skull found at Saint-Césaire	130

Preface

Saint-Césaire and the Debate on the Transition from the Middle to Upper Paleolithic

Lawrence Guy Straus

Each generation of paleoanthropologists witnesses relatively few monumental discoveries that fundamentally alter our conceptions about major aspects of the prehistoric record. Often these phenomena combine a spectacular fossil hominid find in association with archaeological remains and/or materials datable by new techniques. In this generation the discovery of "*Zinjanthropus boisei*" by Mary Leakey, the KNM-ER1470 *Homo habilis* by Richard Leakey, "Lucy"/*Australopithecus afarensis* by Donald Johanson—and the Saint-Césaire Neandertal by François Lévêque—are finds of great magnitude.

In the case of Saint-Césaire, the significance of the 1979 discovery is at least twofold. First, few substantially complete Neandertal skeletons have been discovered under conditions of modern, controlled archaeological excavation. Most were found in the early years of prehistoric research and several of the more recent finds were made under less-than-optimal conditions. Saint-Césaire ranks with Kebara as an exemplary case of excellent archaeological context for a Neandertal—but the specimen from Saint-Césaire is not missing its head! The second reason for which Saint-Césaire is extremely significant is that the skeleton was found in intimate association with an artifact assemblage classified as Castelperronian (also called Chatelperronian, or Lower Perigordian). Until 1979, it was believed that this "hybrid" industry had been the work of anatomically modern (albeit robust) *Homo sapiens sapiens*, based on the discovery of a fossil in supposed association with the Castelperronian at Combe-Capelle (Dordogne) in 1909 by the unsavory Swiss archaeologist Otto Hauser, an agent of the Berlin Museum. Ironically, though much of Hauser's extensive work around Les Eyzies was disdained (or savaged) by contemporary and later French prehistorians, the Combe-Capelle find was more or less accepted at face value, even after André Leroi-Gourhan found taurodont, possibly Neandertal, molars in association with the magnificent Castelperronian at La Grotte du Renne (Arcy-sur-Cure, Yonne). There actually was even a "Combe-Capelle race"!

Until 1979, the Castelperronian was believed to be the incipient "Upper Paleolithic" product of early modern humans—perhaps local prehistoric French humans at that! The majority view followed the late François Bordes in seeing the Lower Perigordian as the early phase of an *in situ* cultural developmental trend that ultimately resulted in the regional Upper Perigordian (also called Gravettian)—and even Magdalenian—despite the "intrusion" of the Aurignacian culture from the east.

Classic Neandertals were relegated to a secondary, peripheral status as cultural dimwits and dead-ends. An irony of this situation was that more-or-less modern hominid skeletal remains were already known to be associated with exclusively Mousterian artifacts at Skhul and Qafzeh, but this anomaly was sometimes dealt with by labeling the Israeli finds as "Neanderthaloid" or "Progressive Neandertals"—progressive in their physique, but not in their technology. Then came the Saint-Césaire bombshell. Bernard Vandermeersch had the remarkable luck to be involved in the discovery and paleontological study of both the later Qafzeh finds and the Saint-Césaire find.

Neandertals (or at least one Neandertal—his back to the Atlantic, like the German soldiers in the southwestern coastal fortress towns of 1944-45, surrounded by the invading/liberating forces) apparently made blades, backed knives, burins, and endscrapers, along with the more customary sidescrapers and denticulates on flakes. Why should this have been a surprise?

In my opinion, the traditional paradigm in Paleolithic prehistory—despite the revolutionary work of François Bordes—tended to minimize variability within the Mousterian and, in the name of simplification and normative classification, glossed over the extent to which blades, burins, and endscrapers could be present in Middle Paleolithic contexts in Europe (and elsewhere). Before the discovery of Saint-

Césaire, we were unprepared by "accepted wisdom" to deal with a supposedly "advanced" technology in the hands of a Neandertal. Perhaps, for me at least, the disappointing thing about the debate that has ensued since the Saint-Césaire discovery is that the "goalposts" of modernity have simply been moved. The vaunted "transition" is now seen as lying essentially between the Castelperronian (or its eastern confrère, the Szeletian) and the Aurignacian—the cultural cachet of true modern humans supposedly coming from the mysterious East (and South). Rather than redefining the nature of our attempts at understanding, Saint-Césaire (so far) has simply led us to postulate a new ad hoc non-explanation: "acculturation." I say non-explanation because the term is simply declared without further analysis and argument as to specifically why and how Neandertals might become (or need to become) acculturated (at least in part) to the ways of the Aurignacian (i.e. Cro-Magnon) "invaders." Yet I am convinced that Saint-Césaire, together with James Bischoff's revolutionary 40,000-year-old "Aurignacian" dates at El Castillo, L'Arbreda, and Romaní in Spain, will ultimately force a fundamental revolution in our understanding of the nature of technological shifts of the Mid to Upper Pleistocene—decoupled, at least partially (and this is an irony), from the biological contrast between the Neandertal and Cro-Magnon ideal types.

This book is a milestone in the publication of the Saint-Césaire discovery. No monographic treatment has thus far been published, and although this is clearly an interim report, it contains not only the essential facts and background, but some truly significant (albeit preliminary) analyses of the hominid, its geological and paleoenvironmental context, the associated artifacts and fauna, and spatial organization of the Neandertal's "living floor." With the exception of the TL dating, little or none of this information has been available in English until now. Indeed the published record even in French has been limited to fairly brief notes without substantive or extended detail on the context of the Neandertal. Thus the title of this book is highly à propos. Anglophone readers are privileged to have access to the essential Saint-Césaire data and interpretations in this book.

In some regards, this book is a standard Paleolithic site report that meets the high standards developed over the past few years in French Paleolithic prehistory. It contains excellent, detailed descriptions of stratigraphy, geochronology, paleoenvironments, palynology, and paleontological remains. But it goes beyond this necessary first step. Also included are interesting interpretations of the lithic reduction processes, taphonomy, and site structure. Although all but one of the authors are French, the volume clearly reflects developments in the interpretation of the archaeological record that sprung in great part from the work of Lewis Binford, in large part as a consequence of his debates with the late François Bordes. This is especially true in the contributions of Anna Backer (the sole American) and Marylène Patou. Although some of their work is still in progress, their preliminary results are intriguing and promising.

Finally, I was struck by one of the possible consequences of François Lévêque's and Michel Guilbaud's analysis of the Castelperronian lithic technology. (American readers used to the Bordesian typology will have to grapple with the less familiar Laplacian systematics. This is essentially an attribute-based analytical method, and a philosophy proud of its logical objectivity in the description of lithic artifacts.)

Lévêque and Guilbaud tell us that there are several Castelperronians. The Saint-Césaire one is neither the most "archaic" nor very "evolved." Some Castelperronian assemblages bear formal similarities to the Aurignacian and the Gravettian. This conclusion supports Georges Laplace's idea of an early Upper Paleolithic "synthétotype." If so, where does this leave the Castelperronian as a "real" thing—as the evolved technology of late Neandertals? Is there any strong reason why, in light of Lévêque's and Guilbaud's conclusions, we should accept the Castelperronian as a "culture," to reify it and to argue its place in the replacement of Neandertal by *Homo sapiens sapiens* in western Europe? Who can say that all the artifact assemblages that we lump into the Castelperronian of western France and northern Spain (or, for that matter, the typologically similar Uluzzian of Italy) were made by Neandertals? No one can. The only significant fossil we have is Saint-Césaire. We do not even know "who" made the Early Aurignacian of France, or, for that matter, Cantabrian Spain, where in fact the distinctions among Mousterian, Castelperronian, and Aurignacian are somewhat blurred.

This is an important tome. We owe a debt to our French colleagues for having provided this critical contribution. We owe a debt to François Lévêque (Principal Investigator of the Saint-Césaire project) and Anna Backer for co-organizing a symposium at the Society for American Archaeology meetings in New Orleans and to both of them as well as to Michel Guilbaud for bringing its proceedings to fruition in published form. Anna Backer spent many days of technical translation and editing. The result of the multidisciplinary work of the Saint-Césaire research team is another milestone not only in paleoanthropological publication but also in international and interdisciplinary collaboration.

1

Le Gisement de Saint-Césaire (Charente-Maritime), France

François Lévêque

Le gisement, situé au lieu-dit "La Roche à Pierrot," se trouve à quelques centaines de mètres au sud-est du village de Saint-Césaire, c'est à dire à une dizaine de km au nord-est de Saintes. Il se présente sous forme d'un abri sous roche effondré, orienté au nord-nord ouest, creusé dans le calcaire du Turonien supérieur. Il a été découvert tout à fait fortuitement en 1976 à l'occasion de travaux de terrassement; une fouille de sauvetage en a été immédiatement entreprise et a donné lieu à 12 campagnes successives jusqu'en 1987.

Le passage du Paléolithique moyen au Paléolithique supérieur reste encore mal connu. Les caractéristiques des industries castelperroniennes demeurent assez imprécises et la disparition de l'Homme de Néandertal tout comme son remplacement par un Homme de type moderne posent encore de nombreux problèmes par suite d'un manque de données.

La région Poitou-Charentes se révèle être aujourd'hui d'une importance capitale pour l'étude de cette transition. Les gisements y sont relativement nombreux; certains bien qu'anciennement fouillés ont apporté, ces dernières années, des éléments nouveaux. Mais surtout des gisements découverts récemments ont permis de mettre au jour des séquences stratigraphiques majeures.

L'importance du gisement de Saint-Césaire tient à plusieurs faits. Tout d'abord ce gisement a permis de mettre en évidence au dessus de plusieurs niveaux moustériens une séquence chronostratigraphique intéressant tout le début du Paléolithique supérieur et se développant de l'interstade des Cottés à celui d'Arcy. Si l'on compare cette séquence à celle de Quinçay on constate que ces deux séquences sont tout à fait comparables ce qui renforce l'intérêt des deux gisements. Ensuite la découverte de restes humains dans le niveaú castelperronien supérieur est d'un plus grand intérêt. En effet ce sont, à ce jour, les seuls restes humains importants recueillis de façon stratigraphique précise dans un niveau castelperronien. Et ces restes sont néandertaliens ce qui permet de penser que l'Homme de Néandertal a pu être, au moins en partie, l'artisan de l'indústrie castelperronienne.

La position de ces restes humains paraît indiscutable dans ce niveau séparé d'une part, au dessous, du dernier moustérien par un second niveau castelperronien sédimentologiquement différent et d'autre part, au dessus, du Protoaurignacien par un niveau stérile. Enfin les datations obtenues par thermoluminescence établissent solidement la présence de néandertaliens au tout début du Paléolithique supérieur.

Introduction to Saint-Césaire

François Lévêque

History of Investigations and Geographic Location

The village of Saint-Césaire is situated about 10 km northeast of the town of Saintes, which is just over 100 km north of Bordeaux and 120 km southwest of Poitiers. The site is located a few hundred meters southwest of the village, at a locality named La Roche à Pierrot. It is a collapsed rockshelter at the base of a cliff measuring 5 to 6 m in height and bordering an extensive, limestone plateau dating to the Upper Turonian. The rockshelter faces roughly north-northwest and fronts the small valley of the Coran, locally known as Le Courant. This stream is a tributary of the Charente, which empties directly into the Atlantic Ocean, about 40 km to the west, at the town of Rochefort.

Turonian limestone has long been quarried for building stone, and this activity, which continued until the last century, has resulted in a network of underground galleries in the plateau. Today most of these underground quarries are being used to grow mushrooms; in several places natural cavities can be detected, and at the back of these caves are remnants of *in situ* levels with associated lithic and faunal materials. This important site must have extended all along the rock face bordering the Coran and was probably gradually destroyed over the years by the quarrying activities. The present-day site at La Roche à Pierrot may therefore represent only a small part of a vast deposit that has now disappeared.

The archaeological site was discovered in 1976 when heavy machinery was used to build an access road to one of the mushroom farms. The site was discovered by accident and partially destroyed. The road work was halted, and what remained of the site was saved from certain destruction. A salvage excavation was begun immediately and continued under good conditions for twelve successive field seasons, from 1976 to 1987.

Background

The Middle-Upper Paleolithic transition is still poorly known. This period, spanning only about 5000 years (from 38,000 to 33,000 BP), is nonetheless one of the most fascinating in prehistory. During the Würm II-III interstadial, Mousterian industries disappeared after having been prevalent in Europe for more than 100,000 years, and shortly afterwards, Neandertals also disappeared, replaced by anatomically modern humans associated with Aurignacian industries. How, why, and under what conditions Neandertals disappeared are questions that to this day remain unanswered, yet these problems are especially intriguing because they touch on the origins of modern humans in Europe.

The characteristics of the first Upper Paleolithic culture, the Castelperronian, at times incorrectly referred to as Châtelperronian or Lower Perigordian, are still rather imprecise. For a long time after the 1909 excavations at Combe-Capelle it was thought that the artisans responsible for these industries were modern humans. More recent investigations have called that interpretation into question. Many of the problems posed by these early Upper Paleolithic industries would no doubt be resolved if we had more data. Castelperronian sites are relatively rare, perhaps because this culture appeared towards the end of the Würm II-III interstadial and therefore these assemblages were covered by only a thin layer of sediments and are in general contained in clayey matrices. The climatic conditions that seem to have accompanied or directly followed their deposition have not facilitated their study. The glacial maximum of Würm III brought with it significant mechanical processes (runoff, and sometimes cryoturbation or solifluction), which have rendered some stratigraphies difficult or impossible to study and have altered these industries in some cases.

The poor or insubstantial nature of these Castelperronian levels relative to the rich or well-

Figure 1.1. The village of Saint-Césaire (photo F. Lévêque).

developed Mousterian levels that precede them and the Aurignacian levels that follow gives an impression of transience. Nevertheless, west-central France and in particular the Poitou Charentes region (Figure 1.2) appears to be a key region for the study of these industries. Not only are the sites relatively abundant, but the sequences preserved and brought to light in this region are quite remarkable. Although a number of these sites were excavated a long time ago and have not yielded comparable or sufficient stratigraphic information, excavations by Dr. Henri-Martin and subsequently by his daughter G. Henri-Martin of the downstream deposits at La Quina, by Dr. L. Pradel at Les Cottés, and by G. Laplace at Belleroche, among others, have underlined the importance of this region. This importance has been confirmed in the past few years by renewed investigations of previously excavated sites, which have provided important information, better control, new or revised stratigraphies, and environmental and chronological data. Especially important are the new discoveries at Saint-Césaire and Quinçay, and important chronostratigraphic sequences, which have contributed a whole set of new elements to our knowledge of the transition from Middle to Upper Paleolithic.

Significance

Because of the overall scarcity of recently documented archaeological remains from the Castelperronian, results from the site of Saint-Césaire become all the more remarkable. Excavation of this site has yielded a chronostratigraphic sequence spanning the period from Les Cottés interstadial to the Arcy interstadial. Above a set of Mousterian levels, and separated from the latter by a hiatus, was found a sequence from the very beginning of the Upper Paleolithic, along with several successive Castelperronian and Aurignacian levels. Sedimentological and palynological studies have aided in the precise definition of a complete climatic sequence from the end of Würm II-III and the beginning of Würm III.

Comparisons with results from La Grande Roche at Quinçay show that the climatic sequences from these two sites are quite comparable, accentuating their importance. The latter was the site of purely Castelperronian occupations, whereas at the former, the Castelperronian was replaced by the Aurignacian. The sequences brought to light at these two sites are among the most complete and the most precise known from this period and thus provide essential information concerning the poorly understood transition from Middle to Upper Paleolithic.

The discovery of human remains in the upper Castelperronian level is of great interest because they are the first to be collected in precise stratigraphic context from a Castelperronian level. These remains are indisputably those of a Neandertal, calling into question the generally accepted chronology and sug-

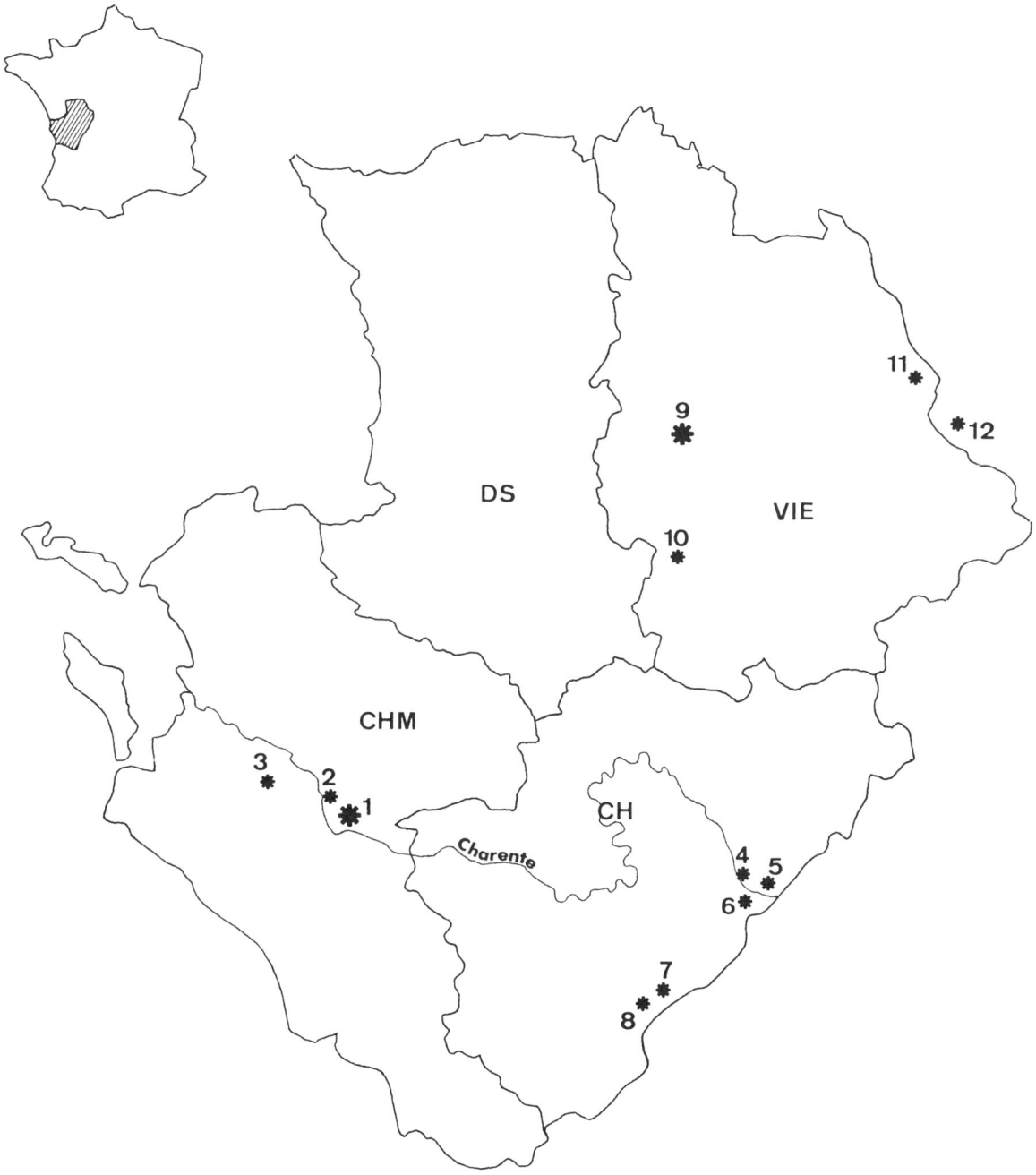

Figure 1.2. Locations of archaeological deposits in the Poitou-Charentes region that have yielded Castelperronian industries. DS = Deux-Sèvres, VIE = Vienne, CH = Charente, CHM = Charente-Maritime. 1: La Roche à Pierrot (Saint-Césaire), two Castelperronian levels; 2: Le Gros Roc (Le Douhet), with one probable Castelperronian level; 3: Le Bouil-Bleu (La Rochecourbon), one possible Castelperronian level; 4: L'Abri du Chasseur (Vilhonneur), one Castelperronian level; 5: Fontéchevade (Montbron), one probable Castelperronian level; 6: La Chaise (Grotte Bourgeois-Delaunay, Vouthon), traces of a Castelperronian level; 7: La Quina (Gardes), one Castelperronian level; 8: Le Trou du Cluzeau (Ronsenac), one possible Castelperronian level; 9: La Grande Roche (Quinçay), eight Castelperronian levels; 10: Belleroche (Vaux), one Castelperronian level; 11: Les Cottés (Saint Pierre de Maille), one Castelperronian level; 12: La Vieille Grange (Mérigny), one Castelperronian level.

gesting that Neandertals did not disappear at the close of the Middle Paleolithic but could have been, at least in part, the authors of the first Upper Paleolithic industry. Thermoluminescence dating of artifacts from Saint-Césaire has solidly established the presence of Neandertals at the beginning of the Upper Paleolithic.

The Neandertal skeleton discovered in one of the Castelperronian levels at La Roche à Pierrot is the best preserved and most complete archaic human found in secure stratigraphic context from this type of level. These human remains were found in a formation separated on top from the Proto-Aurignacian by a sterile layer of fine sediment and on the bottom from the latest Mousterian level by a second Castelperronian level, a fine sediment poor in archaeological remains. The position of the human skeleton is therefore indisputable.

This volume presents data from studies of sedimentology, skeletal biology, stone tool typology, lithic reduction, palynology, paleontology, taphonomy, and site structure at Saint-Césaire, and provides valuable information concerning the environment and adaptation of the last Neandertals and the first anatomically modern humans.

2

Stratigraphie et Etude Sédimentologique de Saint-Césaire: Apports dans L'étude Paléoclimatique

Jean-Claude Miskovsky et François Lévêque

La stratigraphie la plus complète du gisement correspond à la coupe de référence où ont été découverts les restes néandertaliens. Les différents niveaux ont été regroupés en deux séquences, une séquence supérieure ou ensemble jaune comprenant les niveaux de Paléolithique supérieur et une séquence inférieure ou ensemble gris correspondant au Paléolithique moyen.

L'ensemble jaune (EJ) comprend, en partant du haut, les sous-ensembles jaune-jaune (EJJ) et jaune-marron (EJM) caractérisés par un sédiment fin et deux niveaux d'Aurignacien évolué, puis jaune de foyers (EJF) renfermant de nombreux blocs calcaires et de l'Aurignacien ancien. Il se poursuit par le sous-ensemble jaune-orange dont la partie supérieure (EJO sup.) est formée de blocaille de petite dimension et qui comprend une industrie attribuable à un Protoaurignacien. Sa partie inférieure (EJO inf.) formée de sédiment fin est stérile. Au dessous le sous-ensemble jaune-orange pâle, partie supérieure (EJOP sup.) est caractérisé par la présence de nombreux éléments calcaires à angles vifs et une industrie castelperronienne. C'est ce niveau qui a livré les restes humains néandertaliens. Sa partie inférieure (EJOP inf.) comprend un sédiment fin et une industrie pauvre castelperronienne.

L'ensemble gris débute par un très beau sol d'habitat (Moustérien à denticulés, sous-ensemble gris pâle de foyers—EGPF) et se poursuit par les sous-ensembles gris-pâles (EGP) et gris de foyers (EGF) comprenant également du Moustérien à denticulés. La séquence se termine par les sous-ensembles gris clair (EGC) et gris beige (EGB) renfermant deux niveaux de Moustérien de Tradition Acheuléenne.

L'étude sédimentologique montre que pour l'ensemble gris (EG) les sédiments sont caractérisés par la présence de nombreuses pierres et granules avec un pourcentage maximum vers le milieu de la séquence (sommet de EGC) puis une diminution très nette à la partie supérieure (EGPF). Cette séquence apparaît relativement froide et humide surtout à la base, puis très froide et légèrement moins humide, enfin froide et humide au sommet.

L'ensemble jaune (EJ) débute par un ruissellement important (EJOP inf.) puis montre un premier coup de froid associé à une humidité assez forte (EJOP sup. castelperronien). Il se poursuit par un nouvel épisode de ruissellement (EJO inf.) puis le froid se manifeste à nouveau (EJO sup., Protoaurignacien) pour atteindre son maximum à l'Aurignacien ancien (EJF). Au dessus, les niveaux d'Aurignacien évolué (EJM puis EJJ) connaissent une amélioration climatique (Arcy).

The Sediments and Stratigraphy of Saint-Césaire: Contributions to the Paleoclimatology of the Site

Jean-Claude Miskovsky and François Lévêque

Quaternary lithostratigraphic sequences containing industries from the Middle to Upper Paleolithic transition (Castelperronian), dated to between 38,000 and 33,000 BC and corresponding to the end of the Würm II-III interstadial and the early Würm III, are relatively rare. In France, the Poitou-Charentes region appears privileged in that regard, and among the cave and rockshelter deposits, La Roche à Pierrot, Saint-Césaire, in Charente-Maritime, presents a typical stratigraphic sequence for the period (Figure 2.1). In close collaboration with the multidisciplinary research team led by François Lévêque, we have conducted a systematic sedimentological study of these deposits, and the essence of the results of this work is presented here.

Stratigraphy

The stratigraphy of this deposit is remarkably clear and precise; color differences and the alternation of fine and coarse sediments facilitate the recognition of the levels. The archaeological levels from the Paleolithic are covered by a humid layer of variable thickness and by a limestone *éboulis* of considerable size, likely resulting from the collapse of the rockshelter roof after the last Aurignacian occupation. The different levels are grouped into two sequences: an upper, yellow sequence (EJ, levels 3 through 9) corresponding to the early Upper Paleolithic; and a lower, gray sequence (EG, levels 10 through 17) comprising the Middle Paleolithic levels.

Upper, Yellow Sequence (EJ—*ensemble jaune*)

This sequence contains the following levels, from the top down:
- yellow-yellow level (EJJ {dry: 10YR 5/8, wet: 10YR 5/6}), a sediment formed of clayey sand containing limestone elements of small dimensions. In the lower portion of this level is found an industry attributable to an Evolved Aurignacian.
- yellow-brown level (EJM {dry: 10YR 5/8, wet: 10YR 4/4}), with more clay and larger blocks. This level also contains an Evolved Aurignacian industry.

These two formations are characterized by the presence of fine sediment with few pebbles and a relatively high percentage of small carbonate concretions measuring 1 to 2 cm in diameter. The clay portion is smaller than that found in the subjacent level, and the sandy fractions, quite homogeneous, are very fine and are most abundant towards the top.

The percentage of arboreal pollen is higher than in the subjacent level, increasing from 20 to 40%. Pine is the dominant species at the base of these two levels, but mesophilous broad-leafed plants increase in number—in particular, hazel and alder. Oak is present, accompanied by elm, ash, and ivy. The presence of thermophilous taxa is noted, such as the maritime pine.

Various sedimentological indices and the results of pollen analysis point to a wooded landscape, indicating favorable climatic conditions and suggest a possible correspondence with the oscillation evidenced at Arcy.

- yellow level with burning (EJF {dry: 5YR 4/6, wet: 5YR 4/4}). This level is marked by the presence of numerous limestone blocks, heavy burning, and a rich, classic industry of the early Aurignacian (Aurignacian I), comprising carinated endscrapers, strangulated blades, and split-based bone points.

Faunal remains are abundant in this level and are mostly composed of reindeer; mammoth and woolly rhinoceros are also present. The sediment consists of a high proportion of stones, and these rocks show traces of processes that would have occurred during a cold episode. Other indicators of a cold episode include a high percentage of limestone in the fine fractions, round mat quartz grains, and many frost-weathered granules.

The percentage of arboreal pollen from this level is the lowest in the entire pollen diagram (lower than 20%); it is mostly pine, juniper, and alder. For the

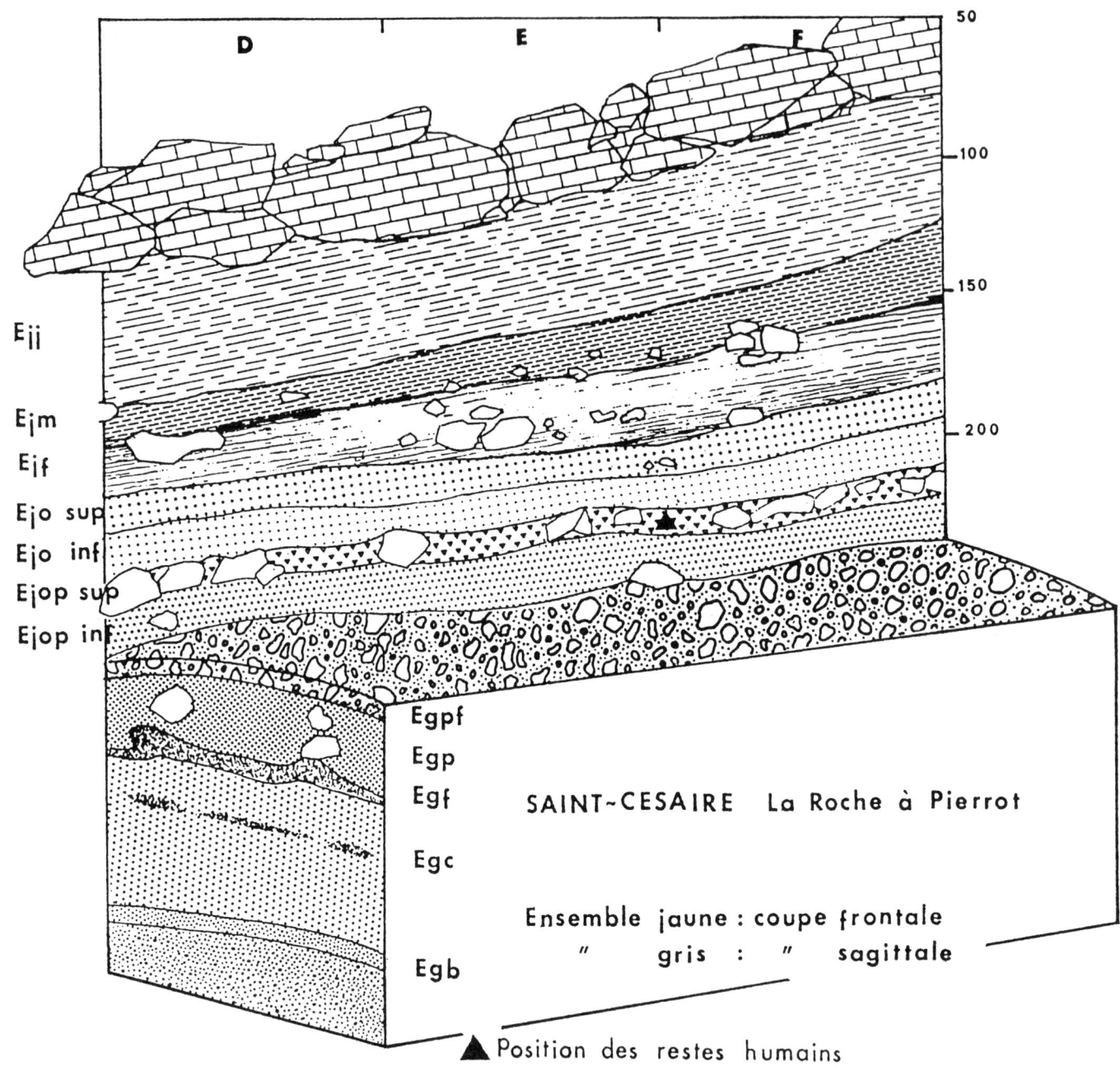

Figure 2.1. Stratigraphy of Saint-Césaire.

herbaceous component, compositae dominate and the classic taxa of a cold steppe appear. All of these elements combine to imply harsh climatic conditions, suggesting a more open landscape dominated by a grassy steppe, as is often noted during the early Aurignacian.

• yellow-orange level, upper stratum (EJO superior {dry: 7.5YR 5/6, wet: 7.5YR 4/4}), characterized by limestone rubble of small dimensions. This level contains an industry corresponding to the Archaic Aurignacian or Proto-Aurignacian (Aurignacian 0).

The cooling trend that reached its maximum in the level above can also be seen in this level, as herbaceous species begin to invade the pollen spectra.

• yellow-orange level, lower stratum (EJO inferior {dry: 7.5YR 5/6, wet: 7.5YR 4/4}). This formation is lighter, more clayey, and practically devoid of blocks. The few blocks that were encountered were situated

Figure 2.2. Stratigraphic profile (photo F. Lévêque).

at the base of the level, which does not contain any lithic artifacts. The sediment is characterized by small pebbles and many granules. Among the fines (sands and clays), sandy fractions with polished, lustrous quartz grains point to the occurrence of runoff.

The pollen spectra show a fluctuating curve for arboreal species and a decrease in arboreal pollen relative to the subjacent level. Evidence for a pine forest dominates, but the increase in alder could indicate a humid climate. This level seems to correspond to an episode of significant runoff belonging to a phase of climatic instability, essentially owing to variations in humidity.

• pale yellow-orange level, upper stratum (EJOP superior {dry: 10YR 5/8, wet: 10YR 5/6}). This level is characterized by a paler color and the presence of numerous angular pieces of limestone. It contains a characteristic Castelperronian industry. A limited

Figure 2.3. The two Castelperronian levels (photo F. Lévêque).

cooling trend appears to be indicated here, with large numbers of rocks and granules, considerable frost-weathering of clasts, a high percentage of limestone, and round, mat quartz grains.

The percentage of arboreal pollen is high, especially pine. Juniper and birch are also noted. The herbaceous stratum is mostly represented by *Cichoriaceae*, with graminates and *Anthemidae* also present. Among the fauna are the three classic "cold indicators": reindeer, mammoth, and woolly rhinoceros. But this cold aspect is tempered by the coexistence of forms generally indicative of a mild climate: large bovines, horse, red deer, megaceros, and boar. Reindeer is represented by shed and unshed antler. Reindeer is clearly dominant in all the upper yellow sequence (Aurignacian), whereas the gray sequence is marked by an abundance of large bovines and horses. The Castelperronian levels appear transitional between these two main chronological sequences.

In 1979 this level yielded Neandertal skeletal remains. Of this skeleton are preserved a major portion of the right half of the cranium, the right hemimandible, a left dental arcade, and part of the postcrania. B. Vandermeersch, who is studying these remains (see Vandermeersch, this volume), believes the skeleton can be classified without hesitation among the western European Neandertals, based on its general design and several aspects of its morphology.

• pale yellow-orange level, lower stratum (EJOP inferior {dry: 10YR 5/8, wet: 10YR 5/6}). This level contains only a few blocks, mostly in its lower part, and appears as a distinctly more clayey matrix. It corresponds to a period of intense runoff. The lithic assemblage, Castelperronian in character, is small.

The expansion of pine is considerable, and this coniferous forest may have covered practically all of the land between the stream and the cliffs. Only a few oaks are present, as well as some junipers. Here we have quite clearly the characteristics of an interstadial phase, which can be tied in to the Les Cottés oscillation.

• pale yellow-orange level, base (EJOP base {dry: 10YR 5/8, wet: 10YR 5/6}). Although sedimentologically similar to the previous one, this level does contain a series of rather large blocks; it is currently under study. The industry includes many scrapers and denticulates but also a number of fashioned tools with abrupt retouch (partially or totally backed).

Lower, Gray Sequence (EG—*ensemble gris*)

We propose to organize the gray sequence in the following manner:

levels 10, 11, 12: Denticulate Mousterian
level 14: Mousterian of Acheulean Tradition
level 17: Mousterian of Acheulean Tradition

The characteristics of this sequence are as follows.
- pale gray level with burning (EGPF {dry: 10YR 4/3, wet: 10YR 3/3}). This level is a beautifully preserved occupation surface. It contains thousands of unretouched flakes, relatively few tools, and abundant faunal remains (primarily large bovines and equids). At its base is a remarkably dense concentration of bone fragments.
- pale gray level (EGP {dry: 10YR 5/4, wet: 10YR 4/4}). This level is marked by the presence of many calcareous elements, some indurated in places. Like the level above it, it contains a Denticulate Mousterian tool assemblage.
- gray level with burning (EGF {dry: 10YR 7/2, wet: 10YR 5/3}). This level is heavily burned, but less so than EGPF. This Denticulate Mousterian level is quite rich in faunal remains.
- light gray levels (EGC {dry: 10YR 8/1, wet: 10YR 8/2}). Both the upper (EGC superior) and the lower (EGC inferior) portions of this unit are practically sterile and have yielded only a few flakes. The middle portion (EGC), at first distinguished by small, isolated patches of burning, was later revealed to be a thin, continuous lens of burning. Although the archaeological materials in this level are scarce, they point to a Mousterian of Acheulean Tradition.
- gray-tan level, upper stratum (EGB superior {dry: 2.5YR 7/2, wet: 2.5YR 6/2}). This level is much sandier and of a lighter color; it is probably at least partially fluvial in origin. The assemblage is not abundant, but it reflects the Mousterian of Acheulean Tradition.
- gray-tan level, lower stratum (EGB inferior {dry: 10YR 7/4, wet: 10YR 5/6}). This level is also essentially light-colored sand but differs from the preceding one in its reddish hue. It contains a few flakes but has only yielded a few fragmentary teeth and bones, with a more or less rolled aspect.

This level was found to lie directly on the bedrock of small limestone slabs. This surface slopes towards the river, and the slope becomes more accentuated as one moves away from the cliff face.

The pollen analysis shows a rupture in the pollen curves between the beginning of the Castelperronian and the latest Mousterian level. This hiatus is probably due to a phase of runoff, which may have removed a part of the deposits, but it appears to have lasted only a relatively short time. Levels 10 and 12 are rich in pollen. The start of a warming trend is noticeable with the expansion of trees, especially pine, alder, and juniper, after a period of extreme cold. The base of the sequence (levels 13 to 17), in contrast, has yielded no pollen.

Sedimentological Analysis

The analytical procedures used at Saint-Césaire were originally established for the study of sediments from cave or rockshelter deposits and have been described in numerous publications. Samples were collected during excavation on an average of every 5 to 10 cm, depending on the thicknesses of the different defined levels, and from different sectors of the site to enable identification of horizontal variations. Techniques used include granulometry (for cobbles, granules, sands, silts, and clays), calcimetry, mineralogy of sands and clays, morphoscopy and exoscopy of quartz, and soil micromorphology.

Two sedimentary and climatic units were identified during excavation and through physical and chemical analysis of the sediments. At the base, resting on limestone bedrock, the first group, 1.20 m thick, contained Mousterian industries. It begins with fine, well-sorted sands and sediments characterized by the presence of numerous cobbles and granules, most of which occur in the middle of the Mousterian sequence (level 13 or EGC superior). These elements decrease very clearly in the upper part (level 10 or EGPF). A very dense concentration of flints and bones was discovered in this upper Mousterian level, indicative of intensive human occupation.

The analysis of the fines shows an important clay fraction (40% of the fines) that contains a high proportion of phosphates, probably owing to decomposition of some of the bones, as well as fine, poorly sorted sands. Especially at the base, in level 13 or EGC superior, these sands contain many blunted, shiny quartz grains, characteristic of a humid climate. This lower sequence, along with its Mousterian industries, appears to have been laid down during relatively cold and humid climatic conditions; at least this inference can be made for the base levels.

To sum up the results from the lower sequence, three climatic episodes characterize the Mousterian deposits: at the base, a cold and humid episode followed by a very cold, slightly less humid episode and, at the top, by a very cold, very humid episode.

The upper levels form another sequence of deposits beginning with a period of heavy runoff, visible during excavation. This sedimentary unit was 1.60 m thick and contained Upper Paleolithic industries.

The base, EJOP inferior and EJOP base, directly overlies the Mousterian levels. It contains a rather high percentage of large clasts (cobbles and granules) and a sandy-clayey fraction with small, well-sorted elements, including quartz grains, many of which show evidence of water action, probably transport by a major episode of runoff. Studies of sediments from the local surroundings show that most of the elements within the deposits of level EJOP inferior originated largely from substratum and local formations close to the site and therefore were transported over very short distances.

Above, level EJOP superior contains many cobbles and granules. Morphoscopic study of these stones shows that some of them came from the rockshelter walls and represent exfoliation during a very cold climatic episode. The fines exhibit very marked characteristics of humid conditions: blunted, shiny quartz grains are found in abundance, and the percentage of limestone is quite high. A few quartz grains show traces of wind action and were later reworked by water action. We are dealing with an initial cold snap associated with relatively high humidity. This level is the one in which the human remains were found.

Above this level, EJO inferior, which is archaeologically sterile, is characterized by a horizon of pebbles less dense than the underlying layer but with many granules and rather large sandy fraction elements. The many blunted, shiny quartz grains are evidence of a renewed episode of runoff. The percentage of limestone is lower than in the underlying layer, suggesting its possible removal by runoff.

Level EJO superior contains an Aurignacian industry. The sediment contains a heavy proportion of stones marked by very clear indices of cold conditions (an abundance of frost-weathered slabs). The fine fractions include quite fine, well-sorted sands, with round, mat quartz grains and some shiny, blunted ones. The percentage of limestone is high. We are dealing with a second cold snap here.

The sedimentological characteristics of the overlying Level EJF show very clearly that the trend towards cold conditions was accentuated: a great number of frost-weathered blocks, few fine sediments, and the presence of round, mat quartz grains typical of wind transport.

This upper group of levels at Saint-Césaire is capped by Evolved Aurignacian levels EJM and EJJ. The sediments are smaller. There is a clear decrease in the number of stones. The fine sediments become sandy and contain many small concretions of gritty limestone conglomerate, from 1 to 2 cm in diameter. Sands are very fine and well sorted, becoming more abundant towards the top. Clays are not abundant and are characterized by a heavy proportion of illite and kaolinite, probably originating in the neighboring formations, very close by.

In general, the sedimentological data show that climatic conditions were becoming milder, and the comparative study of these results with information on flora and fauna leads us to propose a correlation between this period and the increased mild conditions identified at Arcy.

Conclusion

The deposits at the site of Saint-Césaire can be subdivided into two major climatic sequences, in general marked by relatively cold conditions but also characterized by several humid/arid oscillations. The upper levels indicate a clear warming trend. This deposit is crucial because of its contribution to our understanding of this period of transition from Middle to Upper Paleolithic industries, for which few sedimentary sequences are yet known.

3

Datations par Thermoluminescence du Site Préhistorique de La Roche à Pierrot à Saint Césaire

N. Mercier, H. Valladas, J-L. Joron, et J-L. Reyss

Pour dater les niveaux de la fin du Paléolithique moyen et du début du Paléolithique supérieur du site de La Roche à Pierrot à Saint-Césaire, nous avons tenté d'utiliser trois méthodes de datation indépendantes. La méthode du radiocarbone et celle des déséquilibres dans la famille de l'uranium appliquées à des ossements n'ont pas abouti à des résultats fiables en raison du mauvais état de conservation de ces échantillons. La seule méthode utilisable a été la thermoluminescence (TL) appliquée aux silex chauffés dans les foyers préhistoriques. Parmi les cinquante échantillons sélectionnés, 20 seulement avaient été chauffés à une température suffisante (supérieure à 450-500°C) pour être datés par la thermoluminescence: 2 silex proviennent du niveau 6 (Proto-Aurignacien), 6 du niveau 8 (Castelperronien) où ont été découvert les vestiges néandertaliens, et les autres des niveaux moustériens sous-jacents. Les âges moyens obtenus pour les différents niveaux (entre 42 et 32 kans) sont en accord avec la stratigraphie. Les niveaux moustériens à denticulés (10-12) sont placés vers 40 kans tandis que le niveau castelperronien sus-jacent est daté de 36,3 ± 2,7 kans.

Les âges TL de Saint-Césaire sont comparés a ceux obtenus par la méthode du radiocarbone pour des niveaux castelperroniens et aurignaciens anciens d'autres sites paléolithiques d'Europe de l'Ouest. Ces comparaisons suggèrent que les derniers Néandertaliens ont pu être contemporains pendant plusieurs millénaires de sites aurignaciens, attribués à l'Homme moderne.

Thermoluminescence Dating of the Prehistoric Site of La Roche à Pierrot, Saint-Césaire

N. Mercier, H. Valladas, J-L. Joron, and J-L. Reyss

For a long time, the Upper Paleolithic stone tools of western Europe were attributed to modern humans whereas the Middle Paleolithic Mousterian tools were associated with Neandertals. The discovery of Neandertal remains (Lévêque 1989; Lévêque and Vandermeersch 1980; Vandermeersch 1984) alongside Castelperronian (Lower Perigordian) lithic industries in the site of Saint-Césaire (Charente-Maritime) showed for the first time that Neandertals used some innovations associated with the Upper Paleolithic. Few Castelperronian sites have been excavated, so their pivotal position in the transition from Middle to Upper Paleolithic and the fact that none other has yielded indisputable hominid remains (Leroi-Gourhan 1965) make the dating of the Saint-Césaire occupation levels very important (ApSimon 1980; Demars and Hublin 1989; Mellars 1989; Wolpoff et al. 1981). On the other hand, this site offers a rare opportunity for studying the transition from Middle to Upper Paleolithic since it contains occupation levels ranging from Mousterian to Aurignacian.

Different methods of dating were attempted. First the method using disequilibrium in U series was performed on bone samples, indicating an age of about 15,000 years, certainly too young (C. Lalou, personal communication 1990). Second, an attempt was made to radiocarbon date the bone samples, but they did not contain enough collagen to give a reliable date (J. Evin and M. Fontugne, personal communication 1991). It is not surprising that both the U series and the radiocarbon dating methods failed to give satisfactory results, given the poor state of preservation of the bone samples. As yet, no charcoal has been recovered from the site.

The only method that could be used was thermoluminescence (TL) dating of burned flint specimens that were found near the hearth remains in several locations on the site (Mercier et al. 1991). Indeed, numerous studies in our and other laboratories have shown that the heating of flint can be dated reliably by the method of thermoluminescence (Aitken 1985; Valladas 1992; Valladas and Valladas 1987). Approximately 50 pieces of flint of suitable size, all showing evidence of burning, were selected for TL examination. Of these, only 20 had been heated to a temperature high enough to erase the thermoluminescence acquired by the minerals during their geological history and have satisfactory characteristics for TL dating. Two of the 20 were from the Proto-Aurignacian layer 6; six were from the Castelperronian layer 8, where the Neandertal bones were found; and the rest were from the underlying Mousterian strata.

The methods used to treat the samples and to measure their paleodoses have been described in detail elsewhere (Valladas 1992; Valladas and Valladas 1987). The environmental dose rate was measured using 40 dosimeters ($CaSO_4$/Dy) in copper capsules planted in various levels. The external dose rate received by a piece of flint in a given layer was obtained by taking the average dose measured in its vicinity. The gamma dose decreased with depth, which fits well with the mineralogical composition of the field (Miskovsky, this volume), ranging from 60 to 25 mrad/year. The uranium and thorium content in the flint artifacts was measured by epithermal neutron activation inside a cadmium container and the potassium content was measured by neutron activation (Chayla et al. 1973) at the Institut Pierre Süe (CEN, Saclay). The internal radiation dose computed from the concentrations of radioelements represents 40 to 63% of the total annual dose. This reduced the impact on the calculated age of variations in the external dose (which range, depending on the level, from ±15 to ±25%). The results are given in Table 3.1.

The age of burning for each piece of flint and its statistical error are presented as a function of depth in Figure 3.1. The weighted average and the total error (statistic plus systematic; Aitken 1976) calculated for the respective layers are listed on the right. The aver-

Sample	U*	Th*	K*	Internal[a] dose	External[b] dose	Annual dose	Paleodose	Age
	(p.p.m.)			(μGy yr^{-1})			(Gy)	(kyr BP)
Layer 6: EJO superior								
96	0.530	0.491	666	408 ± 25	610	1020 ± 100	31.23 ± 1.20	30.8 ± 3.3
60	0.541	0.237	430	296 ± 20	610	900 ± 100	30.70 ± 1.03	34.0 ± 3.9
Layer 8: EJOP superior								
95	0.687	0.466	1599	510 ± 45	375	890 ± 110	32.39 ± 1.73	36.6 ± 5.0
48	0.836	0.197	178	374 ± 26	395	770 ± 100	29.35 ± 1.04	38.2 ± 5.3
103	0.485	0.106	378	291 ± 18	407	700 ± 100	23.48 ± 1.33	33.7 ± 5.4
53	0.614	0.029	240	441 ± 31	402	850 ± 100	30.82 ± 1.38	36.6 ± 4.9
54	0.510	0.069	430	370 ± 26	402	770 ± 100	28.86 ± 0.93	37.4 ± 5.2
82	0.719	0.397	484	460 ± 33	418	880 ± 110	31.30 ± 1.08	35.6 ± 4.6
Layer 10: EGPF								
75	0.529	0.188	274	277 ± 20	351	630 ± 60	27.06 ± 1.26	43.1 ± 4.8
107	0.946	0.260	732	565 ± 38	352	920 ± 70	36.20 ± 1.95	39.5 ± 3.9
106	0.400	0.415	1206	341 ± 20	359	700 ± 60	27.29 ± 1.75	39.0 ± 4.5
83	0.616	0.270	292	359 ± 22	281	640 ± 60	21.40 ± 1.38	33.5 ± 3.8
66	0.461	0.120	440	282 ± 21	315	600 ± 50	25.35 ± 1.18	42.4 ± 4.4
105	1.051	0.212	864	555 ± 36	318	870 ± 60	37.92 ± 1.25	43.4 ± 3.4
111	0.652	0.289	780	447 ± 33	315	760 ± 60	29.64 ± 1.02	38.9 ± 3.4
112	0.603	0.342	842	348 ± 25	336	680 ± 70	31.19 ± 1.39	45.6 ± 4.8
25	0.472	0.389	610	344 ± 23	310	650 ± 60	30.82 ± 1.56	47.1 ± 4.9
Layer 11: EGP								
84	0.746	0.384	472	353 ± 24	257	610 ± 60	24.22 ± 0.91	39.7 ± 3.9
78	0.452	0.337	364	286 ± 19	284	570 ± 50	20.96 ± 0.74	36.8 ± 3.7
Layer 12: EGF								
86	0.629	0.272	320	340 ± 24	251	590 ± 60	25.06 ± 1.00	42.4 ± 4.3

* The values of U, Th, and K were measured by neutron activation at the Institut Pierre Süe (CEN, Saclay), and each have an error of ±6%.

[a] The internal dose includes the alpha and beta annual dose computed from the radioelement contents of the flint.

[b] The external dose includes a cosmic contribution ranging from 0.10 to 0.13 μGy·yr^{-1}. It has been calculated using the data given by Prescott and Stephan (1982). The uranium series radionuclides are essentially at equilibrium in the sediment: the activities of ^{234}Th, ^{226}Ra, ^{214}Bi, and ^{210}Pb measured by gamma spectrometry are 1.13 ± 0.09, 0.99 ± 0.08, 0.90 ± 0.05, and 1.05 ± 0.14 d.p.m. g^{-1}, respectively.

Table 3.1. Thermoluminescence results and radioactivity data for the flints from Saint-Césaire.

ages, ranging from 42,000 to 32,000 BP, fit the stratigraphic evidence. The denticulate Mousterian layers (10-12) cluster around 40,000 BP, suggesting that they were deposited within a short time interval. The flint artifacts found near the Neandertal remains yielded a date of 36,300 ± 2700, making this specimen the youngest Neandertal dated thus far. The gap of more than 2000 years separating the uppermost Mousterian from the dated Castelperronian can be partially explained by a stratigraphic discontinuity apparently caused by erosion of the layers overlying the surviving Mousterian (Leroi-Gourhan 1984; Lévêque and Miskovsky 1983). The Proto-Aurignacian layer, for which only two datable flint artifacts were available, had an age of 32,000 ± 3000.

The TL date for the Castelperronian stratum at Saint-Césaire appears older than the radiocarbon dates reported for the same industry at Arcy-sur-Cure in Yonne (GrN 1742: 33,860 ± 250; GrN 1736: 33,500 ± 400 and GrN 2163: 33,000 ± 1400; Girard et al. 1990) and Les Cottés in Vienne (GrN 4333: 33,300 ± 500 and GrN 4510: 31,900 ± 430; Vogel and Waterbolk 1967). This age difference may not be as significant as it appears in view of recent evidence (Bard et al. 1990; Bell 1991) that radiocarbon dates within this time period might be systematically too young by as much as 10%. The same evidence would make the TL results from Saint-Césaire younger than the radiocarbon date (OxA 1443: 38,000 ± 2000; Hedges et al. 1990) obtained for the Castelperronian stratum at Le Roc de Combe (in Lot).

Otherwise, the surviving Neandertal of Saint-Césaire could be a contemporary of the occupants of several radiocarbon dated Aurignacian sites, such as

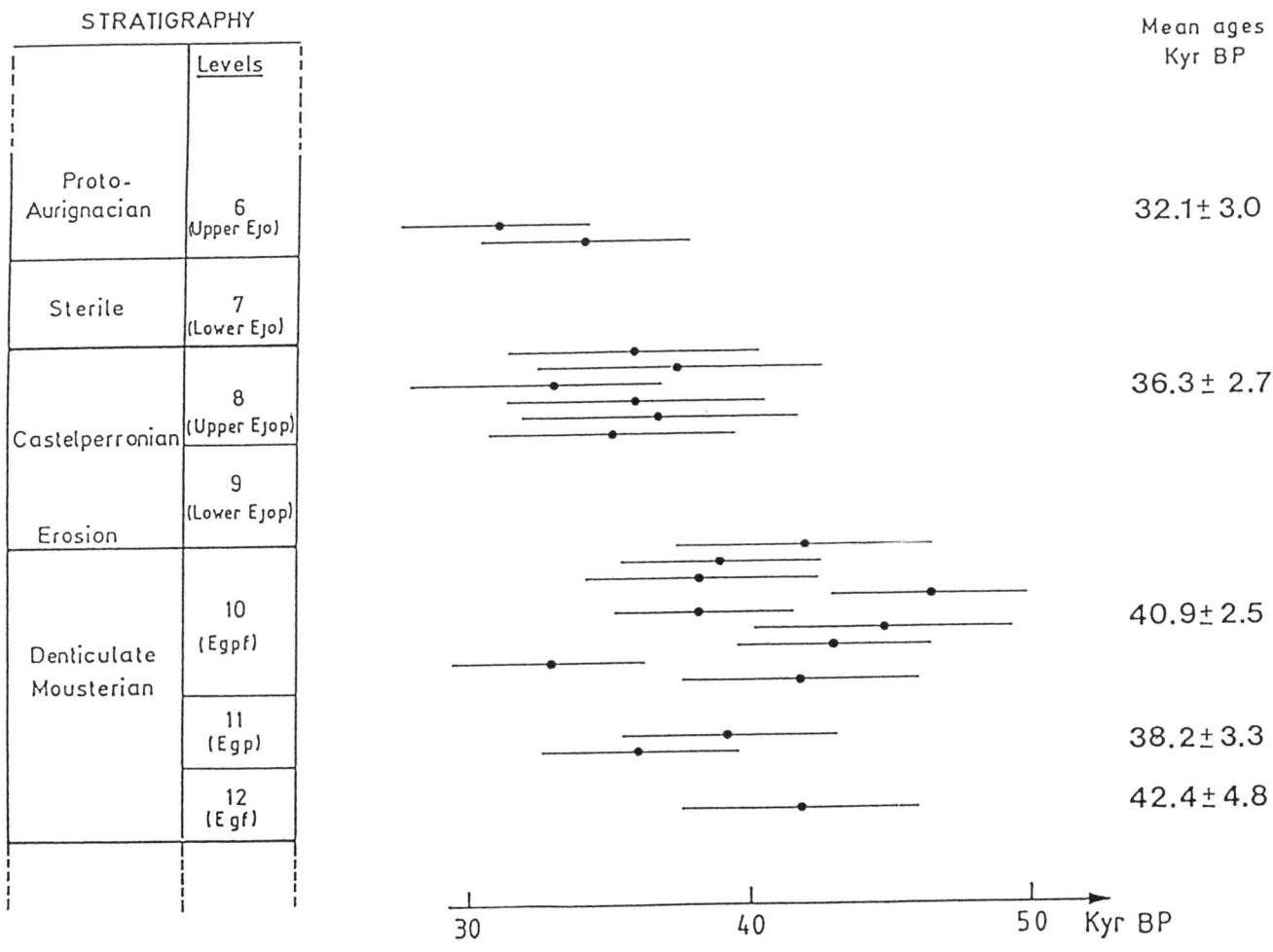

Figure 3.1. Horizontal lines represent the TL ages of burned flint from Saint-Césaire. Weighted average ages deduced by level are listed on the right. Errors (statistical plus systematic) have been assessed at the 68% confidence level, following Aitken 1976. A systematic error of ± 7% has been assumed for the external dose to take possible past variations in the water content of archaeological sediments into account.

L'Abri Pataud in Dordogne (GrN 4507: 34,250 ± 675, GrN 4720: 33,300 ± 410, GrN 4719: 33,260 ± 425; Vogel and Waterbolk 1967); Le Flageolet in Dordogne (OxA 598: 33,800 ± 1800; Gowlett et al. 1986); Le Roc de Combe in the Lot (OxA 1262: 33,400 ± 1100 and OxA 1263: 34,800 ± 1200; Hedges et al. 1990); and La Ferrassie in Dordogne (Gif 4279: >35,000 BP and GrN 5751: 33,200 ± 570; Delibrias 1984).

The Aurignacian layers of these sites are currently believed to have been occupied by modern humans (Gambier 1989). Moreover, even if the recently reported radiocarbon dates for the Aurignacian levels at El Castillo Cave (38,700 ± 1900; Cabrera-Valdès and Bischoff 1989) and L'Arbreda Cave (38,500 ± 1000; Bischoff et al. 1989) in Spain are not adjusted, the TL date of the Saint-Césaire Neandertal suggests that members of this population might have survived several millennia *after* the arrival of the people responsible for the Aurignacian industries of western Europe.

Despite its late date, the Saint-Césaire skull exhibits classical Neandertal features (Vandermeersch 1984) with no evidence of evolution in the direction of modern humans. Therefore the age and the morphology of the Saint-Césaire hominid should remove any remaining doubts that the western European Neandertals were replaced by an intrusive population of modern humans instead of evolving into succeeding populations.

References Cited

Aitken, M. J.
1976 Thermoluminescent Age Evaluation and Assessment of Error Limits: Revised System. *Archaeometry* 18:233-238.
1985 *Thermoluminescence Dating*. Academic, New York.

ApSimon, A. M.
1980 The Last Neandertal. *Nature* 287:272-273.

Bard, E., B. Hamelin, R. G. Fairbanks, and A. Zindler
1990 Calibration of the 14C Timescale Over the Past 30,000 Years Using Mass Spectrometric U-Th Ages from Barbados Corals. *Nature* 345:405-410.

Bell, W. T.
1991 Thermoluminescence Dates for the Lake Mungo Aboriginal Fireplaces and the Implications for Radiocarbon Dating. *Archaeometry* 33:43-50.

Bischoff, J. L., N. Soler, J. Maroto, and R. Julia
1989 Abrupt Mousterian/Aurignacian Boundary at ca. 40 ka BP: Accelerator Radiocarbon Dates from L'Arbreda Cave (Catalunya, Spain). *Journal of Archaeological Science* 16:563-576.

Cabrera-Valdès, V., and J. L. Bischoff
1989 Accelerator C-14 dates for early Upper Palaeolithic (basal Aurignacian) at El Castillo Cave (Spain). *Journal of Archaeological Science* 16:577-584.

Chayla, B., H. Jaffrezic, and J. L. Joron
1973 Analyse par activation dans les neutrons épithermiques: Application à la détermination d'éléments en traces dans les roches. *Compte rendu de l'Academie des Sciences* (Paris) 277:273-275.

Delibrias, G.
1984 La datation par le carbone 14 des ossements de La Ferrassie. In *Le grand abri de La Ferrassie*, sous la direction de H. Delporte. *Etudes Quaternaires* 7:105-107.

Demars, P. Y., and J.-J. Hublin
1989 La transition néandertaliens/hommes de type moderne en Europe occidentale: Aspects paléontologiques et culturels. In *L'homme de Néandertal*, vol. 3: *L'extinction*, edited by Marcel Otte, pp. 23-37. Eraul 34. Liège.

Gambier, D.
1989 Les caractères "néandertaliens" des premiers hommes modernes du Paléolithique supérieur français. In *L'homme de Néandertal*, vol. 3: *L'extinction*, edited by Marcel Otte, pp. 67-84. Eraul 34. Liège.

Girard, M., J. C. Miskovsky, and J. Evin
1990 La fin du Würm ancien et le début du Würm supérieur. Précisions paléoclimatiques et chronostratigraphiques d'après les remplissages des grottes d'Arcy sur Cure. *Mémoires du Musée de Préhistoire d'Ile de France* 3:295-303.

Gowlett, J. A. J., R. E. M. Hedges, I. A. Law, and C. Perry
1986 Radiocarbon Dates from the Oxford AMS System: Archaeometry Datelist 4. *Archaeometry* 28:206-222.

Hedges, R. E. M., R. A. Housley, I. A. Law, and C. R. Bronk
1990 Radiocarbon Dates from the Oxford AMS System: Archaeometry Datelist 10. *Archaeometry* 32:101-108.

Leroi-Gourhan, A.
　1965 *Préhistoire de l'art occidental*. Ed. Mazenod, Paris.
　1984 La place du Néandertalien de Saint Césaire dans la chronologie würmienne. *Bulletin de la Société Préhistorique Française* 81(7):196-198.

Lévêque, F.
　1989 L'Homme de Saint Césaire: Sa place dans le Castelperronien de Poitou-Charentes. In *L'homme de Néandertal*, vol. 3: *L'extinction*, edited by Marcel Otte, pp. 99-108. Eraul 34. Liège.

Lévêque, F., and J. C. Miskovsky
　1983 Le Castelperronien dans son environnement géologique. Essai de synthèse à partir de l'étude lithostratigraphique du remplissage de la grotte de la Grande Roche de la Plématrie (Quinçay, Vienne) et d'autres dépôts actuellement mis au jour. *L'Anthropologie* 87(3):369-391.

Lévêque, F., and B. Vandermeersch
　1980 Découverte des restes humains dans un niveau castelperronien à Saint-Césaire (Charente-Maritime). *Compte rendu de l'Academie des Sciences* (Paris) 291:187-189.

Mellars, P.
　1989 Technological Changes Across the Middle-Upper Palaeolithic Transition: Economic, Social and Cognitive Perspectives. In *The Human Revolution*. Edited by P. Mellars and C. B. Stringer, pp. 338-365. Edinburgh University Press, Edinburgh.

Mercier, N., H. Valladas, J. L. Joron, J. L. Reyss, F. Lévêque, and B. Vandermeersch
　1991 Thermoluminescence Dating of the Late Neanderthal Remains from Saint-Césaire. *Nature* 351:737-739.

Prescott, J. R., and L. G. Stephan
　1982 The Contribution of Cosmic Radiation to the Environmental Dose for TL Dating. Latitude, Altitude and Depth Dependences. *Second Seminar on TL Dating*, PACT 6:17-25. Conseil de l'Europe, Strasbourg.

Valladas, H.
　1992 Thermoluminescence Dating of Flint. *Quaternary Science Reviews* 11(1/2):1-5.

Valladas, H., and G. Valladas
　1987 Thermoluminescence Dating of Burnt Flint and Quartz: Comparative Results. *Archaeometry* 27:214-220.

Vandermeersch, B.
　1984 A propos de la découverte du squelette néandertalien de Saint-Césaire. *Bulletin et Mémoires de la Société d'Anthropologie de Paris* 1(XIV):191-196.

Vogel, J. C., and H. T. Waterbolk
　1967 Gröningen Radiocarbon Dates. *Radiocarbon* 19:107-155.

Wolpoff, M. H., A. M. ApSimon, C. B. Stringer, and R. G. Kruszynski
　1981 Allez neanderthal. *Nature* 289:823-824.

4

L'industrie Castelperronienne de Saint-Césaire: Le Niveau Supérieur

François Lévêque

L'étude du matériel lithique a été effectuée suivant la grille de 1986 de la typologie analytique. L'industrie de ce sous-ensemble est caractérisée par l'importance du groupe des racloirs et à un degré moindre par celle du groupe des denticulés. Les pièces à dos (pointes et lames) sont en nombre relativement important (un peu plus de 13% de l'industrie) mais les pointes à dos sont assez peu diversifiées. Les groupes burins et grattoirs sont à peu près en nombre équivalent.

Un certain nombre de pièces ne sont pas sans rappeler un Moustérien de tradition acheuléenne terminal avec la présence d'un petit biface foliacé et de grands racloirs plats. Souvent des retouches d'amincissement intéressent la face interne des pièces. On note également un caractère foliacé assez fréquent intéressant différents types d'outils.

Cet ensemble de caractères paraît évoquer un Castelperronien de type certainement assez ancien et par certains aspects archaïque. Le remontage de plusieurs outils trouvés en plusieurs fragments au cours de la fouille indique que ces pièces ont subi peu de déplacement.

L'étude sédimentologique de Saint-Césaire et de Quinçay permet d'établir avec précision le cadre chronostratigraphique pendant lequel les dépôts de ces deux gisements se sont formés. Leur succession est tout à fait comparable et il semble bien que le niveau castelperronien supérieur de Saint-Césaire (EJOP sup.) puisse être comparé à l'ensemble noir (EN) correspondant au sommet de la séquence inférieure de Quinçay. L'industrie du niveau EJOP sup. de Saint-Césaire se rapproche par certains points, en particulier par le type de pointes à dos, de l'industrie de cet ensemble noir de Quinçay (Castelperronien ancien) mais semble également présenter des caractères plus archaïques par son nombre plus élevé de racloirs et de denticulés et la présence de foliacés. On serait donc tenté de le placer comme intermédiare entre les phases anciennes et archaïques. On peut considérer aussi qu'il est contemporain de l'ensemble noir de Quinçay mais qu'en plus d'un fonds commun il présente des caractéristiques propres.

Si cette première étude apporte quelques précisions sur les caractères de cette industrie, elle montre aussi la complexité du phénomène castelperronien. En effet celui-ci comprend très certainement plusieurs stades successifs, mais sans doute faut il envisager également l'existence de plusieurs unités castelperroniennes contemporaines et plus ou moins différentes.

The Castelperronian Industry of Saint-Césaire: The Upper Level

François Lévêque

This study concerns the lithic materials from EJOP superior (pale yellow-orange subset, or level 8) where the Neandertal remains were discovered (Lévêque and Vandermeersch 1980, 1981; Vandermeersch 1984). We know that this level, characterized by the presence of numerous angular limestone blocks, is capped by a sterile level of sandy clay (EJO inferior, yellow-orange subset [inferior], or level 7) and in turn overlies a level containing relatively few artifacts, also attributable to the Castelperronian (EJOP inferior, pale yellow-orange subset [inferior], or level 9) (Lévêque 1989a). The lower Castelperronian level again consists of sandy clay but lacks limestone blocks except at the base (EJOP base), where rather large scattered boulders are found directly overlying the most recent Mousterian level, a rich occupation surface (EGPF, pale gray subset with burning, or level 10).

The materials discussed here do not include the totality of the assemblage recovered during excavation but do cover all lithic artifacts from a 32 m^2 area, enough to give a general picture of the characteristics of this industry. It should be noted as well that some of the lithics, especially those from the vicinity of the cliff wall, often exhibit a lustrous polish and traces of mechanical action, with steep, simple, or alternate retouch from natural processes at times superimposed on previous retouch owing to tool fashioning. In other sectors of the site, however, materials were not affected by these weathering processes. Only the indisputable retouched tools were selected for the counts reported here.

Typology

The notion of typology was a logical outgrowth of the earliest prehistoric research. One direct consequence of excavation was the need for systems geared to recognizing, defining, and classifying the different kinds of tools encountered at sites. Numerous typologies were therefore drawn up to study and understand the different Paleolithic industries. The criteria that served as the basis for different typological classifications can be summarized as follows:

- criteria derived from functional interpretations— for example, burins, knives, arrowheads
- criteria of form, emphasizing the general aspect of the piece—for example, fluted becs, laurel leaf points—or particular characteristics of the pieces (beveled, protruberant)
- criteria of fashioning techniques—for example, steep or scalar retouch

The designations thus obtained can be further qualified either by adjectives derived from the classification of industries, such as Aurignacian endscrapers; by a place name, such as Abri Audi points; or by a person's name (e.g., Lacorre dart points). At times, the industry is described according to the relative size of the pieces: *coutelas* - cutlass, *couteau* - knife, *canif* - penknife; *perçoir* - punch, *microperçoir* - micropunch.

These different criteria are often used simultaneously, resulting in mixed nomenclature that can be complex because these different typologies may interfere with one another. The proposed "types" therefore tend to be vague, poorly defined, and sometimes cumulative. "In this way, for example, despite similar dimensions and arrangement of retouch, a piece called an Azilian point in France becomes a Tjonger point in Holland and a bladelet with arched backing in the Maghreb" (Vilain 1966:47). Gaps in these type lists require the introduction of additional epithets, such as "atypical, crude, pseudo-," leading to "atypical" types, a contradiction in terms. These different typologies can be referred to as empirical typologies, and thus essentially reflect three constituent tendencies (Laplace 1972):

- a "functional descriptive tendency." This tendency is the oldest, and it has deeply influenced the beginnings of typology, through the efforts of Boucher de Perthes to create a functional typology that de Mortillet attempted to rationalize, with "cutting, grinding, crushing, pounding, and perforating" tools.

- a "strictly descriptive constituent" that deals with the complementary domains of form and fashioning technique, but without reaching any generalizing principles; this trend is of comparative persuasion, and it paves the way for typometry.
- a "stratigraphic constituent" came later, resulting from new knowledge gained from discoveries of cultural sequences while at the same time leading to the development of theories attempting to explain these sequences. This constituent is at the root of the notion of *fossiles directeurs* and the multiplication of designations derived from place names diagnostic of a site, a culture, or a period.

Empirical typologies have had the definite merit of advancing our knowledge of prehistoric industries. Attempts in this direction have broadened our knowledge in successive stages. Nevertheless, it appears today that a new, more rigorous, more rational, more systematic, computer-assisted orientation of typological studies is needed for a new stage of research. Analytical typology, drawn up by Laplace from 1957 onwards, does not rely on place names, stratigraphy, cultural affiliation or relative size. On the contrary, it is profoundly different from empirical typologies, in that it is a strictly morphotechnic method of analysis. This work has resulted in attempts to group forms that are similar to each other. For example, retouch techniques are used to fashion the products of reduction. Therefore, one form of typological analysis concentrates on recognizing retouch modes (constituting the systematic level of the order), on determining the extent of retouch, its direction, the outline of the retouched edge, the orientation of retouch, its form and placement. Hierarchical, structured associations of attributes are thus created, based at the simplest level on the retouch mode and increasing in complexity with optional ramifications involving typological groups, classes, primary types, and secondary types (see Laplace 1985-7). Each level of analysis integrates more and more complex associations. At each level of analysis the prehistorian determines the most pertinent attributes as a function of the desired analytical goal. If one so desires, the analysis can stop at a simple description of the industries, but it is also desirable to attempt to "delineate distributions of similar assemblages, and to study their evolutionary development using statistical and multivariate analyses" (Livache 1989:30).[1]

Assemblage Characteristics

Counts were carried out using the latest version of the analytical typology of Georges Laplace (1966, 1972, 1985-7) on 305 tools, categorized as sidescrapers (Figure 4.1), points (Figure 4.2a), endscrapers (Figure 4.2b), denticulates, retouched flakes (Figure 4.4b), becs, backed points (Figure 4.3), backed blades (Figure 4.4a), foliates (Figure 4.5), burins, and tools with scalar retouch[2]. Scrapers are the dominant group, with 122 pieces accounting for 40% of the assemblage. Carinated scrapers are poorly represented (only 7, or less than 6% of the total number of scrapers). An important majority of the scrapers are of the lateral type (84%) (Figure 4.1), whereas transverse and lateral-transverse scrapers account for only 8% and 7%, respectively. Fashioning by marginal retouch is slightly more common than invasive retouch (56% vs. 44%). Four percent of the scrapers were fashioned by retouch on the ventral face. In general form, convex scrapers (48%) are slightly more frequent than straight scrapers (44%); concave scrapers are rare. More than 20% of the scrapers are double tools—usually double scrapers, but sometimes a scraper exhibits a denticulate edge. Some of the pieces exhibit thinning removals on the ventral face, and in some cases retouch tends toward the foliate type.

The eight points (2.6% of the tools) are primarily simple points; one is shouldered. Retouch on two of them tends toward the foliate type; one exhibits bifacial retouch.

Endscrapers are represented by 18 pieces, nearly 6% of the assemblage. Usually thin and flat, only four are carinated. Rounded endscrapers are predominant relative to nosed ones. The rounded pieces include simple and lateral retouch in roughly equivalent proportions. The nosed endscrapers are equally divided between ogival and distinctly projecting forms.

Fifty-nine denticulates (slightly more than 19% of the assemblage) form the second typological group. Most are thin; carinated forms account for less than 17% of these tools. The denticulates consist of denticulate scrapers (approximately 41%), notches (32%), spines (22%), and points (slightly less than 5%). An overwhelming number of the denticulates (nearly 90%) are fashioned by summary retouch.

Steep or abrupt retouch is found on 12 pieces (less than 4% of the tools). Ten of these tools exhibit continuous retouch and two others exhibit denticulations. Marginal retouch is dominant. One piece with steep retouch of the invasive type is latero-transversal and is identical to a piece from La Grande Roche, Quinçay. One circular piece with invasive, steep retouch on the ventral side is fashioned on a Levallois blank (Figure 4.4b).

Together, the 13 becs represent only slightly more than 4% of the tool assemblage. Truncation drills are dominant (12 examples), usually fashioned by alternate retouch.

Backed points number 26, a little more than 8% of

the assemblage. Two of these tools were found broken into two or three pieces, which we were able to conjoin; in each case the fragments were found close to each other, suggesting that these objects underwent little lateral movement. These pieces form a homogeneous group. Only one exhibits a truncated base. The others are classic, fully backed points; in one case, the back is angulated. Only four have fashioned bases. Bipolar retouch was relatively seldom used, and when found, it is limited to the point itself. None of the backed points were made by the trihedral technique *à piquant trièdre*.

Fourteen backed blades were found, a little less than 5% of the entire assemblage. Most (11 examples) are simple, one is shouldered, and two are truncated. Marginal retouch dominates; only three show invasive retouch. Five exhibit ventral retouch and only one is retouched on both sides.

Foliates account for less than 2% of the tools, but their very presence is worthy of interest since thin, flat retouch removals can be found as a secondary characteristic on some of the other tool types. One of the foliates is a small cordiform biface. Another is a point exhibiting invasive retouch as well as ventral removals and basal thinning.

Fourteen burins (including one double burin) were included in this study (4.6% of the assemblage). Flat surfaces dominate as the point of origin for the detachment of the burin spalls. These surfaces can be flake scars or breaks, present in equal proportions. Dihedral burins are fewer and are mostly laterotransversal. Finally, burins formed by the detachment of spalls from a retouched portion of a tool only number two. In both cases, a lateral removal was made on a transversely retouched edge.

Scalar retouch is rare (slightly more than 4% of the assemblage) but noteworthy. In all cases, this retouch affects the surface of the tool.

In summary, the Castelperronian assemblage from level 8 is characterized by high proportions of scrapers and to a lesser degree by denticulates. It is important to remember, however, that these counts were carried out after a strict selection process and that, in some squares, many pieces with alternate retouch that might otherwise have been included were removed from the sample, at least for this study, with the result that percentages of denticulates and steep, abrupt retouch are significantly decreased. Backed pieces (points and blades) are relatively frequent (13% of the assemblage). These backed points do not exhibit much diversity in form.

Finally, some pieces are reminiscent of a terminal Mousterian of Acheulean Tradition, with the small bifaces exhibiting foliate retouch, the presence of large flat scrapers, and the occurrence of ventral thinning.

Different types of tools exhibit a distinctly similar kind of foliate retouch.

The burin and endscraper groups are about equal in number.

Taken together, these attributes give an archaic appearance to this Castelperronian assemblage.

Placement of Saint-Césaire in the Broader Context of the Castelperronian from Poitou-Charentes

The most complete Castelperronian sequence known to date has been studied at the site of La Grande Roche of Quinçay, about 15 km from Poitiers (Lévêque and Miskovsky 1983). This site contains a succession of eight Castelperronian levels within four sedimentary units deposited from the end of the Würm II-III interstadial to the beginning of Würm III. The study of these industries, in progress, shows not one but several Castelperronians over time. In fact, four different phases can be distinguished (Lévêque 1979):

1) Archaic or proto-Castelperronian, with large numbers of sidescrapers, slightly fewer denticulates, and foliate bifaces. It also contains some burins, endscrapers (some of which are blades), and backed pieces fashioned by marginal and invasive backing.

2) Early or typical Castelperronian, with high percentages of backed points, mostly fashioned by unipolar retouch in the lower level but more often by bipolar retouch in the later levels.

3) Evolved Castelperronian, with fewer backed points. These points are more or less straight, they can be very light and streamlined, and their bases are often worked into highly diverse forms.

4) Castelperronian with regressive characteristics: an apparent reversal to even fewer backed points, usually unipolar. These points tend to be smaller and less elaborate than earlier ones.

The sedimentology of Saint-Césaire and Quinçay establishes with precision the chronostratigraphic framework of these two deposits, and the sequences are quite comparable (Lévêque and Miskovsky 1987). This observation is important, since the period is as yet poorly known. Quinçay can be used as a yardstick for comparisons with the Castelperronian from level EJOP superior at Saint-Césaire.

First, EJOP superior at Saint-Césaire, by its position and its nature, is referable to EN (the black level) at the top of the lower sequence at Quinçay. The assemblage from level EN at Quinçay is Early Castelperronian. The industry at Saint-Césaire is similar to it in some aspects, especially the backed point types, but it seems to have some archaic qualities (the high number of sidescrapers, some denticulates, and the presence of foliates). It is tempting to place it as intermediate between the Archaic and the Early Castelperronian and to consider the Saint-Césaire assemblage closer to the lowest Early Castelperronian level of Quinçay (the top of the gray set, EGF). Furthermore, we are led to view it as contemporary with the black set at Quinçay, but despite some basic similarities it retains unique aspects.

A second point should be stressed: at all four sites in the Poitou-Charentes region with well-known stratigraphic sequences (Saint-Césaire, Les Cottés [Pradel 1961; Bastin, Lévêque, and Pradel 1976], La Quina [Henri-Martin 1962; Lévêque 1967], and La Grande Roche, Quinçay), the maximum cold oscillation of Würm IIIa is marked by levels containing rockfall. At three sites (Saint-Césaire, Les Cottés, and La Quina), these levels contain Early Aurignacian industries. At Quinçay, however, the corresponding sedimentary unit (EJ, the yellow level) continues to yield a Castelperronian industry. In other words, whereas at Saint-Césaire the proto- and Early Aurignacian follow the Castelperronian, at Quinçay during the same time period the Castelperronian endures for several phases (Lévêque 1989b, 1991).

This initial study, preliminary to thorough publication of the site, contributes some details on the characteristics of the Castelperronian. At the same time, it raises several questions and reveals the complexity of the Castelperronian phenomenon. The Castelperronian includes several successive stages, some of which, at some points in time, were contemporary with the Aurignacian (Lévêque et al. 1992). On the other hand, several contemporary Castelperronian variants can be envisaged. Guilbaud's study of the debitage seems to point in this direction (Guilbaud 1985, 1987).

Notes

[1] "à définir les répartitions d'ensembles industriels semblables et à étudier leurs processus évolutifs grâce à la mise au point d'analyses statistiques basées sur les calculs de probabilité et l'analyse des correspondances."

[2] *retouche écaillée.*

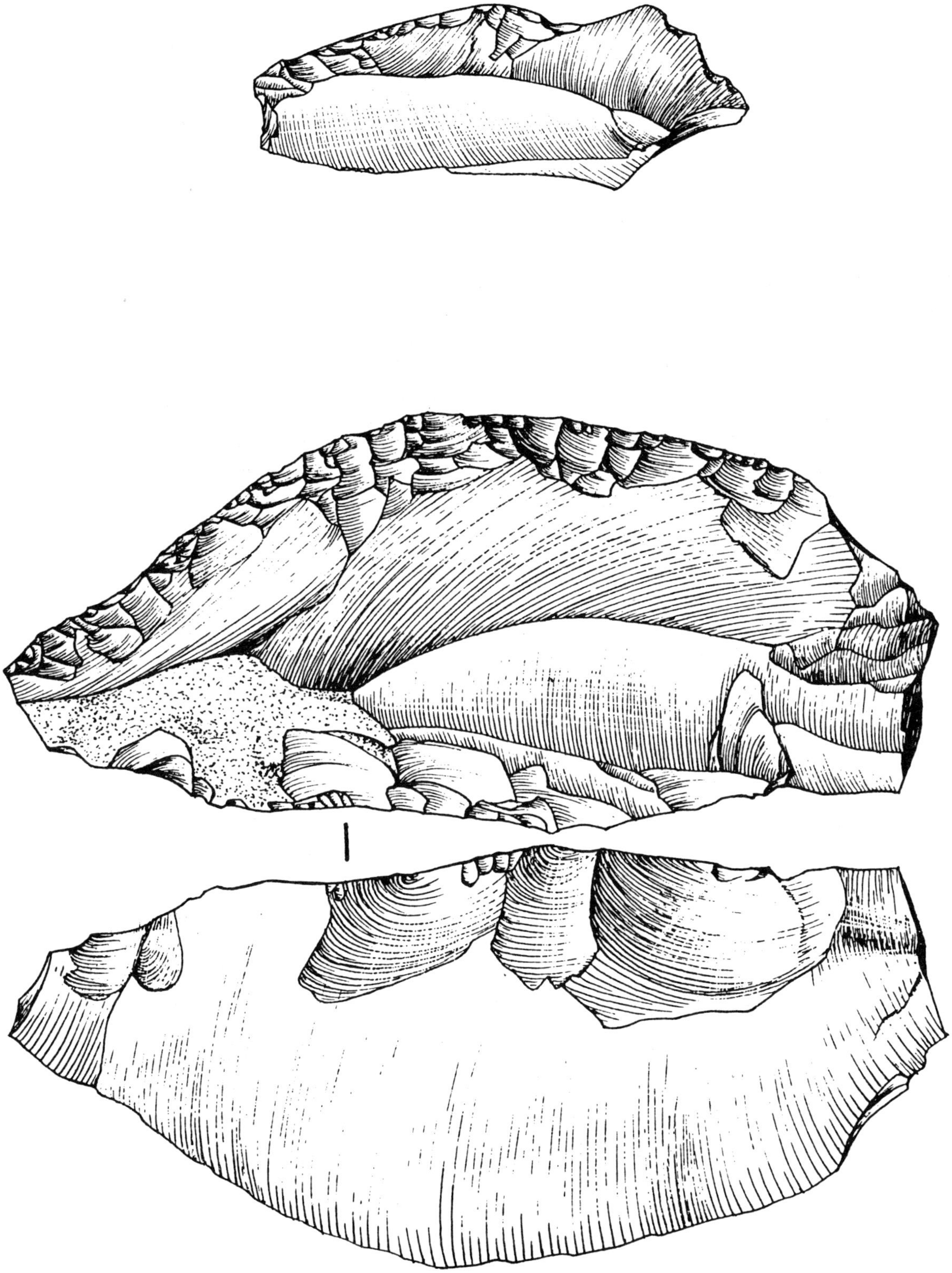

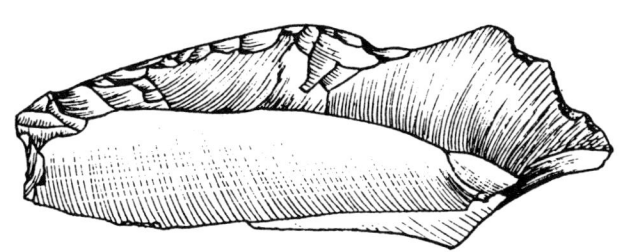

Figure 4.1. Sidescrapers (All drawings by Audoin).

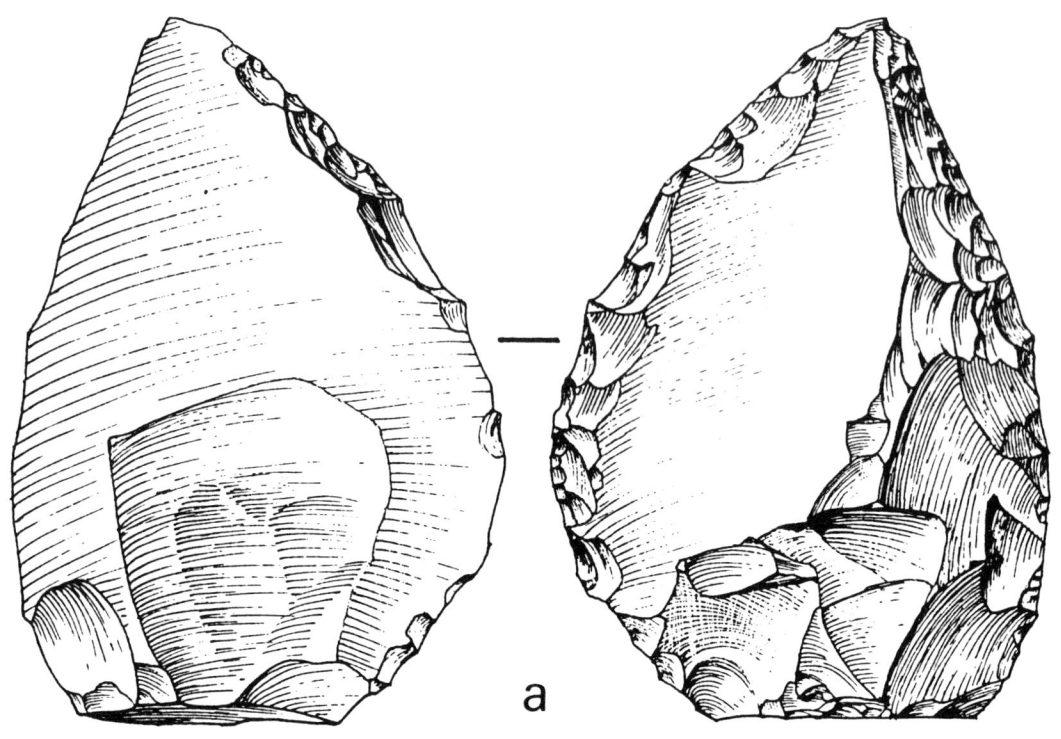
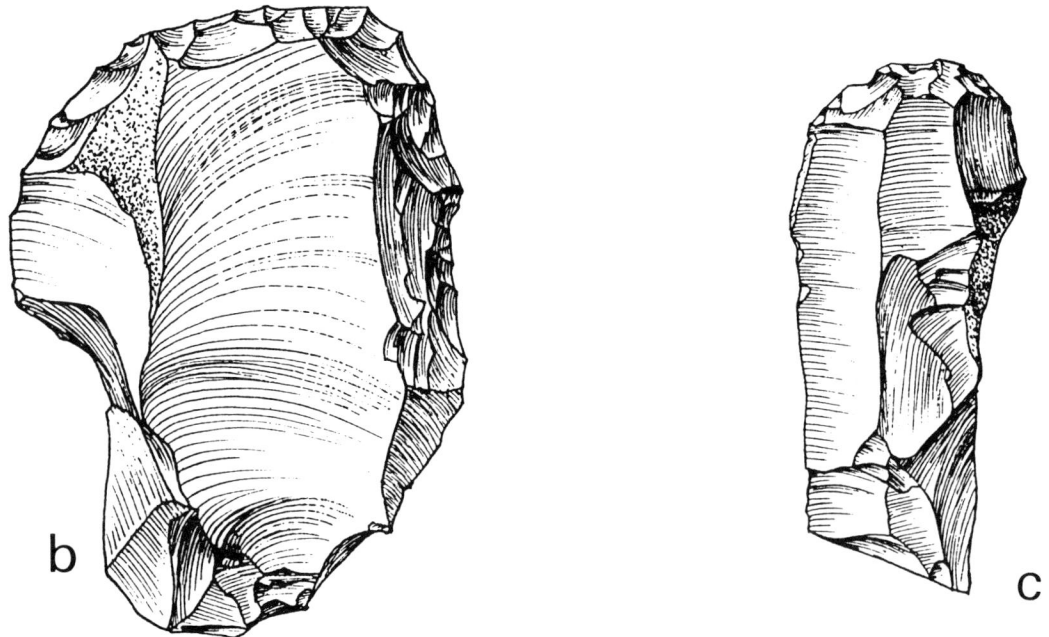

Figure 4.2. a: Point; b, c: endscrapers.

The Castelperronian Industry of Saint-Césaire 31

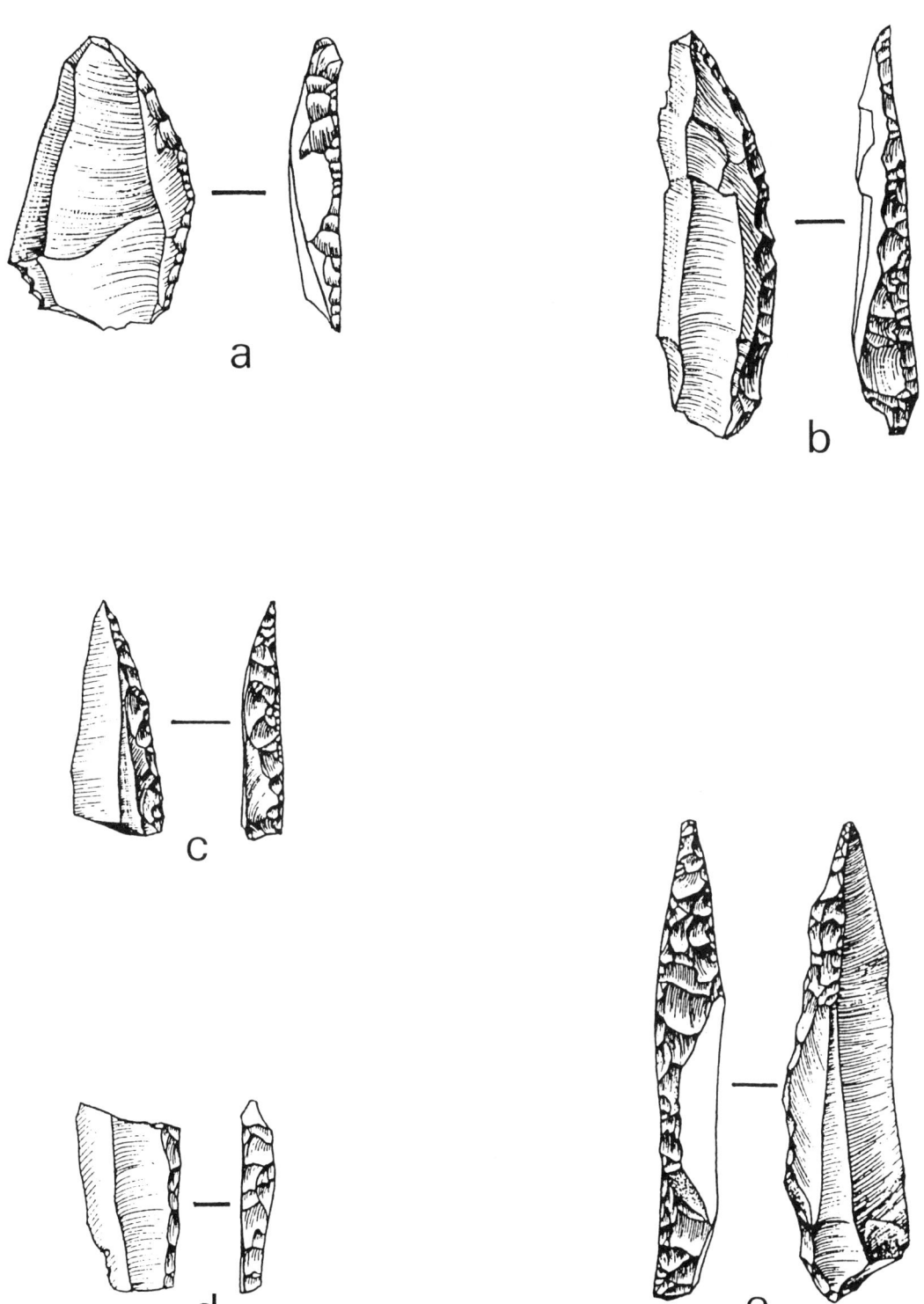

Figure 4.3. Backed points. a, b, c, d: totally backed; e: truncated backing.

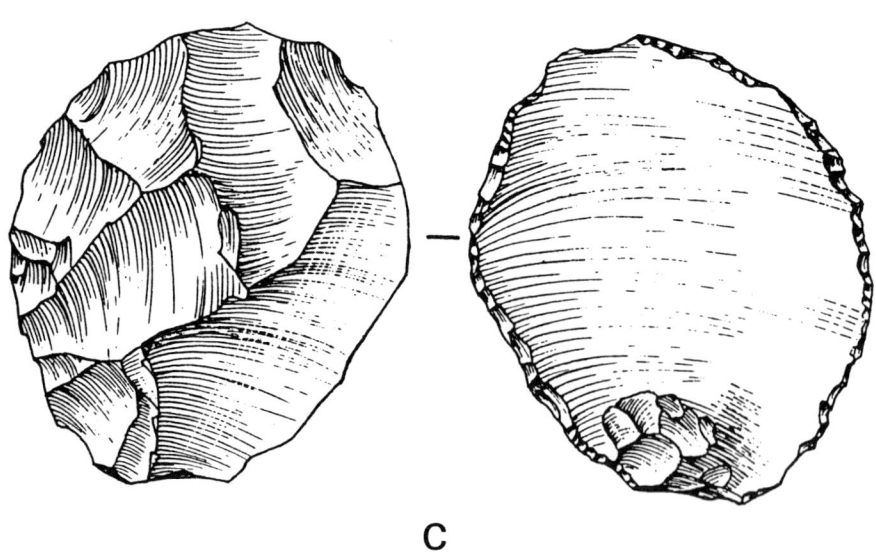

Figure 4.4. Backed blades. a: direct retouch; b: inverse retouch; c: Levallois flake, modified by steep retouch.

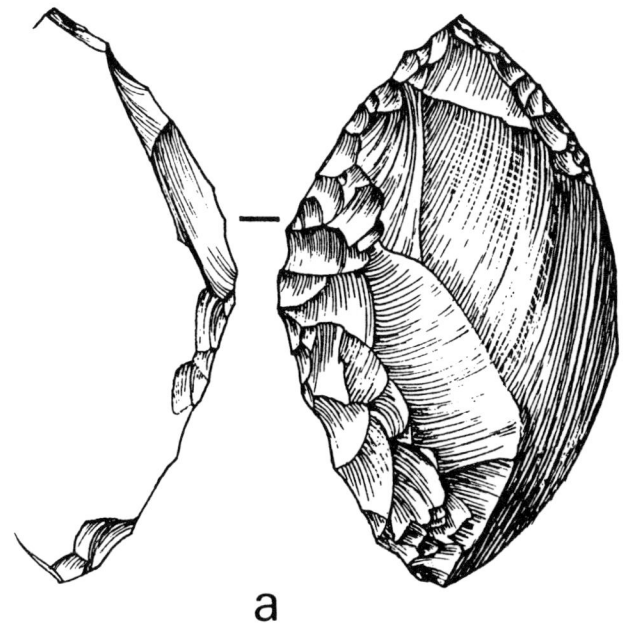

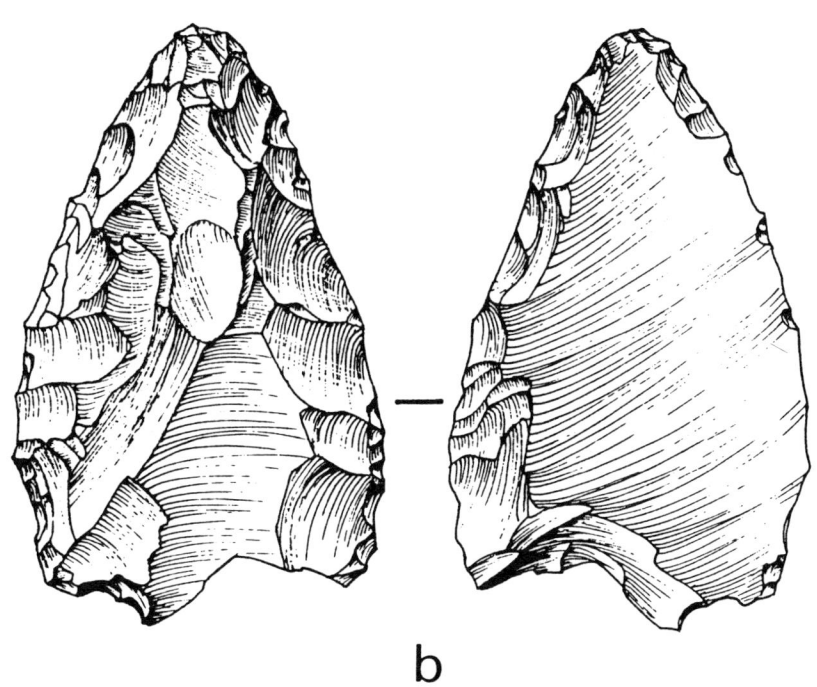

Figure 4.5. Foliates. a: foliate point; b: foliate point with retouched base.

References Cited

Bastin, B., Lévêque, F., and L. Pradel
    1976 Mise en évidence de spectres polliniques interstadiaires entre le Moustérien et le Périgordien ancien de la grotte des Cottés (Vienne). *Compte Rendu de l'Académie des Sciences de Paris* 282(D):1261-1264.

Guilbaud, M.
    1985 Elaboration d'une Méthode d'Analyse pour les Produits de Débitage en Typologie Analytique et son Application à quelques Industries des Gisements de Saint-Césaire (Charente-Maritime) et de Quinçay (Vienne). Unpublished Ph.D. dissertation, Museum National d'Histoire Naturelle, Université de Paris VI.
    1987 Elaboration d'un cadre morphotechnique par l'étude du débitage en typologie analytique des gisements de Saint-Césaire (Charente-Maritime) et de Quinçay (Vienne). In *Préhistoire de Poitou-Charentes, Problèmes Actuels*, Editions du Comité des Travaux Historiques et Scientifiques, Actes du 111ème Congrès National des Sociétés Savantes (1986, Poitiers), pp. 103-113, Paris.

Henri-Martin, G.
    1962 Le niveau de Châtelperron de La Quina (Charente). *Bulletin de la Société Préhistorique Française* 58(11-12):796-808.

Laplace, G.
    1966 *Recherches sur l'origine et l'évolution des complexes leptolithiques*. Ecole française de Rome, Supplément 4. Editions de Boccage, Paris.
    1972 La typologie analytique et structurale. Base rationnelle d'étude des industries lithiques et osseuses. In *Banques de données archéologiques*, Colloques Nationaux du CNRS 932:91-143, Marseille.
    1985-7 Un exemple de nouvelle écriture de la grille typologique. *Dialektiké, Cahiers de Typologie Analytique*, Centre de Palethnologie Stratigraphique "ERURI":16-21, Pau.

Lévêque, F.
    1967 Analyses pédologiques et parapédologiques appliquées à l'étude des gisements préhistoriques. Gatzarria (Suhare, Basses-Pyrénées), La Quina (Gardes, Charente). Dipôme d'Etudes Approfondies, unpublished thesis, Université de Poitiers.
    1979 Note à propos de trois gisements castelperroniens de Poitou-Charentes. *Dialektiké, Cahiers de Typologie Analytique*, Centre de Palethnologie Stratigraphique "ERURI":25-40, Pau.
    1989a L'homme de Saint-Césaire: sa place dans le Castelperronien de Poitou-Charentes. In *L'Homme de Néandertal*, Vol.7:L'Extinction, edited by M. Otte, pp. 99-108. Etudes et Recherches Archéologiques de l'Université de Liège 34, Liège.
    1989b Les débuts du Paléolithique supérieur en Poitou-Charentes. *Le Temps de la Préhistoire* I-Les Millénaires de la Préhistoire, 23ème Congrès Préhistorique de France:264-268, Dijon.
    1991 Les débuts du Paléolithiqiue supérieur. *Les Archéologiques de Poitou-Charentes* 1991. Bilan et perspectives sur la recherche régionale, edited by the Service de l'Archéologie, Direction Regionale des Affaires Culturelles de Poitou-Charentes et Association desArchéologues de Poitou Charentes, Poitiers:17-24.

Lévêque, F., and J. C. Miskovsky
    1983 Le Castelperronien dans son environnement géologique. Essai de synthèse à partir de l'étude lithostratigraphique du remplissage de la grotte de la Grande Roche de la Plématrie (Quinçay-Vienne) et d'autres dépôts actuellement mis au jour. *L'Anthropologie* 87(3):369-391.

    1987 Les apports de la sédimentologie dans l'étude des gisements castelperroniens de Quinçay (Vienne) et de Saint-Césaire (Charente-Maritime). In *Préhistoire de Poitou-Charentes, Problèmes Actuels*, Editions du Comité des Travaux Historiques et Scientifiques, Actes du 111ème Congrès National des Sociétés Savantes (1986, Poitiers), pp. 99-102, Paris.

Lévêque, F., N. Mercier, H. Valladas, and B. Vandermeersch
    1992 Saint-Césaire: le dernier néandertalien. *La Recherche* 239(23):112-113.

Lévêque, F., and B. Vandermeersch
    1980 Découverte de restes humains dans un niveau castelperronien à Saint-Césaire (Charente-Maritime). *Compte Rendu de l'Académie des Sciences de Paris* 291:187-189.
    1981 Le Néandertalien de Saint-Césaire. *La Recherche* 119(12):242-244.

Livache, M.
    1989 La typologie analytique. Une dialectique. In *Le Temps de la Préhistoire*, Vol. 1, La Découverte du Temps. Succession des Systèmes Appliqués. Société Préhistorique Française et Editions Archeologia, Dijon.

Pradel, L.
    1961 La grotte des Cottés, Saint-Pierre de Maillé (Vienne). *L'Anthropologie* 65(3-4):229-270.

Vandermeersch, B.
    1984 A propos de la découverte du squelette néandertalien de Saint-Césaire. *Bulletin et Mémoires de la Société d'Anthropologie de Paris* 1(XIV):191-196.

Vilain, R.
    1966 Le gisement de Sous-Balme à Culoz dans l'Ain et ses industries microlithiques. Diplôme d'Etudes Supérieures, Department of Geology, Université de Lyon.

5

Le Débitage du Niveau Supérieur Castelperronien à Saint-Césaire

Approches Méthodologiques et Implications pour La Transition Paléolithique Moyen à Supérieur

Michel Guilbaud

Les observations nous ont conduit, pour l'étude technologique présentée ici, à discerner explicitement deux aspects essentiels du travail de la pierre: l'aspect physique et l'aspect psychique. Cette distinction permet de nuancer et d'affiner l'analyse par la recherche d'une part des thèmes opératoires propres au Castelperronien de Saint-Césaire, et d'autre part des liens dans cette industrie entre des conceptions technologiques à priori fondamentalement différentes les unes des autres: les "conceptions moustériennes" du débitage et les conceptions laminaires qui caractérisent le Paléolithique supérieur. Malgré l'influence incontestable des techniques laminaires, ce Castelperronien est technologiquement "archaïque" car les thèmes "moustéroides" sont dominants, et les caractères propres au Paléolithique supérieur n'atteignent pas la spécialisation aurignacienne ou gravettienne. La présence d'un néandertalien dans ce niveau pourrait alors être directement liée à l'aspect "moustéroide" très marqué de cet ensemble lithique.

La comparaison sommaire du Castelperronien de Saint-Césaire avec celui des Tambourets (zone 3) et celui du niveau EN de Quinçay indique clairement des tendances technologiques très différentes d'une industrie à l'autre. Cela signifie qu'il n'y a pas un Castelperronien unique mais que, comme l'ont déjà montré les travaux de G. Laplace (1958) et ceux de F. Lévêque (1979), la notion de Castelperronien se compose de plusieurs éléments allant d'ensembles à caractères archaïques (comme à Saint-Césaire) à des industries plus "avancées" dans la voie du Paléolithique supérieur, comme à Quinçay ou aux Tambourets.

Ces résultats sont peut-être l'indice d'une évolution à partir d'une souche ancienne (Castelperronien de "type Saint-Césaire") mais ils peuvent tout aussi bien exprimer des activités fonctionnelles différentes d'un même système culturel (Binford et Binford 1966; S. Binford 1972).

Debitage from the Upper Castelperronian Level at Saint-Césaire

Methodological Approaches and Implications for the Transition from Middle to Upper Paleolithic

Michel Guilbaud

This study is an introduction to the by-products of reduction from the upper Castelperronian level (EJOP superior), Saint-Césaire. Only a few essential links with the findings from the study of retouched tools will be made here. A complete, in-depth examination of the entire data set, including refitting studies, is in progress. Nevertheless preliminary results enable the presentation of a methodological approach that requires a renewal of the basic technological elements used in studying the transition from Middle to Upper Paleolithic.

Two main goals guide this research: first, to determine the character of the technological system of EJOP superior as clearly as possible through observation of the archaeological materials, and second, to place this system within the framework of the transition, to get a better grasp of the concept of the Castelperronian from the standpoint of debitage. Since the beginning of my research on Saint-Césaire, I have focused on relationships between lithic objects and on understanding the role of a number of pieces that would usually be considered atypical or uncharacteristic. This strategy was influenced by the work of Carbonell and his research team (Carbonell 1985; Carbonell, Guilbaud, and Mora 1983-1984, 1985; Carbonell et al. 1988) and gradually led to the use of a vocabulary and a methodology designed for technological analysis of the evolution from Middle to Upper Paleolithic (Guilbaud 1985; Backer and Guilbaud 1989).

The Reduction Field

Observations on the debitage from Saint-Césaire have led me to discern explicitly two aspects of reality: the physical aspect and the psychic aspect. This means simply that material objects and physically definable events (the working of siliceous rock, for example) are distinct from the images, concepts, ideas, and intentions involved in the manufacture and utilization of prehistoric tools. The interaction between the memory of the knapper and his current stone-working activities, influenced by the social and natural environment, has prompted the concept of reduction field.[1] From pieces of an industry we may attempt to reconstitute physical events, strictly ordered through time into reduction sequences (the manufacture and use of objects), while noting the complex influence of morphological and technical conceptual associations.

For example, at Saint-Césaire, products of Castelperronian core reduction often incorporate conceptual elements of form and technique commonly associated with endscraper, biface, or burin manufacture. Some objects combine the use of such different technical concepts that these objects would ordinarily be classified as atypical and would therefore be excluded.

Distinctions made between types of objects in a classical typology are in a certain sense attempts to reconstruct the conceptual models that guide the production of prehistoric tools. This endeavor is only partly rewarding, because typology often tries to make industries conform to a preestablished list of general types.[2] The concept of reduction field attempts to create a more balanced view rather than a generalizing theory of artifacts, since it does not systematize normative, object types but rather, seeks the conceptual themes appropriate to a particular industry:[3] these themes will be referred to as morphotechnic themes or reduction themes.

Figure 5.1 is a schematic illustration of the primary elements of the reduction field that can be reconstituted for level EJOP superior. The physical aspect, organized through time and space (natural environment) by discrete actions and objects into reduction sequences, is represented by the white dots connected to one another. Each white dot symbolizes a material object before or after an elementary action (removal of a flake). The psychic aspect is the hatched area or

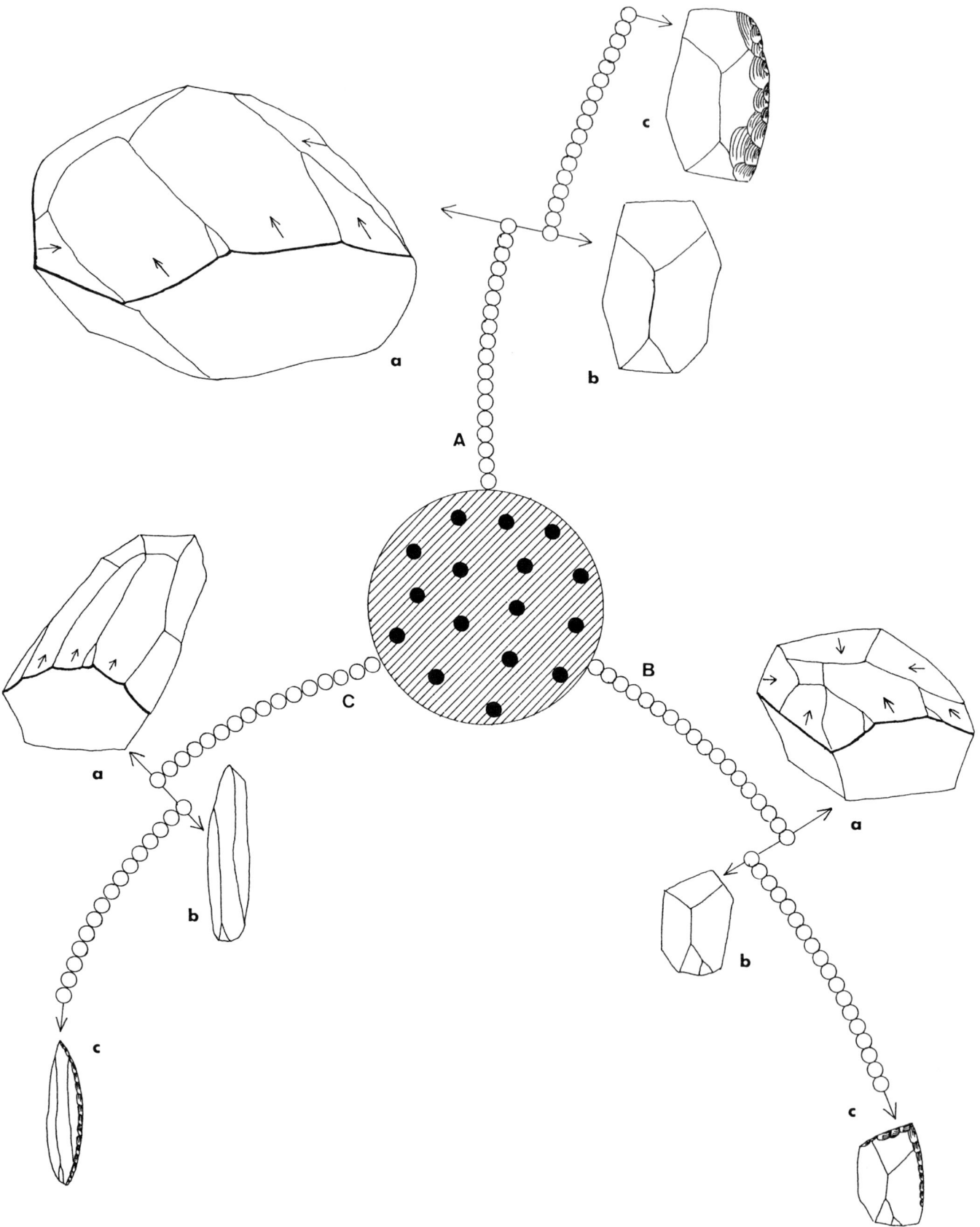

Figure 5.1. Model of reduction process in EJOP superior, the Castelperronian level, showing the physical (white dots) and psychic (black dots) domains.

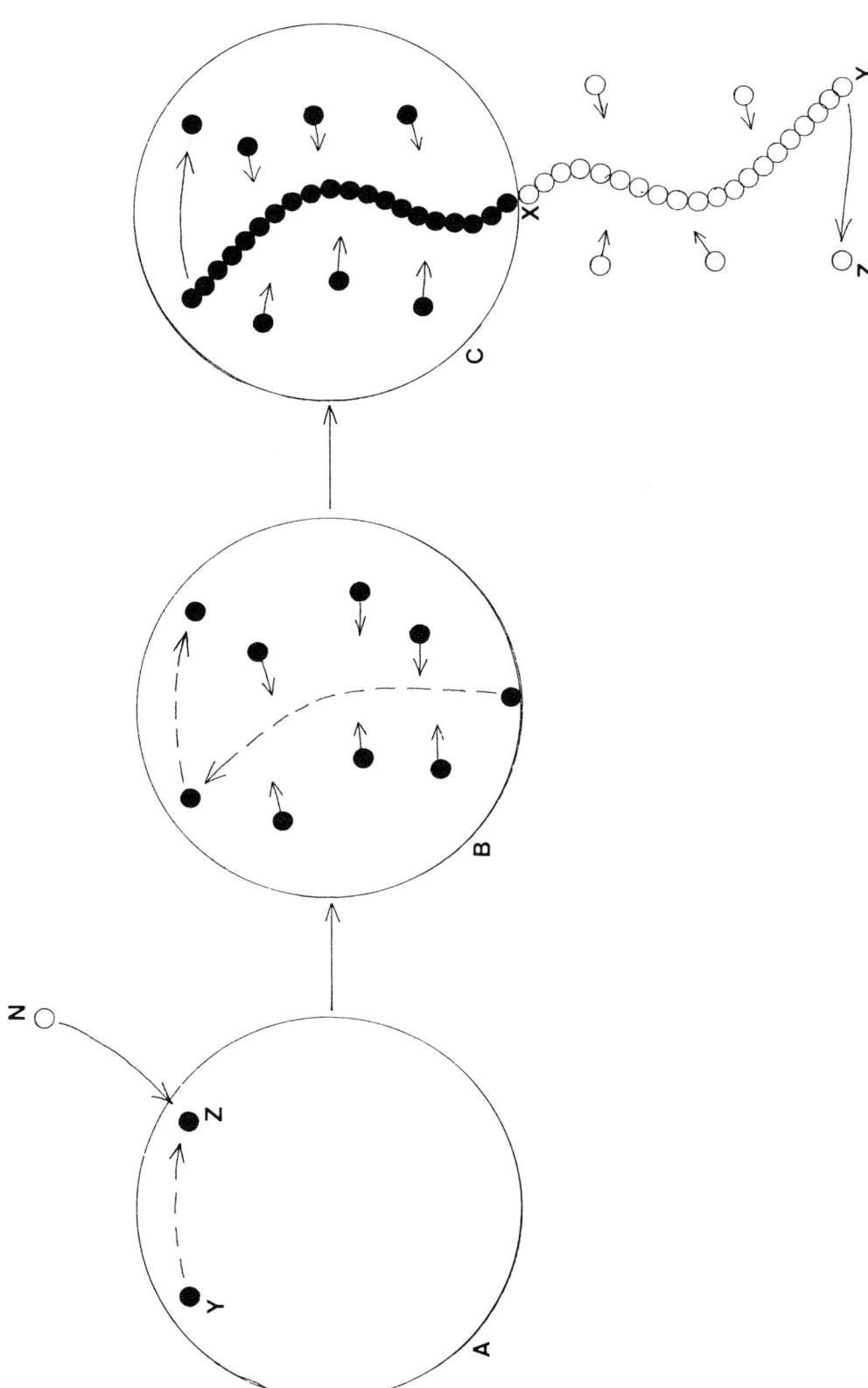

Figure 5.2. Model sequence illustrating the concept of reduction field.

reduction center. It groups the conceptual technological and morphological associations observed on objects. These associations can belong to one or several prehistoric knappers and are, naturally, "filtered" by our own knowledge and modern-day representations of reality. This subjectivity is always present in any typology or technological approach, whenever we identify objects, analyze them, or perform experiments.

The black dots in Figure 5.1 represent conceptual reduction themes found in EJOP superior, through observation (detailed in Figure 5.4). These themes approach "pure" morphotechnic elements and serve as guideposts in defining what we can learn about the technical potential of this industry. Observation shows that each object from EJOP superior approximates, to varying degrees and in different ways, a particular reduction theme or a combination of several conceptual themes.[4] The immediate consequence is that an object can no longer be analyzed on its own, as a simple material and statistical unit. A complete study must seek the internal characteristics of each piece in light of its particular links with all the other objects of the industry under study.

Interaction among several conceptual themes on many of the pieces from level EJOP superior supports the view that reduction sequences are not only guided by a linear impulse imprinted by a precise objective, but also that they are permanently under the influence of the psycho-physical context of the moment. This context can manifest itself by a change in objectives during stone working, by constraints of the raw material or other environmental aspects, by an accident or error in knapping, by the conscious or unconscious influence of psycho-physical factors in the social environment, and so on. For example, faced with a particular technical difficulty, a knapper may resort to certain reduction themes held in memory or passed on by a person of his/her entourage.

Figure 5.2 illustrates the concept of the reduction field, where two pressures (psychic and physical) can be seen to influence a technological sequence. The natural environment, factor N, puts constraints on an individual who conceives of an objective Z to be accomplished. This goal cannot be achieved without first manufacturing object Y (Figure 5.2A). To this end, the individual conceives of a particular reduction sequence (a mental reduction sequence shown in the figure as a broken line), with more or less precision, with the help of the different morphotechnic themes (black dots with arrows) in his/her memory: this is the phase of predetermination (Figure 5.2B). The raw material X is consequently chosen, and the stone knapper begins working toward goals Y and Z in a linear predetermined fashion (Figure 5.2C: the physical reduction sequence is represented as white dots; its perception and mental representation by the knapper are indicated as black dots). Throughout the work, superimposed on the linear impulse is pressure from the psychic (black dots with arrows) and physical (white dots with arrows) context. From general experimental knowledge, it can be stated that raw material constraints and technical difficulties will orient the stone worker towards several alternative solutions. In this way, a sort of competition begins between the reduction themes in memory (black dots with arrows), which are acquired through experience and enable the knapper to find and choose the best solution to technical problems being posed. For example, learning the Levallois technique can serve directly or indirectly, depending on the situation, to thin a biface by removal of wide flakes. It is also possible that by economizing or taking advantage of an opportunity relating to raw material economy might result in an object that reflects several technical concepts that would otherwise be independent,[5] involving several themes because the object served more than one function.

It is therefore not surprising to find different attributes associated on a single object. Artifacts that don't appear characteristic, classically referred to as "atypical," can hold important information on the links between themes of a lithic series. The interaction of predetermination factors, memorized reduction themes, and materials used for working, on the one hand, versus the objective to be achieved on the other, seems to be one of the major causes of the multiple interactions observed not only on Castelperronian artifacts from Saint-Césaire, but also on industries from diverse periods that I have thus far had the opportunity to study.

Technology of Level EJOP Superior

Reduction Sequences

During my research I examined every artifact from the level and within time constraints have conjoined as many pieces as possible to reconstruct as many reduction chains as possible.[6] From single observations, when all possible theoretical conjoins are taken into account, three groups of fragmentary reduction sequences have been detected (Figure 5.1A, B, and C). The first group (A sequence) starts with a large core (about 10 to 15 cm in length; Aa), and yields large flakes with tapered edges (Ab) or large, flat scrapers with retouch that often tends to be invasive (Ac). These flakes and scrapers exceed 6 cm in length. (Note that the cores themselves are not found in level EJOP superior.) The second group (B sequence)

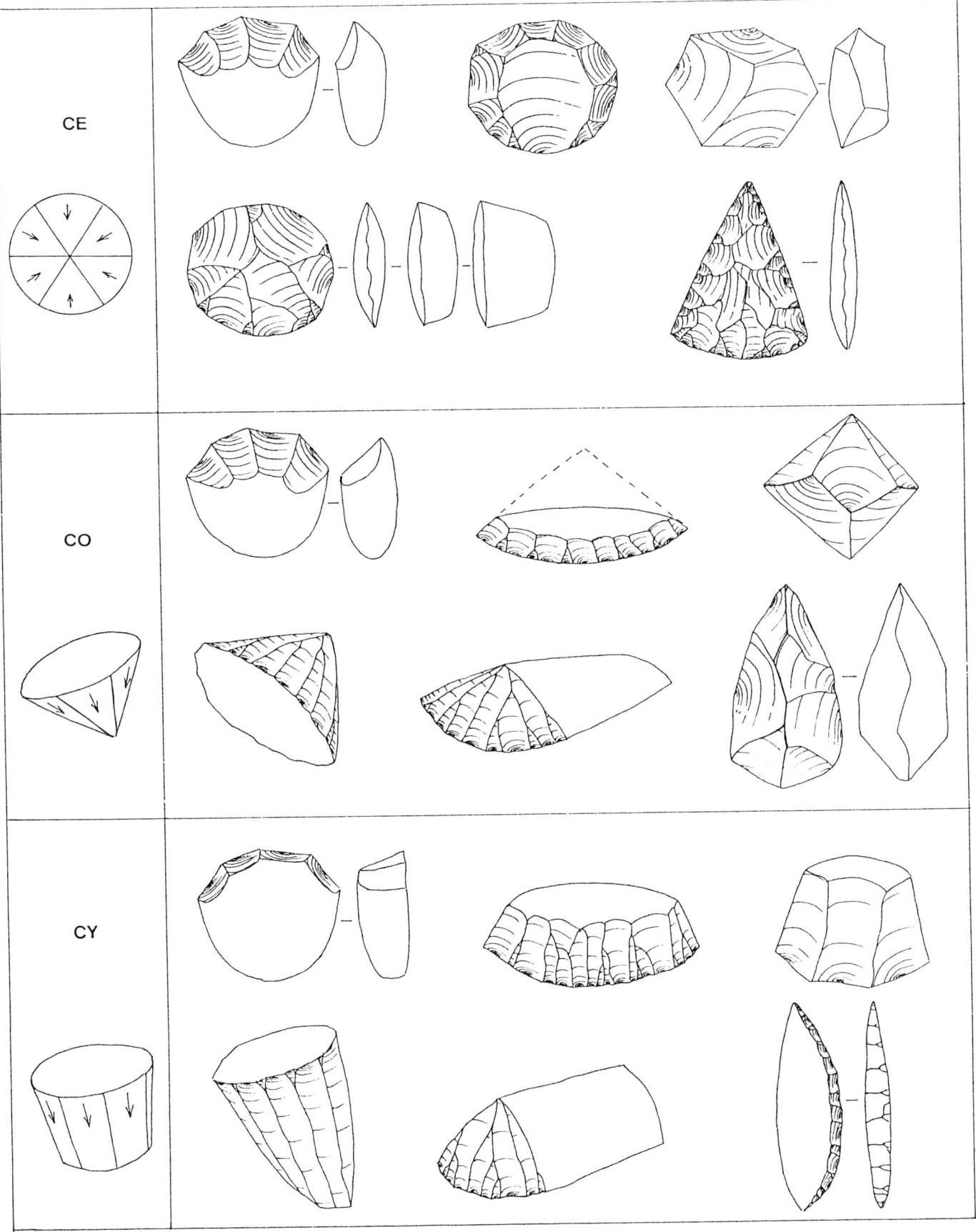

Figure 5.3. Three elementary reduction sequences: centripetal (CE), conical (CO), and cylindrial (CY). A few examples (tools or cores) illustrate each of these different reduction modes.

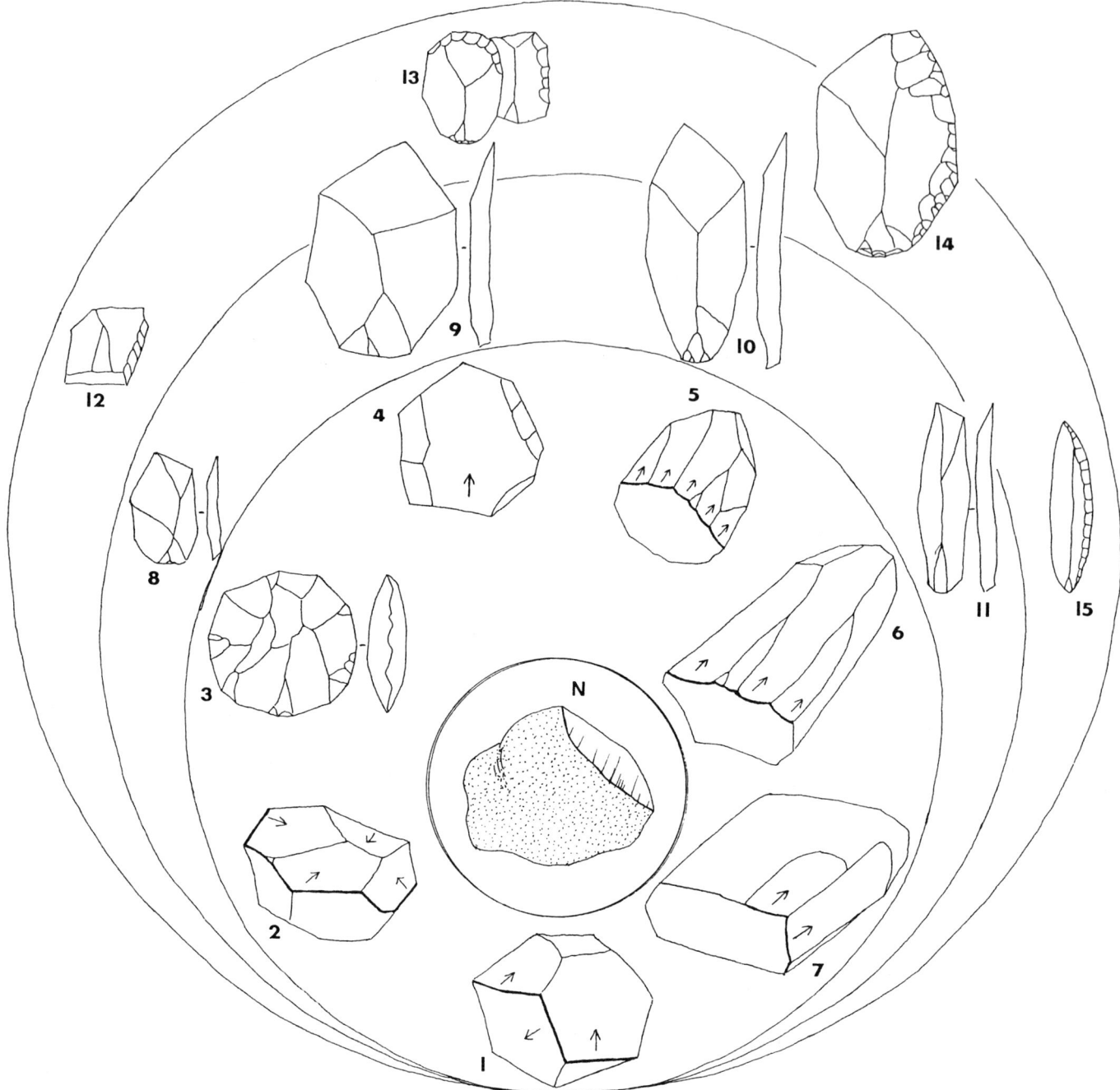

Figure 5.4. The reduction center of level EJOP superior with its sixteen reduction themes (theme N to theme 15): these themes correspond to the black dots in Figure 5.1 model.

includes short flakes of small dimensions (between 2 and 6 cm; Bb) that may be differentially fashioned into scrapers, denticulates, becs, steeply retouched tools, or endscrapers (Bc); sometimes the retouch is summary and accompanied by breaks. Whether or not these breaks were the result of intentional, human action remains to be verified. Some of these pieces could have been broken by natural crushing.

The third group (C sequence) leads to the manufacture of points or backed blades (Cc) generally typical of the Castelperronian. These pieces, as well as certain large flakes and scrapers from the A sequence, are sometimes broken too, just as many B sequence materials are. Backed points and backed blades are made on blade blanks (Cb) that come from cores reduced in a cylindrical manner (CY in Figure 5.3).[7] These cores can be elongated or short; the reduction is cylindrical and longitudinal in the case of elongated cores (Ca in Figure 5.1), or cylindrical in the case of short cores. B sequence tools and unretouched flakes are apparently most often made by cen-

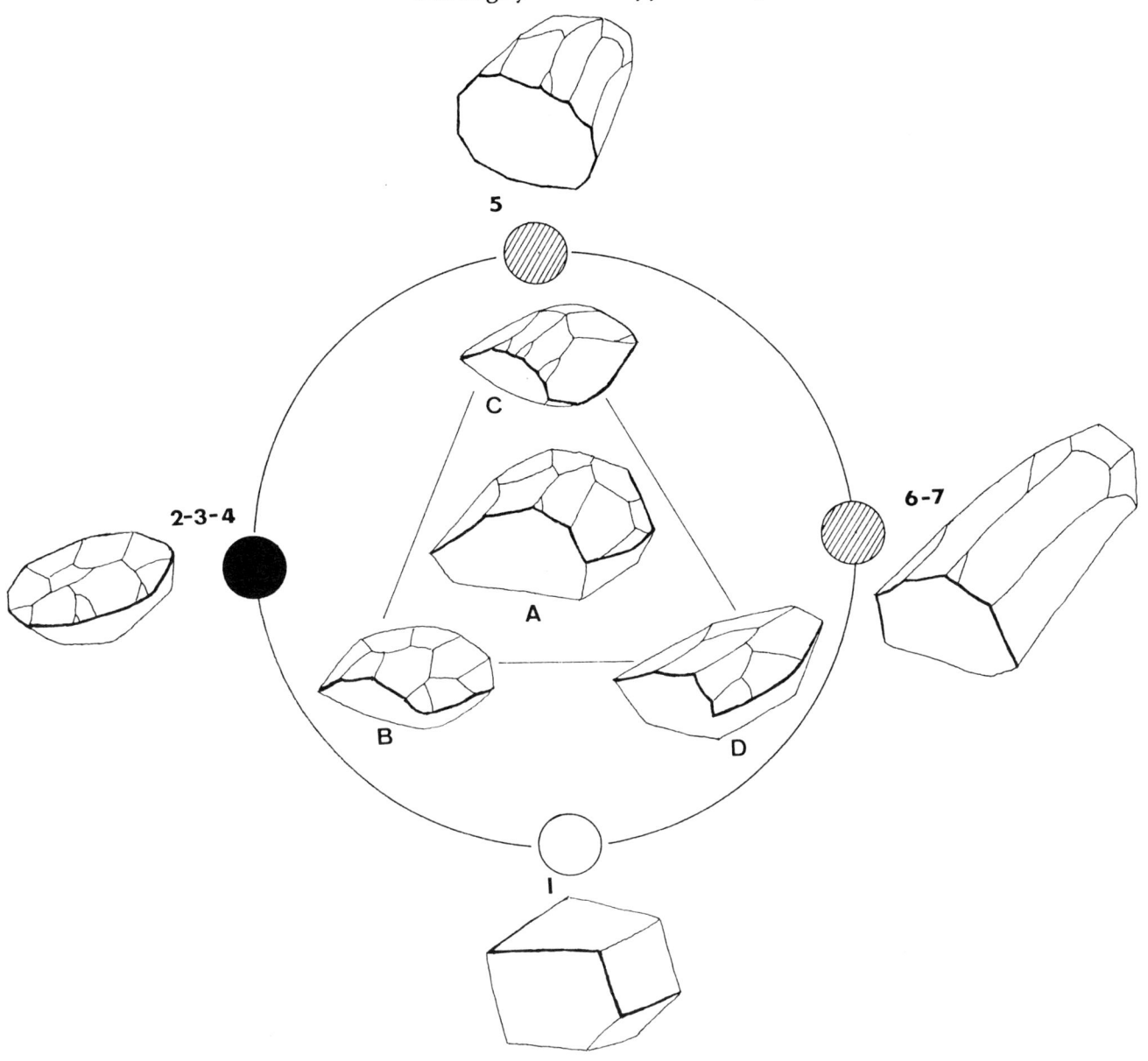

Figure 5.5. Quantitative estimate of the dominant themes 1 to 7 in level EJOP superior. Black blob: theme present in high frequencies; hatched blob: theme present in medium frequencies; white blob: theme present in low frequencies. A, B, C, D: different forms of theme 0.

tripetal or undifferentiated reduction of short cores (Ba in Figure 5.1). As for the big flakes and scrapers, they probably correspond to a flat or centripetal (rarely cylindrical) reduction mode (Aa in Figure 5.1). These three groups of reduction sequences reflect three major intentions: manufacturing large, flat, wide tools with a maximum of cutting edge; producing small, short retouched tools of different shapes; and fashioning narrow, more or less slender forms with cutting edges opposite partial backs with steep retouch.

Reduction Themes

During the exhaustive analysis of reduction sequences and general examination of the industry as a whole, 16 main reduction themes were noted. Figure 5.4 orders these themes into four levels from the smallest to the largest circle: natural raw materials, cores, unretouched flakes, and differentiated, retouched forms.

Raw Material and Cores

The raw material at Saint-Césaire (theme N) consists of nodules of brown and black chert which are abundant in the vicinity of the site. Although we do not know the exact locations of sources of chert available in the past, we are certain that prehistoric humans supplied themselves at least in large part with material from close by the site. Today, flint can

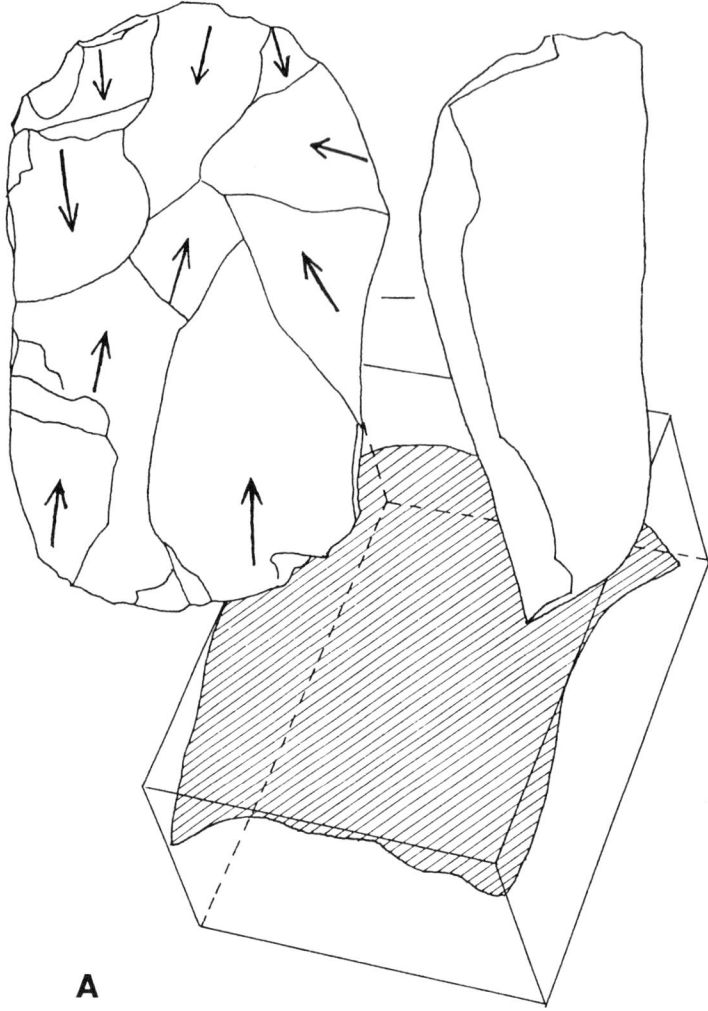

Figure 5.6 A, B, C. Three examples of conceptual associations on cores of level EJOP superior

be found just above the cliff overhanging the rockshelter deposit.

The dimensions of the 202 cores recovered from level EJOP vary mostly between 4 and 8 cm. These cores have enabled the characterization of seven reduction themes. Theme 1 represents angular, chunky forms and is due to knapping techniques that tend to be multidirectional; negative removals are wide and overlap the edge of the core. With theme 2, the overall shape becomes flatter relative to cores in theme 1, and knapping is organized around the centripetal technique; removals are rather wide and sometimes overlapping, and the edge of the platform is quite sinuous. Theme 3 accentuates the centripetal character of theme 2 by way of the discoidal technique; here the flake scars are closely spaced and rarely overlapping, corresponding to the extraction of narrow flakes. With themes 4 and 5 we see a disruption of the balance described above: theme 4 consists of a large scar removed by Levallois technique or not, and in theme 5 the centripetal technique is replaced by a cylindrical reduction mode that is at times laminary, and some of the cores become chunkier. Theme 6 reflects an elongation of volume and a longitudinal, sometimes laminary or slightly laminary reduction of the core. Theme 7, rather rare at Saint-Césaire, is the concept of blade removals from the edge of flat blanks; this technique is close to that used to produce burins.

In order to simplify observations and to facilitate subsequent comparative work, themes 2, 3, and 4 are grouped on the one hand, and 6 and 7 on the other, to form two synthetic themes, each with common traits: theme 2-3-4 is a centripetal conception on a flattish core, and theme 6-7 represents blade reduction on an elongated core or on the edge of a thinned blank. As mentioned above, these themes do not have the same meaning as types in the classic sense. They represent conceptual elements that can occur together to differing degrees. That is, an object can be tied to a single theme, or it can combine two or more themes. As a

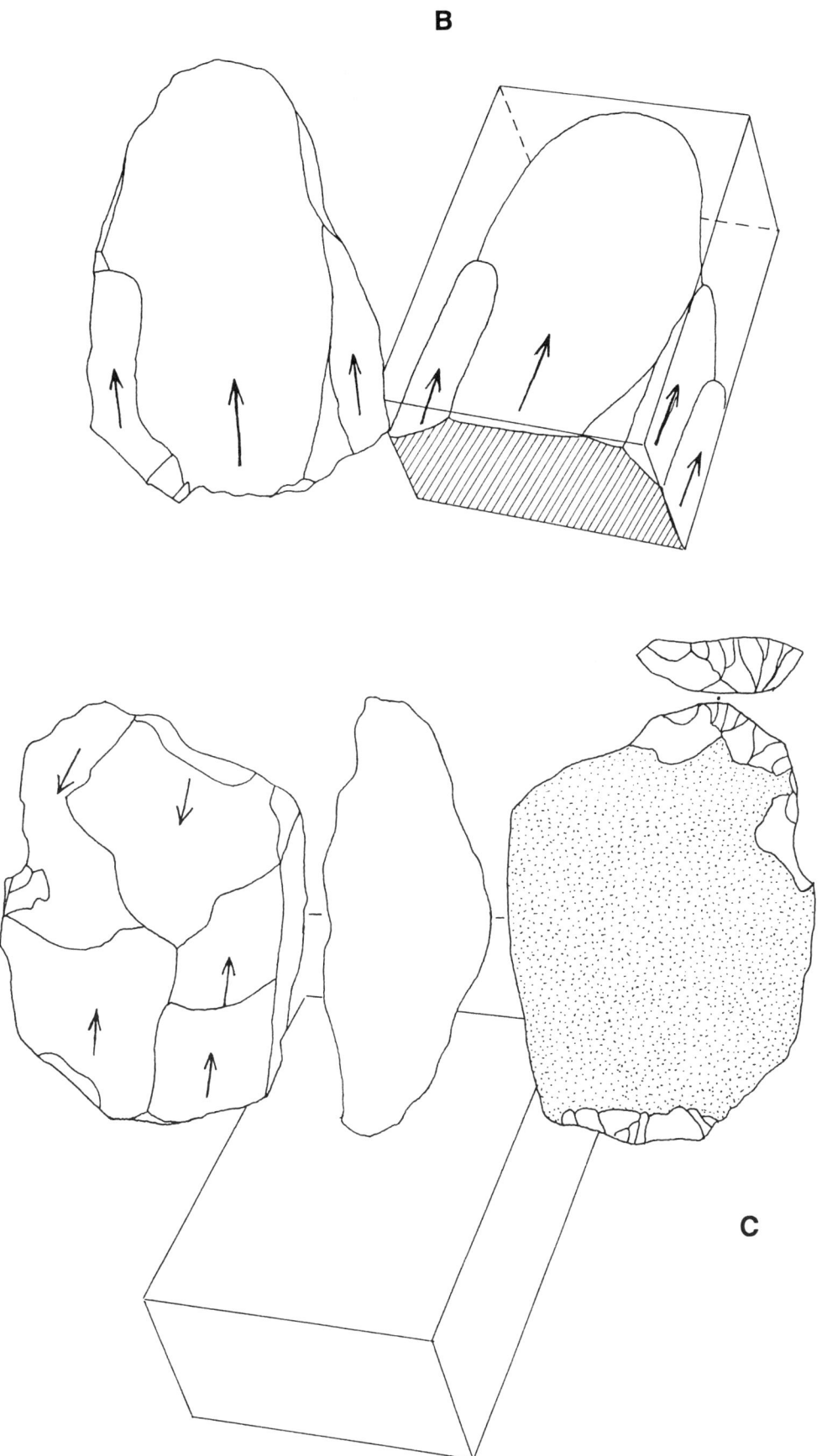

consequence, the resulting theme counts are different from type list counts. A full exposition of this quantification and ensuing statistical analysis is outside of the scope of this article; in my view, it is enough that these preliminary results provide a simple estimate (low, medium, and high) of the number of dominant themes represented on each object.

Figure 5.5 shows high frequencies of theme 2-3-4 (approximately 60%), medium frequencies of themes 5 (approximately 20%) and 6-7 (approximately 15%), and low frequencies of theme 1 (approximately 5%). The technique in level EJOP superior oscillates, therefore, between two poles: a heavily centripetal pole, generally characteristic of many Mousterian industries, and a cylindrical pole that is quite bladey with short or elongated cores, suggestive of the Upper Paleolithic. The influence of theme 2-3-4 appears to intervene in groups of reduction sequences A and B (Figure 5.1), while themes 5 and 6-7, in their pure form, appear more specific to the manufacture of backed points and blades (C reduction sequence, Figure 5.1). A very large number of objects combines these two conceptual extremes to differing degrees. Many of these composite objects form a guidepost equidistant to all others that I call theme 0, the central theme. These relatively undifferentiated objects combine technical elements common to two, three or all the themes seen in this industry. Figure 5.5A, B, C and D show some variations of theme 0. Its major characteristics are a twisted platform edge and a centripetal-cylindrical aspect (Guilbaud 1985).

Many other conceptual associations can be found in addition to theme 0. For example, the theme illustrated in Figure 5.6A combines the flattening of the blank and the preferential removal scar of theme 4 with the elongation and the cylindrical tendency of theme 6. Figure 5.6B superimposes theme 2 (centripetal), theme 4 (one large removal), and theme 6 (elongation of the blank, associated with a slightly cylindrical tendency in the reduction mode). Figure 5.6C combines conceptual themes 4 and 6, and it is interesting to note that the manufacture of an endscraper (theme 13) can serve as the preparation of a striking platform for a series of removals. We therefore see a combination of themes, each one belonging in its "pure" form to different technical and probably functional choices.

Unretouched Flakes and Retouched Pieces

For the purposes of this study, flakes measuring more than 2 cm (maximum length) were selected. The 4770 unretouched flakes (> 2 cm) are largely short and thin and when whole, have a high proportion of cutting edge (theme 8). Among them, faceted platforms and centripetal technique appear in relatively high frequencies and fit in well with the importance of theme 2-3-4 among the cores. The Levallois technique *sensu stricto* is present, but it remains to be seen what the influence and the exact limits of the Levallois concept really are, and to what measure it melds with the other reduction themes, because it seems very difficult, in many cases, to determine whether a flake is Levallois or not. As far as the cores are concerned, for the time being it can only be said that theme 4, in its typical Levallois form (marked preparation of the Levallois surface), represents approximately 5% of themes in level EJOP superior.

Theme 8 is associated with small or medium-sized flakes (<6 cm). Other flakes can measure from 6 to 14 cm (theme 9), and some of these tend to be bladelike (theme 10). These large flakes (approximately 2% of flakes and blades) belong to the A group of reduction themes and, when retouched, correspond to the large simple, double, and convergent scrapers (theme 14).

True blades (theme 11), relatively infrequent in the Castelperronian of Saint-Césaire, are of modest dimensions (mostly between 4 and 6 cm). In general, the technique of blade reduction is not very systematic. Some pieces, however, show a high degree of systemization but are much less spectacular than Aurignacian or Gravettian industries. Indicators of both hard- and soft-hammer percussion are present on flakes and blades.

Figure 5.4 shows the principal themes of retouched pieces: short, broken pieces with simple or steep retouch (theme 12) (intentional or natural retouch and breaks); various short or medium- sized tools of different shapes (scrapers, denticulates, points, becs, endscrapers, and so on) (theme 13); the one biface found in the level; large scrapers with flat or simple retouch (theme 14); and finally backed points and blades (theme 15). The study of the retouched pieces was done by Lévêque (this volume). Themes 12 (of questionable anthropic origin) and 13 are part of the B reduction sequence, theme 14 is part of the A sequence, and theme 15 is part of the C sequence.

Discussion

Preliminary results of technological analysis undeniably point to the archaic character of the Castelperronian at Saint-Césaire—high frequencies of Mousteroid themes, moderate differentiation of themes that can be more or less ascribed to the Upper Paleolithic (themes 5, 6 and 7 do not reach the degree of specialization observed for the Aurignacian or the Gravettian), and the limited development of systematic blade production.

The use of reduction themes as a research tool, explicitly taking into account the conceptual aspect of technology, enables the enumeration and explication of links between different reduction techniques present in the Castelperronian assemblage from Saint-Césaire.

Theme 0, for example, indicates a possible relationship between "Mousteroid" themes and themes common to the Upper Paleolithic, but none of the results of this analysis prove that level EJOP superior, stratigraphically very distinct, does not contain the results of successive, different activities that spanned several centuries, even millennia (Backer, this volume). This discussion implies that the concept of reduction field, specific to a particular industry, can include a time factor of some magnitude and that it is associated with several generations or relatively distinct human groups.

A detailed study of interaction between themes and between reduction sequences is currently being integrated with artifact spatial distributions, with a view to discerning possible techno-spatial patterns in the assemblage from EJOP superior.

A Research Perspective on the Transition from Middle to Upper Paleolithic

Quadripolar Orientation

For a clearer picture of the evolutionary/functional variability of the Castelperronian, some general technological orientations should be outlined that serve as guideposts throughout the Paleolithic. Four main poles that appear to be important throughout prehistory have been chosen in an attempt to place the Castelperronian of Saint-Césaire in the framework of the transition from Middle to Upper Paleolithic (Guilbaud 1985): pole 1 (chunky forms), pole 2 (flat or thin forms), pole 3 (elongated forms), and pole 4 (curved forms and rounded ends) (Figure 5.7).[8]

It is quite clear that many intermediary cases can be found among these four main orientations, and often an industry articulates several components of two, three, or all four poles. A more detailed presentation of the quadripole is beyond the scope of this article because it would require a consideration of ancient chopper industries as well as some highly specialized industries of the Neolithic or Paleoindian periods. The elements indicated in Note 8 suffice to establish simple comparisons in studying the technological transition from Middle to Upper Paleolithic.

A Brief Comparative Study

Figure 5.8 situates three different Castelperronian assemblages based on the quantitative estimates derived above of themes in their generic form: level EJOP superior at Saint-Césaire, Zone 3 at Les Tambourets,[9] and level EN at Quinçay.[10] Although the importance of the "Mousteroid" theme 2-3-4 is notable at Saint-Césaire, at Les Tambourets and at Quinçay this theme is rare or less characteristic. On the other hand, theme 5 is very frequent at Les Tambourets and theme 6-7 largely predominates at Quinçay. At Les Tambourets, the central theme (theme 0) is very frequent, enabling more detailed observation than at Saint-Césaire of similarities between themes.

If these attributes are examined in light of quadripolar orientation, each of the Castelperronian industries is oriented around a different pole: Saint-Césaire clearly tends towards poles 1 and 2 ("Mousteroid" themes 2, 3, and 4 are present in high frequencies), Les Tambourets towards pole 4 (with theme 5 present in high frequencies and varying forms), and Quinçay towards pole 3 (with predominant themes 6 and 7). The notion of Castelperronian, therefore, encapsulates at least three different technological designs. One is directed towards the manufacture of thin, tapered flakes; the second concentrates on and around theme 0, using the cylindrical reduction mode with rounded ends, proper to the Aurignacian; and the third consists of an enhanced production of rectilinear, extremely well streamlined blades. The orientation of technology at Les Tambourets towards pole 4 is reinforced by the presence among the tools of some well-differentiated endscrapers and some pieces with partially rounded or subcircular ends, sometimes obtained by steep or semi-steep removals. As Meroc and Bricker indicate, "the endscrapers are the most important tool class at Les Tambourets," "scrapers evoking the Mousterian are rare" (1984:62) and "the whole foliate biface ... is an unusual object" (1984:64).

Figure 5.8 translates the polarity of the three Castelperronian assemblages into a quadripolar space delineated by four specialized industries: the Denticulate Mousterian of level EGPF at Saint-Césaire (with many polyhedrons, many forms that are close to theme 2, and thick, short, overlapping flakes); a Mousterian assemblage with systematized reduction of short, thin flakes on flat blanks (a very common technique during the Middle Paleolithic and especially in some assemblages of the Mousterian of Acheulean Tradition); a Gravettian like the one from level D at La Ferrassie (with straight, very streamlined blades and forms similar to themes 6 and 7);[11] and finally an Aurignacian like the early Aurignacian of level EJF at Saint-Césaire (with forms with rounded ends, and curved, slender blades). These four specialized industries represent poles 1 through 4, respectively (in their differentiated form).

Technologically, therefore, the Castelperronian assemblages of Saint-Césaire, of Les Tambourets, and of Quinçay (level EN) had a similar polar orientation, respectively, as a Mousterian with thin flakes (and to a certain extent, as a Mousterian like the one from level EGPF), as an Aurignacian like the early Aurignacian of Saint-Césaire, and as a Gravettian like that of La

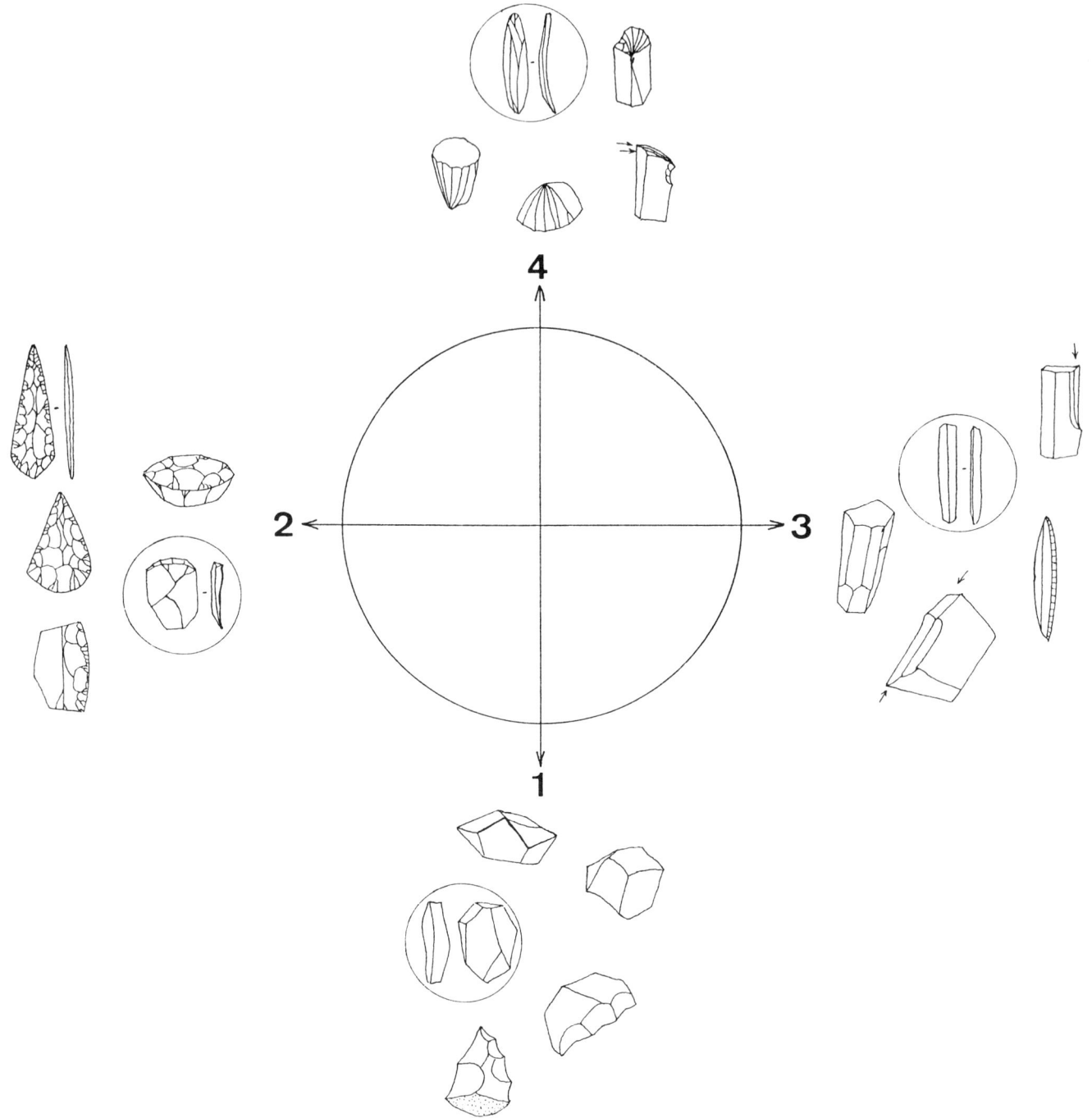

Figure 5.7. Quadripolar orientation. Pole 1: chunky forms; Pole 2: flat or thin forms; Pole 3: elongated forms; Pole 4: curved forms with rounded ends.

Ferrassie (level D), though the three former assemblages do not display the degree of specialization of the three latter ones.[12] For example, at Les Tambourets, curved blade reduction typical of the Aurignacian is not very differentiated at all, and rounded ends, though very abundant, are often mixed with other reduction themes (theme 0). In addition, in level EN at Quincay, the streamlining and slender quality of the blades do not often reach the specialization of the Gravettian. As for the Castelperronian of Saint-Césaire, themes 0, 5, and 6-7 temper the influence of the "pure" themes from poles 1 and 2. This lack of specialization corroborates the central, relatively undifferentiated position of the Castelperronian in Figure 5.8 as compared to the more specialized industries represented by the four poles.[13]

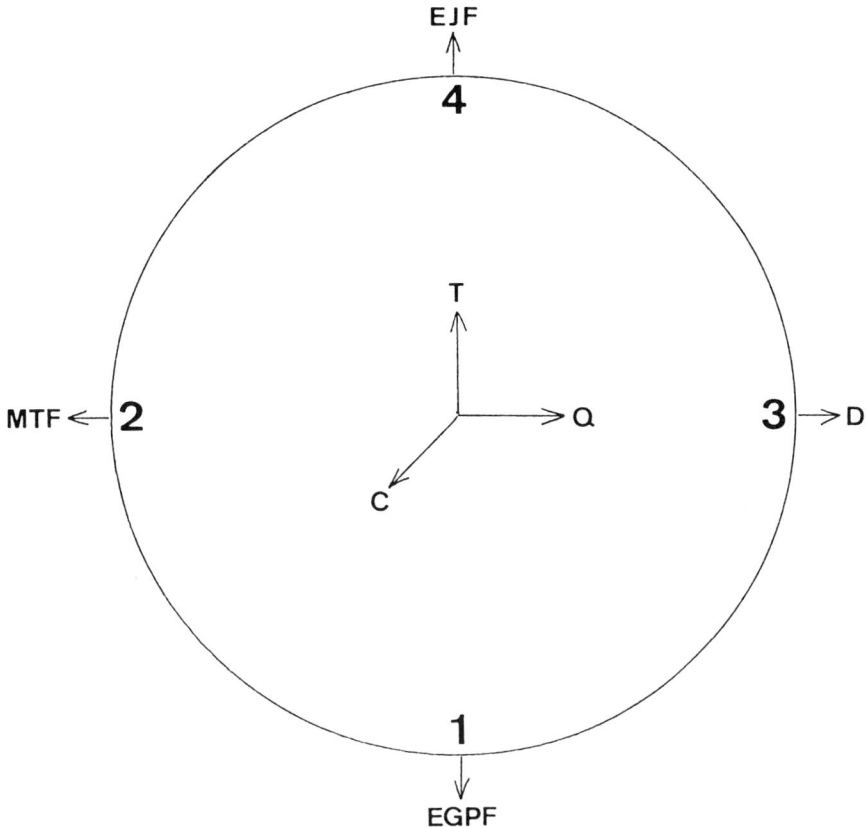

Figure 5.8. Three different Castelperronian orientations in reference to the quadripole: C: Castelperronian of Saint-Césaire (level EJOP superior); T: Castelperronian of Les Tambourets (Zone 3); Q: Castelperronian of Quinçay (level EN); EGPF: Denticulate Mousterian from level EGPF at Saint-Césaire (pole 1); MTF: Mousterian with thin flakes (pole 2); D: Gravettian from level D at La Ferrassie (pole 3); EJF: Early Aurignacian from level EJF at Saint-Césaire (pole 4).

Before conclusions can be drawn from this preliminary technological study it must be placed in the context of a more far-reaching body of work, one dealing essentially with retouched tools that was begun in 1957 by Laplace as an attempt to explain the origin of the leptolithic complexes of the Upper Paleolithic.

Laplace's Theory of the *synthétotype*

After minutely examining the theories of Breuil and Peyrony on Aurignacian levels (Breuil 1912; Breuil and Lantier 1959; Peyrony 1933, 1936), as well as the interpretations proposed by various authors (Delporte 1954a, 1954b; Lacorre 1959; Cheynier 1967; Combier 1951; Sonneville-Bordes 1955, 1960; Bordes and Sonneville-Bordes 1966), and also after having studied more than a hundred industries dating from different periods (Mousterian, Castelperronian, Protoaurignacian, Aurignacian, Gravettian, Szeletian) distributed throughout central and western Europe, Laplace (1958, 1966, 1968) presented his theory of the synthétotype supported by the typological data, a structural research based on various chronological data. This theory proposes a structured evolutionary scheme for the industries spanning the Middle and Upper Paleolithic. During this transitional phase, the undifferentiated synthétotype constituted by the early and subevolved Castelperronian is succeeded by the differentiated synthétotype, which brings together the evolved Castelperronian and the Proto-Aurignacian. According to Laplace, the complexes of the synthétotype appear to be differentiated in western Europe and to be correlated with a radial movement from the area where the early Castelperronian technique appears, mostly in the Périgord, into the other areas. In central Europe, the undifferentiated synthétotype constituted by the early Szeletian could have given rise to the essentially differentiated Aurignacian-like and Szeletian-like complexes.

It is possible that certain industrial assemblages assigned to the undifferentiated and the differentiated synthétotypes might be synchronous: such occurrences could be explained by a phenomenon of survival of the undifferentiated synthétotype, the genetic center assuming the function of center of conservation. (Laplace 1968:158)[14]

According to Laplace, the essential traits of the synthétotype complexes are made up of a large substrate of forms common to the various Mousterian facies (Mousteroid cores, scrapers, steep retouch, denticulates); of ancient, evolved forms (backed pieces for the Castelperronian, foliates for the Szeletian); and of Aurignacian-like materials.

Technological and Typological Data

The research on changes in lithic technology summarized here appears to be in accord, in some respects, with the work of Laplace on the origin and the evolution of leptolithic complexes, and the distinction made by Lévêque from his typological studies of a series of different Castelperronians at Quinçay and Saint-Césaire (Lévêque 1979-80 and this volume).

In the framework of Laplace's theory, the central portion of Figure 5.8 representing the Castelperronian would correspond to the undifferentiated synthetotype (early or subevolved Castelperronian), situated between poles 1, 2, 3, and 4. Pole 2 is seen here as one of the possible Mousterian origins of the Castelperronian, beginning with the Castelperronian industries like EJOP superior of Saint-Césaire, but it can also, in a more differentiated form, provide alternatives that can take the shape of a specialization like the Szeletian or the Solutrean (in which the fashioning of very thin objects approaches the extreme limits of this pole).

From the technological data, the Castelperronian of Saint-Césaire exhibits many archaic, "Mousteroid" characteristics. In spite of a very distinct differentiation towards pole 3, the Castelperronian of Quinçay (level EN) does not reach the specialization of the Gravettian. This supports Lévêque's findings that the industry from level EJOP superior is typologically intermediate between the archaic Castelperronian (level EG at Quinçay) and the early or typical Castelperronian. According to Lévêque, level EN at Quinçay contains an early Castelperronian. The industry of zone 3 at Les Tambourets has not been typologically compared to the assemblages from Quinçay and Saint-Césaire, but studies of reduction from this site show that it might also be a relatively undifferentiated Castelperronian (with very high frequencies of theme 0 and the undifferentiated production of curved blades).

Synthesis and Conclusion

The distinction of the physical and the psychic in the analysis of lithic objects has led to the establishment of the concept of reduction field, making the refinement of intricate observations of lithic materials possible, through the search for particular reduction themes present within an industry and the detailed examination of the mutual influences of these themes. The explicit inclusion of the mental aspect of stone working facilitates the distinction and the understanding of certain "continuities" between objects that could appear à priori to be mutually exclusive.

The reduction field of the Castelperronian of Saint-Césaire blends "Mousteroid" technological themes with themes proper to the Upper Paleolithic: the centripetal reduction of short flakes is associated with a longitudinal reduction that is more or less laminary. Equally significant is the importance of the influence of undifferentiated theme 0, which associates "Mousteroid" attributes and Upper Paleolithic morphotechnic elements on the same piece (different varieties of cores with twisted striking platforms). Theme 0 can be considered a transitional or intermediary form between "archaic" themes and more "evolved" themes, through time or within a single reduction sequence. Although it seems to be a relatively important characteristic of the Castelperronian in general, forms similar to this theme can be found in various industries spanning the prehistoric period from the Lower Paleolithic to the Mesolithic.

In spite of the presence of the blade technique, the Castelperronian of Saint-Césaire is technologically archaic because the "Mousteroid" or undifferentiated themes are dominant, while the Upper Paleolithic characteristics do not reach an Aurignacian or Gravettian specialization. From a typological point of view, this industry is very close to an archaic Castelperronian (Lévêque, this volume). The presence of a Neandertal in level EJOP superior could therefore be directly linked to the very marked "Mousteroid" aspect of this Castelperronian.

Although the concept of reduction field is essentially an attempt to understand stone objects on a time scale that is as close as possible to the short term (immediate transformations of stone according to reduction sequences in the context of the everyday life of prehistoric humans), it must also take into account the temporal component and the possibility that the long-term transformation of objects (diachronic evolution) could eventually occur in a stratigraphically homogeneous matrix. It may be that several geologically indistinguishable "cultural levels" were superimposed over the centuries to form EJOP superior.

The brief comparison of the Castelperronian of Saint-Césaire with that of Les Tambourets (zone 3) and level EN at Quinçay shows clearly that these industries have very different technological tendencies. This means that there is not just one Castelperronian, but that as Laplace and Lévêque have shown, the very concept of Castelperronian is composed of several elements, from archaic assemblages to industries that were farther "advanced" along the path of the Upper Paleolithic. The Castelperronian of Les Tambourets has an undifferentiated Aurignacian technological color, whereas that of level EN at Quinçay is organized around some undeniable Gravettian themes. These results may be an indicator of an evolutionary divergence from a common archaic origin (like the Castelperronian of Saint-Césaire); however, it could also be expressing functional differences of a single adaptive system (Binford and Binford 1966; S. Binford 1972).

In sum, the preliminary study presented in this article seeks to contribute to a research orientation that can enhance interpretations of archaeological remains dating to the transition from Middle to Upper Paleolithic. Although prehistorians are legitimately concerned with synthesizing data pertaining to problems of the evolution of lithic industries and human groups in general, it behooves us to pay special attention to the significance of an industry by searching for the concrete links of the reduction field, encompassing two scales: the everyday life of prehistoric humans and techno-typological change through time as documented by archaeologists, suffused with abstract changes.

Acknowledgments

I wish to thank Monsieur François Lévêque, Curator of Historic and Prehistoric Antiquities of Poitou-Charentes, for allowing me to study the stone reduction from Saint-Césaire.

I wish also to thank Anna Backer for translating my text, and June-el Piper for editing and clarifying. Discussions with them were helpful.

Dr. Henri Delporte, Head Curator of French National Antiquities, kindly allowed me to study artifacts from La Ferrassie, for which I am very grateful, as well as for his encouragement.

I would also like to thank Dominique Buisson for facilitating my access to the Ferrassie lithic collection.

Dr. Jean Clottes, Director of Prehistoric Antiquities, Midi-Pyrénées, and his coworkers kindly allowed me to study the lithic assemblages from Les Tambourets in 1986.

Notes

[1] The reduction field concept does not exceed the finite framework of a particular assemblage, generally spatially and temporally circumscribed. A group of reduction themes characteristic of a specific industry and its specific context does not constitute a type list usable for another industry. Reduction themes in their generic form, however, can be found in different industries, enhancing comparative studies. Only in this case does the notion of theme converge on the notion of type.

[2] Some classical or neoclassical typological and technological studies are exaggeratedly systematic and repetitive because they require that all objects be classified à priori according to "objective" systems and models, which are difficult to modify: a chipped stone object has to fit exclusively into one single type anticipated by the classificatory system, as an identifiable bone is attributable to a precise part of an animal's body. This procedure, taken to the extreme, favors the proliferation of some uncontrolled and falsely rigorous statistical analyses. It has the advantage of facilitating comparisons and quick syntheses, but it tends to erase the particularities of each industry, which are indispensable for a solid comparative study.

[3] This way of looking at objects from an ideational angle, as a mental representation or image, is not new; it has been used by several archaeologists, in particular by Deetz (1967:45-49) in his elaboration of his theory of mental templates. The present article does not espouse any particular school of theory. My main concern is to limit study as much as possible to the realm of artifactual materials and to bring to the fore concrete and detailed observations, using a few simple concepts, to deal with specific lithic industries. The role of the mental image in prehistoric technology is mentioned by Collina-Girard (1987) in his study of archaic Catalonian industries, spanning the ancient Mindel to the Riss. At the end of the study, the author concludes that "a tool is a mental object, a mental image elaborated by the prehistoric human, and as such, it follows, in its evolution, laws that are closer to those of language and symbolism than those of paleontological evolution" (1987:130).

Another study (Airvaux 1987), centered around the establishment and the rigorous analysis of the formal potentials of lithic tool kits (morphodynamic potential of penetration of matter by tools), also emphasizes the importance of the mental aspect of stone working by asserting that "the evolution of lithic tools and the very concept of a tool is part of a psycho-genetic mechanism" (1987:18) and that "formal concepts of tools and of work are narrowly linked on the symbolic level" (1987:64).

[4] In my opinion, this phenomenon has already been formulated indirectly in different ways by prehistorians like Laplace (1972:134), when he speaks of tendencies of primary types towards others; Carbonell (1985), who stresses the evolution of contradictory elements on an object; Collina-Girard (1987), whose modal pieces are surrounded by more complex pieces resulting from the combination of two or even three reduction modes, or within a different perspective; and Dibble (1984), who underlines gradual changes between tool types through utilization and resharpening.

[5] For example, the discovery of an exceptional conjoined set of approximately 40 flakes predating 200,000 years BP at Tourville-la-Riviere (Seine-Maritime, France). This refitting has shown that the final core bears the marks of two different, sequential reduction concepts that could indicate the superpositioning and the succession of two different intentions (Carpentier, Guilbaud, and Descombes 1992).

[6] Some actual conjoins but the majority are refitting by analogy. Refitting by analogy is the refitting of a flake A on a negative imprint left by a flake B that is similar to flake A.

[7] With a view to studying chipped stone from a three-dimensional, volumetric perspective, some elementary reduction developments are chosen for study (Guilbaud 1985). Three of these are used in the present article: centripetal (CE), conical (CO) and cylindrical (CY). In centripetal reduction, the edge of the platform is quite convex, delimiting a planar or convex surface where flake scars converge; this is the case for radial and converging reduction mentioned by Shchelinskï (1983:80-82, cited in Plisson 1988). Reduction of Levallois and discoidal cores utilizes the centripetal mode to different degrees. In conical reduction, the edge of the platform is more or less convex and the place of origin of removals is higher than in centripetal reduction, converging along a cone or a portion of a cone to a real or virtual point on the core. Finally, cylindrical reduction with a more or less convex platform edge delimits a reduction face with parallel or very slightly converging removals; in this last case, the cylindrical detachment of curved blades can accentuate this convergence. Pyramidal cores oscillate between conical and cylindrical concepts. When the striking platform does not follow a curve in any particular direction, or if we are dealing with a single removal, the reduction is termed neutral. All these criteria can be combined with other attributes, like flat reduction, in which scars are arranged on the broadest faces of a flattened core, and longitudinal reduction, in which scars are oriented along the long axis of faces of an elongated or flattened core; the technique of the burin spall is an example of the latter method of flake extraction that is often laminary.

[8] Pole 1: Chunky forms. This pole constitutes the most ancient orientation adopted by prehistoric stone workers. Its main element is the creation of thick, short lithic objects; debris; unmodified and retouched flakes; and cores. The cores resulting from the removal of thick, short flakes are often polyhedrons or prismatic cubes with several striking platforms and wide scars from removals of the core edge (*enlèvements débordants*). During core reduction, when a core begins to exhibit wide removals, deep bulbar scars, and deeply denticulated, sinuous or angular crests with few fine regularizing retouch scars, its orientation tends towards pole 1. Multiple, disorderly breakage of a single block into chunky pieces (one of the simplest types of fracture) is one of the main characteristics of this pole. An important consequence of this kind of morphotechnic choice, whether by breakage, reduction, or retouch, is the production on flakes or cores of significant proportions of robust edges with edge angles between 40 and 90 degrees. We can therefore already see that the choice of technological orientation depends, to a certain extent, on precise functional choices. Clactonian flakes, many choppers and chopping tools, Abbevillian bifaces, denticulates with Clactonian removals, thick or unstreamlined points, carinated endscrapers and crudely shaped *rabots*, and many polyhedrons and angular cores are all typical examples of pole 1. The Denticulate Mousterian of level EGPF of Saint-Césaire, directly below the Castelperronian levels, is heavily influenced by this pole.

Pole 2: Flat or thin forms. This pole represents a technological specialization in which the essential criteria are the extension of the surfaces and a reduction of the object's thickness. Unlike in the preceding pole, flakes typical of pole 2 have much less robust edges with few edge angles wider than 40 degrees. These sharp cutting edges cover a large proportion of the perimeter of flakes, which do not usually extend over the core's edge (they are seldom *débordants*). Very little of the edge of the original core-blank from which they are struck is removed. A series of removals of numerous thin flakes, "peeling" the flattened core and resulting in slender cutting edges, constitutes the basic character of this pole.

Specializing in flat things should be distinguished from tendencies towards elongation (see pole 3). In the former we are dealing essentially with flat rather short objects, which underscore two important morphotechnic aspects: extreme differentiation of tapered cutting edges and a mastery in fashioning extensive, regular, planar or slightly convex surfaces. This kind of reduction is very often accompanied by fine, regularizing retouch or preparation and usually adopts a centripetal development. It uses a grazing strike, often by soft-hammer percussion.

The "thin technique" of pole 2 begins to appear as early as the Acheulean and begins to really develop toward the end of the Lower Paleolithic and during the Middle Paleolithic, and reaches a high degree of specialization in the Solutrean industries and the American Paleoindian. Short flakes produced by the Levallois method, disks, foliate scrapers, most bifaces, and laurel leaf points follow this technological orientation.

Pole 3: Elongated forms. This pole favors above all the elongation of cores and flakes to the detriment of extensive surfaces and quite often of tapered edges. In this respect, the process of development towards pole 3 differs completely from that of pole 2. The knapping of rectilinear, very elongated blades by cylindrical reduction is the major characteristic of this pole. These blades can often exhibit some of the essential aspects of pole 1, if they are very thick, if the cores have wide scars, or if the scars frequently extend onto the edge of the core. They can also integrate, to a certain degree, some of the essential qualities of pole 4, like thinning and curvature. It is not rare to see some concepts of pole 2 represented in this blade production (core form and preparation).

The simplest and easiest strategy for the production of very long, rectilinear blades is to extract them from blanks that are also very long. One can knap flat cores longitudinally, along the edge, a process that eventually destroys the cutting edges and creates robust, narrow edges (similar to the bevel of burin edges). If the stone worker repeats this longitudinal knapping process to its logical end, the core tends to become cylindrical, thick, and very elongated.

The pole 3 blades have the almost exclusive advantage of furnishing blanks ideal for the fashioning of very streamlined points like Gravette points, with steep retouch. Some prismatic burins or burins with very straight scars are reminiscent of this longitudinal reduction technique.

Pole 4: curved forms and rounded ends. This pole refers to the production of blades and bladelets with concave ventral faces. This technique of laminary detachment accompanies the appearance, on the cores, of convex forms, resulting both from the curvature of the blades, and from the cylindrical or conical development of the core (Figure 5.3). The term "rounded end" (*front*) is a good description for these convex forms, which are often retouched. The manufacture of curved blades calls into play the chunky technique, for the preparation of striking platforms by detaching thick, overlapping flakes (*avivages*). Although pole 4 is the complete opposite of pole 1, the repetitive curved blade technique, when fully developed, sooner or later produces chunky cores, whatever the form of the original block of raw material. This chunky aspect is naturally linked to the appearance of rounded ends on cores. At this stage the cores can be maintained in an extreme laminary specialization or else they can become irregular with wide scars that are not elongated; they thus rejoin the orientation of pole 1.

The manufacture of rounded ends and the detachment of curved blades reveal a semiconical, semicylindrical progression and are very common in Aurignacian industries. The early Aurignacian of level EJF at Saint-Césaire is typical of the pole 4 specialization. The flattened or carenated endscrapers and the burins with curved bladelet scars are good examples of tools strongly linked to this pole. Here again, the type of orientation can be heavily influenced by precise functional choices.

Each of the four reduction modes described here can create quite precise tool types or tool components: rounded ends; thin edges; streamlined points; tapered, denticulate, or robust cutting edges; polyhedrons; prismatic cores; and so on.

[9] The industry of Les Tambourets was collected by Louis Méroc on the quaternary alluvial terraces of the Garonne and the Volp (southwest France). Since 1973, an international team led by Harvey Bricker has been investigating these terraces (Meroc and Bricker 1984).

[10] The site of Quinçay (Vienne, France), excavated by Lévêque, has yielded the most complete Castelperronian sequence known to date. Level EN, which concerns us here, is underlain and overlain by other Castelperronian levels (Lévêque 1983).

[11] Discovered and excavated at the beginning of this century, La Ferrassie (Dordogne) was recently reexcavated by the team led by Delporte (1969, 1984).

[12] In spite of their little-differentiated, central position, the Castelperronian assemblages of Les Tambourets and Quinçay (EN) are technologically more specialized in the direction of the Upper Paleolithic than the Castelperronian of Saint-Césaire.

The rarity of theme 2-3-4 in these two industries is a direct indicator of this fact. For Les Tambourets, Bricker even asserts that "the previously published diagnosis [by Meroc, based on an earlier excavation] according to which the industry represents an Evolved Chatelperronian clearly differentiated from its Mousterian predecessors, remains unchanged by more recent examinations" (Meroc and Bricker 1984:71).

[13] The relative quadripolar arrangement of the industries from levels EGPF (pole 1), EJOP superior (tending towards poles 1 and 2), EN (towards pole 3), and EJF (pole 4) is the result of statistical analysis of approximately 15 attributes on cores and a sample of flakes from each industry (Guilbaud 1985).

[14] "Il n'est pas exclu que certains ensembles industriels rapportés au synthétotype indifférencié et au synthétotype différencié soient synchrones: de tels faits pourraient s'expliquer par un phénomène de survivance du synthétotype indifférencié, le centre génétique assumant la fonction de centre de conservation."

References Cited

Airvaux, J.
    1987 Les potentialités morphologiques. Annals of the Premiére Rèunion Internationale sur les Systmes d'Analyse en Archéologie (1986). Center for Prehistoric Eco-social Research, Girona.

Backer, A., and M. Guilbaud
    1989 Spatial distributions, debitage and microdebitage in Aurignacian and Castelperronian levels of Saint-Césaire, Charente-Maritime. Paper presented at the 54th Annual Meeting of the Society for American Archaeology, Atlanta, Georgia.

Binford, L. R., and S. R. Binford
    1966 A Preliminary Analysis of Functional Variability in the Mousterian of Levallois Facies. *American Anthropologist* 68:238-295.

Binford, S.R.
    1972 The Significance of Variability: A Minority Report. In *Origines de l'Homme Moderne,* Actes du Colloque de l'UNESCO:199-210, Paris.

Bordes, F. and D. de Sonneville-Bordes
    1966 Protomagdalénien ou Périgordien 7? *L'Anthropologie* 70:112-122.

Breuil, H.
    1912 Les subdivisions du Paléolithique supérieur et leur signification. CIAAP, Geneva.

Breuil, H. and R. Lantier
    1959 *Les Hommes de la Pierre Ancienne.* Payot, Paris.

Carbonell, E.
    1985 Construction du systeme logico-analytique: applications à la structure lithique des gisements Pleistocenes du Massif du Montgri (Catalogne, Espagne). Ph.D. dissertation, Université de Paris VI, Paris, France.

Carbonell, E., J. Collina-Girard, M. Guilbaud, R. Mora and R. Sala
    1988 Le gisement Pleistocene moyen de Puig d'en Roca (Espagne). *Bulletin de la Société Préhistorique Française* 7(85):204-209.

Carbonell, E., M. Guilbaud and R. Mora
    1983-84 Elaboration d'un système d'analyse pour l'étude des éclats bruts de débitage. *Dialektikê,* Cahiers de Typologie Analytique, Université de Pau:22-31.

Carbonell, E., R. Mora and M. Guilbaud
   1985 Application of the Logical Analytical System to the Middle Paleolithic Period. The Technocomplex of Saint-Césaire, Charente-Maritime and Abric Romani, Catalunya. Cahier Noir 2:11-70. GIPES, Girona.

Carpentier, G., J-C. Descombes, and M. Guilbaud
   1992 Un cimetière de mammouths en Normandie. *Archeologia* 277:60-66.

Cheynier, A.
   1967 *Comment vivait l'homme des cavernes à l'age du renne?* Eds. Arnoux.

Collina-Girard, J.
   1987 Grille descriptive et évolution des industries archaiques: le modèle Catalan. Première Réunion Internationale sur les Systèmes d'Analyse en Archéologie (1986). Center for Prehistoric Eco-social Research, Girona.

Combier, J.
   1951 Gisements paléolithiques de Roclaine à Romanéche-Thorins (Seine-et-Loire) I: Le rendez-vous de chasse Périgordien 2. *Revue Archéologique de l'Est et du Centre-Est* II:27- 39.

Deetz, J.
   1967 *Invitation to Archaeology*. Natural History Press, New York.

Delporte, H.
   1954a Le Périgordien. BSPF LI:44-48.
   1954b Les faciès Castelperroniens et leur répartition géographique. Annals of the Fourth International Congress of the Sciences Préhistoriques et Protohistoriques. Madrid:225-229.
   1969 Les fouilles du Musée des Antiquités Nationales à La Ferrassie. *Bulletin des Antiquités Nationales* 1:15-28.

Delporte, H., Ed.
   1984 *Le Grand Abri de la Ferrassie:* Fouilles 1968 à 1973. Etudes Quaternaires 7, Paris.

Dibble, H.
   1984 Interpreting Typological Variation of Middle Paleolithic Scrapers: Function, Style or Sequence of Reduction. *Journal of Field Archaeology* 11:431-436.

Guilbaud, M.
   1985 Elaboration d'une Méthode d'Analyse pour les Produits de Débitage en Typologie Analytique et son application à quelques industries des gisements de Saint-Césaire (Charente-Maritime) et de Quinçay (Vienne). Ph.D. dissertation, Université de Paris VI, Paris, France.

Lacorre, F.
   1959 Tableau chronologique du Périgordien et de l'Aurignacien et de leurs complexes. BSPF lVI:53-57.

Laplace, G.
   1958 Recherches sur l'origine et l'évolution des complexes leptolithiques. Le problème des Périgordiens I et II et l'hypothèse du synthétotype Aurignaco-Gravettien. Essai de typologie analytique. *Quaternaria* V:153-240.
   1966 *Recherches sur l'Origine et l'Evolution des Complexes Leptolithiques*. Ecole Française de Rome, Mélanges d'Archéologie et d'Histoire. Supplément 4 (XII), Rome.

1968 Les niveaux Aurignaciens et l'hypothèse du synthétotype. In *L'Homme de Cro-Magnon*, Arts et Métiers Graphiques, Paris:141-163.

1972 Banques de données archéologiques. CNRS National Colloquia 932, Marseille:91-152.

Lévêque, F.
1979-80 Note à propos de trois gisements Castelperroniens de Poitou-Charentes. *Dialektikê*, Cahiers de Typologie Analytique, Pau:25-40.
1983 Le Castelperronien dans son environnement géologique. Essai de synthèse à partir de l'étude lithostratigraphique du remplissage de la grotte de La Grande Roche de la Plématrie (Quinçay, Vienne) et d'autres dépôts actuellement mis au jour. *L'Anthropologie* 87(3):369-391.

Méroc, L., and H. Bricker
1984 L'industrie lithique Châtelperronienne des Tambourets (Col. Méroc) à Coulardère et Saint-Christaud (Haute-Garonne). *Bulletin de la Société Préhistorique de l'Ariège* XXXIX:43-83.

Peyrony, D.
1933 Les industries "aurignaciennes" dans le bassin de la Vézère. Aurignacien et Périgordien. BSPF XXX:543-559.

1936 Le Périgordien et l'Aurignacien. Nouvelles observations. BSPF XXXIII:616-619.

Plisson, H.
1988 Technologie et tracéologie des outils lithiques en Union Soviétique: les travaux de V.E. Shchelinskiï. In *L'homme de Neandertal* Vol.4: La Technique, edited by L.R. Binford and J-P. Rigaud, pp.121-168. Etudes et Recherches Archéologiques de l'Université de Liège.

Sonneville-Bordes, D. de
1955 La question du Périgordien II. BSPF LII:187-203.
1960 *Le Paléolithique Supérieur en Périgord*. Delmas, Bordeaux.

6

L'analyse Pollinique de Saint-Césaire

Chantal Leroyer et Arlette Leroi-Gourhan

L'analyse pollinique de Saint-Césaire repose sur trois colonnes, complétées par des prélèvements sur les restes humains. Cet échantillonnage multiple nous a conduit à reconsidérer l'interprétation initiale développée à partir de l'étude d'un seul profil.

La première séquence, prélevée en 1980, englobe toute la stratigraphie du site. Un hiatus se marque nettement entre les dépôts moustériens (carré C 4) et les niveaux castelperroniens (carré E 3/4) où les taux de pollens d'arbres atteignent 78%. Les sédiments recueillis sur le Néandertalien s'intègrent parfaitement au sein de cette séquence.

En 1981, des prélèvements sont réalisés dans le carré F 3/4; ils couvrent le passage des niveaux moustériens à castelperroniens. La hausse des pollens d'arbres entrevue au sommet des niveaux moustériens est confirmée, mais aucun hiatus ne se marque puisque les fréquences de pollens arboréens ne dépassent pas 48% dans l'ensemble castelperronien.

La troisième colonne, prélevée en 1982 dans le carré G 5, ne prend en compte que les couches castelperroniennes. Les pollens d'arbres régressent progressivement de 13,6 à 5,3% puis s'élèvent à 21%.

Les diagrammes des niveaux castelperroniens, pourtant corroborés par ceux des restes humains, se différencient donc par des fréquences de pollens arboréens qui varient de 80 à 50% puis 20%. Mais l'organisation interne des cortèges polliniques reste assez proche; le pin est toujours majoritaire, accompagné par le genévrier et sporadiquement par quelques feuillus mésophiles tandis que les herbacées sont largement dominées par les liguliflores.

Ces différences peuvent s'expliquer en terme de dispersion pollinique (certaines zones auraient été favorisées naturellement ou non par la pollinisation du pin) ou en terme de sédimentation (les niveaux castelperroniens ne seraient pas homogènes). Quelle qu'en soit l'origine, ces variations soulèvent des problèmes d'interprétations climatique et chronologique.

L'attribution initiale de ces dépôts à un épisode tempéré ne trouve sa justification que dans les taux très élevés de pollens d'arbres en E3/E4, mais s'avère controversée par les deux autres profils. Le rattachement désormais classique du castelperronien à l'oscillation des Cottés ne peut donc être retenu, à Saint-Césaire, que par la seule prise en compte de la séquence de 1980. La considération des deux autres diagrammes nous conduit à douter de l'existence de cet épisode tempéré, tout au moins à Saint-Césaire (séquence continue), ou à rattacher l'occupation castelperronienne à une période froide antérieure ou postérieure au réchauffement (existence d'un hiatus).

Pollen Analysis at Saint-Césaire

Chantal Leroyer and Arlette Leroi-Gourhan

The pollen analysis at La Roche à Pierrot, Saint-Césaire, was done by Arlette Leroi-Gourhan. This study is based on three sample columns collected in 1980, 1981, and 1982 from different locations across the site. In addition, targeted samples from on and around the human remains complement the stratigraphic sampling (Figure 6.1). This multiplicity of pollen sequences at Saint-Césaire has led us to reconsider our initial interpretation, which was based on a single profile (Leroi-Gourhan 1984; Leroyer 1987, 1989).

The First Sequence

In 1980 the entire stratigraphic sequence of the site was sampled, from Mousterian deposits in square C4 to the Upper Paleolithic levels in E3/4 and F3. The diagram published in 1984 (Figure 6.2) is based on that initial sample. Although pollen was present in low densities, and the samples from the lowest Mousterian levels (EGB and EGC) were completely sterile, this first diagram covers almost the entire stratigraphic sequence of the site. Also in 1980, at the laboratory of Prof. B. Vandermeersch, A. Leroi-Gourhan collected sediments surrounding the Neandertal skeleton discovered the year before (Lévêque and Vandermeersch 1980). The results obtained from the pollen around and on the human remains (Figure 6.3) can be perfectly integrated with those from the initial sample column (Figure 6.4).

Six pollen groups have been identified, two before and four after a hiatus. The first group was recognized at the top of EGF and the base of EGP (Figure 6.4). The proportion of arboreal pollen is low and even nonexistent in one of the samples. The pollen spectra are largely dominated by liguifloral compositae. The second group of pollen was noted at the top of the Mousterian levels (EGP and EGPF). Proportions of arboreal pollen increase from 14 to 30%. This change is essentially the result of the marked increase in pine (*Pinus*) accompanied by a smaller but still significant increase in juniper (*Juniperus*) and some sporadic broadleaf trees.

The landscape appears to have been open country at first, corresponding to a rigorous climatic episode, whereas a warming trend apparently began toward the end of the Mousterian. After this time, there is clear evidence for a hiatus between the underlying Mousterian and the overlying Castelperronian. The hiatus is probably accentuated by the fact that the sample columns were taken from different locations (a shift from C4 to E3/4) because a slope in the levels was observed on the site.

The first pollen group distinguishable after the hiatus consists of the pollen spectra from the Castelperronian levels (EJOP inferior and superior) and those from the base of the overlying, archaeologically sterile level (EJO inferior). It is characterized by high percentages of arboreal pollen, first progressing from 69 to 78% and then stabilizing at around 55%. These high percentages are almost entirely due to the occurrence of pine. Broadleaf mesotherms are practically absent: only sporadic oak (*Quercus*) and birch (*Betula*) pollen are present. Only juniper is represented by a continuous curve, but it appears in weak proportions (in the vicinity of 3%). The herbaceous stratum is mostly represented by liguliflora with some graminates and tubulifloral compositae.

The second group corresponds to the archaeologically sterile level and to the base of the Proto-Aurignacian occupation (EJOP superior). It is isolated from the rest of the sequence by two gaps, one at the base and the other at the top. The pollen spectra present an arboreal pollen curve that progresses from 36 to 50%. Pine pollen is still in the majority within the arboreal stratum, which also contains juniper and sporadic oak, birch, and alder (*Alnus*). Liguliflora are still the dominant herbaceous form.

The third group consists of the pollen spectra from the top of the Proto-Aurignacian level (EJOP superior)

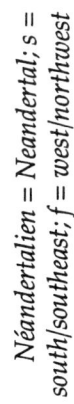

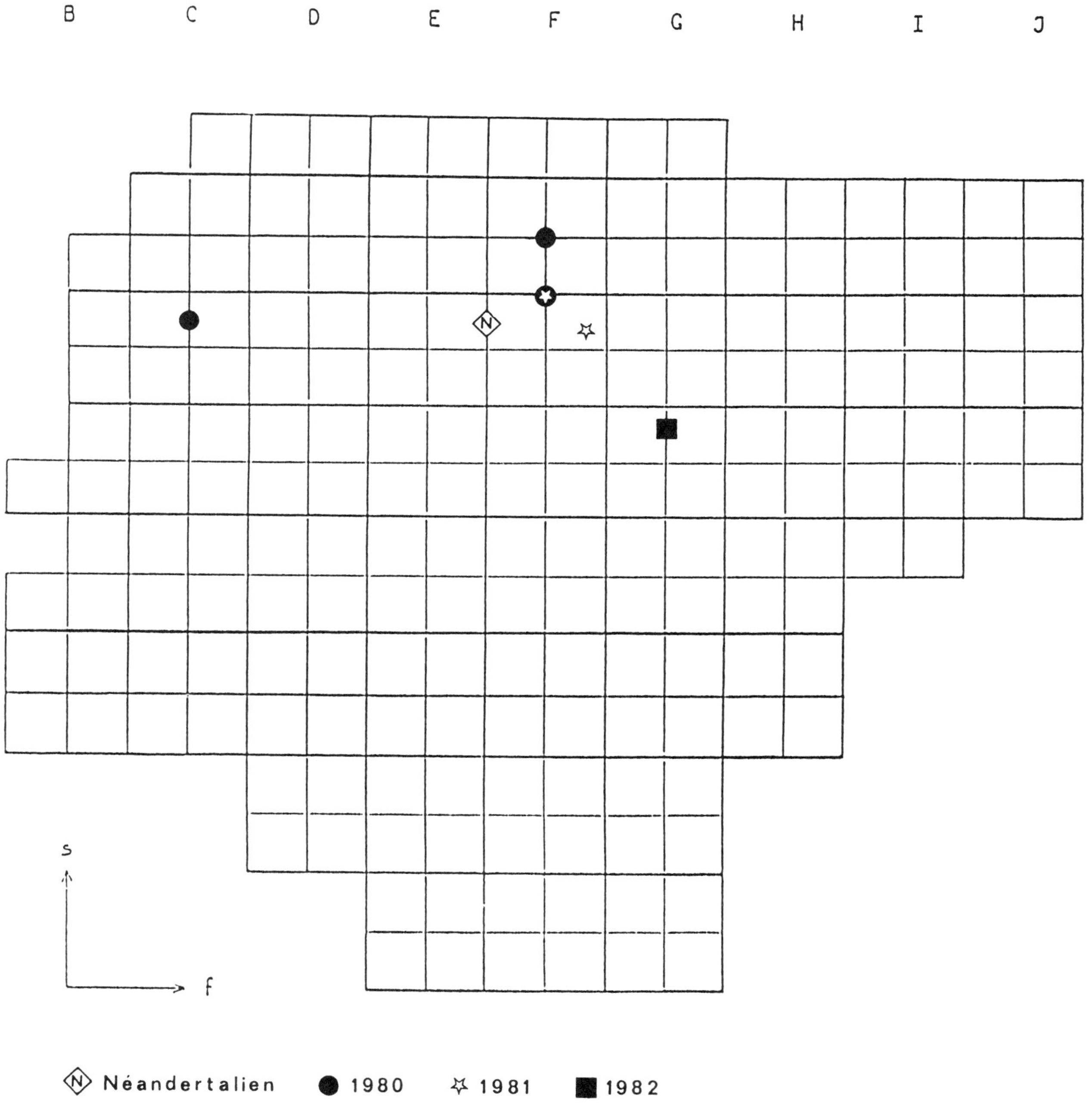

Figure 6.1. Localization of sample columns at the site of Saint-Césaire: 1980, 1981, 1982

Néandertalien = Neandertal; s = south/southeast; f = west/northwest

Figure 6.2 (facing page). Complete diagram of the first pollen sequence obtained at Saint-Césaire (Arlette Leroi-Gourhan 1984).

Datation palynologique = pollen dating; industrie = industry; couches = levels; altitude en F3 = depth in square F3; arbres soulignés = trees underlined; Interstade d'Arcy = Arcy Interstadial; froid = cold; instabilité climatique = climatic instability; Interstade des Cottés = Les Cottés Interstadial; Aurignacien évolué = Evolved Aurignacian; Aurignacien ancien = Early Aurignacian; Proto-Aurignacien = Proto-Aurignacian; industrie très pauvre (1 pointe de Châtelperron) = very few tools (1 Châtelperron point); Castelperronien = Castelperronian; pauvre = with few tools; Moustérien = Mousterian; Néandertalien = Neandertal.

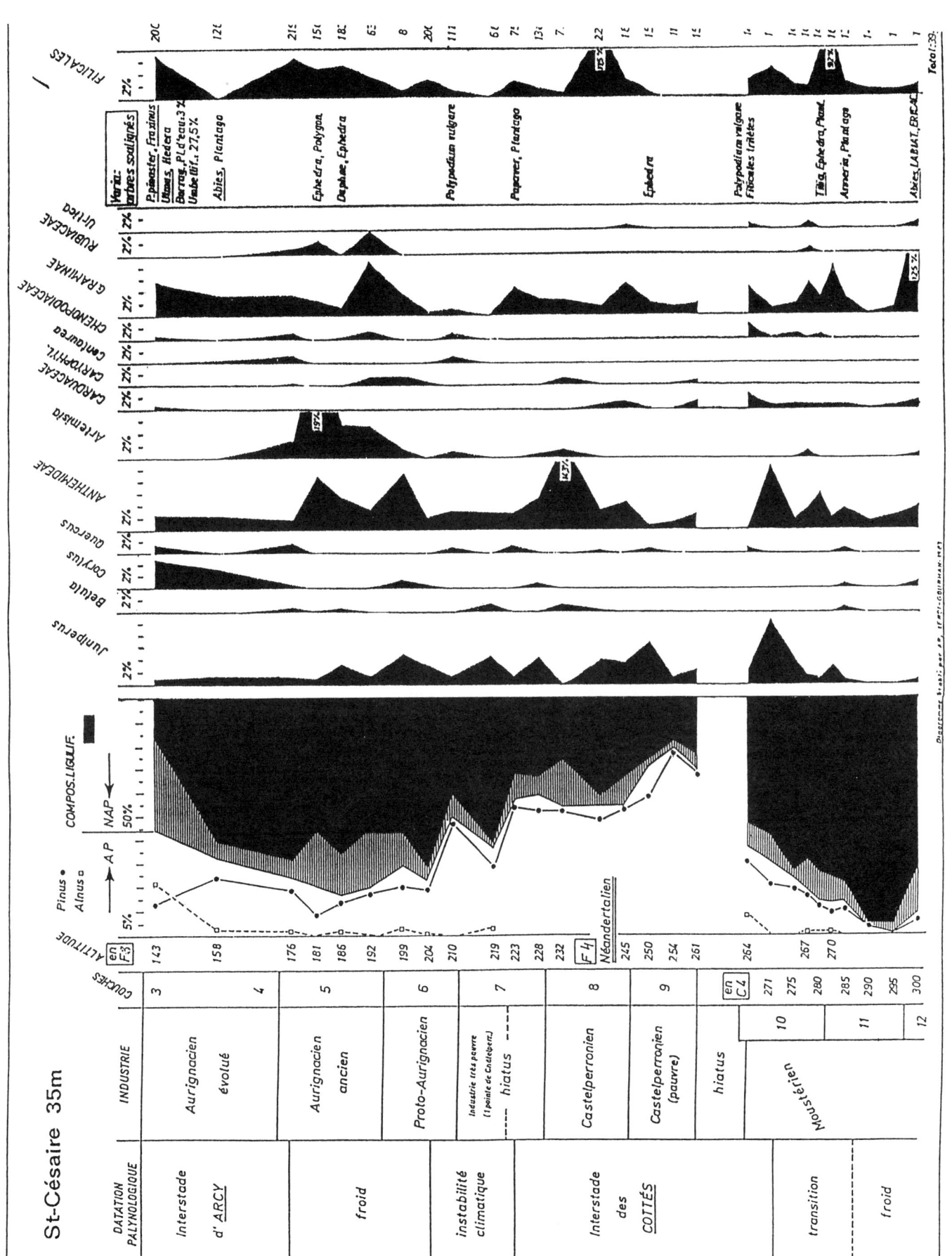

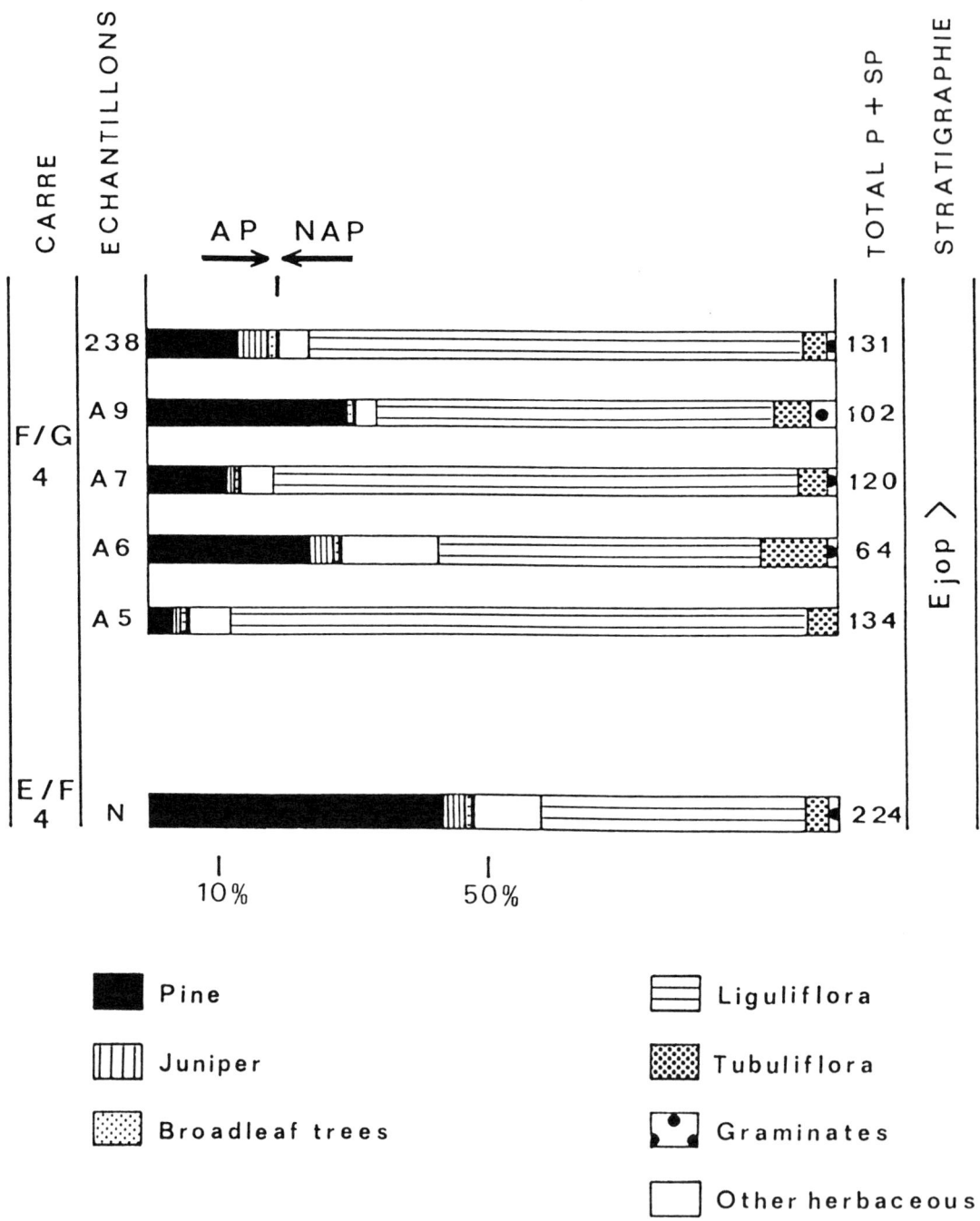

Figure 6.3. Simplified diagram of results obtained from pollen samples collected near the human remains: the Neandertal (N) in E/F4 and the hand in F/G4.

Restes humains = human remains; carré = grid square; échantillons = samples; stratigraphie = stratigraphy.

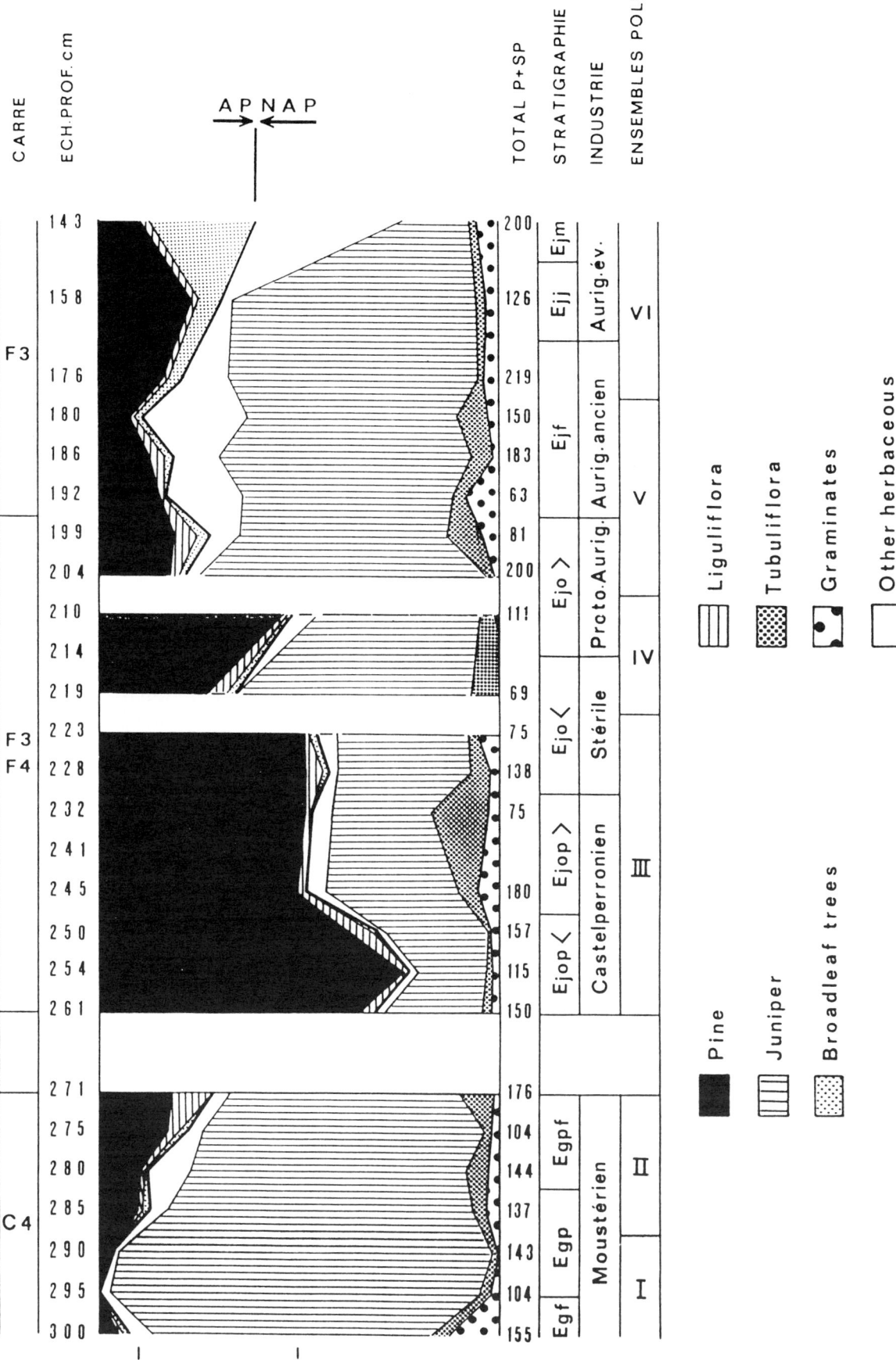

Figure 6.4. Simplified diagram of the first pollen sequence at Saint-Césaire sampled in 1980.

Carré = grid square; Ech. prof. cm = sample depth (cm); stratigraphie = stratigraphy; industrie = industry; ensembles poll. = pollen assemblages; Moustérien = Mousterian; Castelperronien = Castelperronian; Proto.Aurig. = Proto-Aurignacian; Aurig. ancien = early Aurignacian; Aurig. ev. = evolved Aurignacian.

and from the Early Aurignacian (EJF). It is characterized by the lowest arboreal pollen percentages in the upper sequence, around 20%. The herbaceous stratum is more diversified as indicated by the presence of steppe-adapted taxa, such as *Artemisia* and *Ephedra*, among others.

The fourth group gathers together the pollen spectra of the Evolved Aurignacian levels (EJJ and EJM). Arboreal pollen percentages are on the increase (from 21 to 40%). Although pine is still dominant, the proportions of broadleaf trees develop considerably until, finally, alder is in the majority.

These four groups determine four climatic episodes: first a temperate oscillation followed by a transitional phase, which leads to a cold period. Last, the top of the sequence corresponds to a temperate, humid episode.

On the basis of this diagram, Leroi-Gourhan has been able to integrate the Saint-Césaire sequence into her chronobotanical framework of the late glacial period (Leroi-Gourhan 1968, 1980). She attributes the top of the Mousterian levels and the Castelperronian sequence to the Les Cottés oscillation (Bastin et al. 1976). The level containing the Neandertal remains corresponds to the second half of this oscillation, after the climatic optimum. The Evolved Aurignacian levels are placed within the Arcy oscillation (Leroi-Gourhan and Leroi-Gourhan 1965).

The Second Sequence

In 1981, several new samples were collected. A small profile was scraped down in F3/4 and used for a continuous sample spanning from levels EGPF (Mousterian) to EJOP (Castelperronian) in order to verify the possible existence of a hiatus between these two stratigraphic units. A further set of samples was collected on a horizontal level between each of the fingers of the human hand discovered in squares F4/G4, and another vertical series was collected across the Castelperronian levels above and below these human remains.

The pollen spectra from the samples collected around the hand are different from each other (Figure 6.3). Although the palynological representation of the pollen spectra is identical (i.e., predominance of pine and liguifloral compositae), the taxa are represented in extremely variable proportions. The percentages of arboreal pollen fluctuate between 5 and 31%, largely because of changes in the amount of pine. Juniper is absent from one of the samples, while some broadleaf trees—alder, birch, and ash (*Fraxinus*)—are present in low proportions. The pattern for herbaceous plants is more or less diversified, showing a predominance of liguifloral compositae but in varying proportions (from 52 to 65%).

Arboreal pollen is not very strongly represented in any of these samples, unlike the one recovered from the complete sequence sampled in 1980 or the sample collected from the skeleton. From this finding, Leroi-Gourhan has proposed the hypothesis that sediments have leached from the Aurignacian levels in this sector of the site. This interpretation is corroborated by the variations recorded between the four pollen spectra.

The pollen sequence spanning the transition between the Mousterian deposits (EGPF) and the Castelperronian levels (EJOP) can be subdivided into two groups (Figure 6.5). First, an increase in arboreal pollen from 12.7 to 48% is observed at the top of the Mousterian deposits and at the base of the Castelperronian. Pine is in the majority, accompanied by juniper and alder, both of which occur in relatively unvarying frequencies. Oak is also present in low proportions in the final sample from the Mousterian (EGPF), but no broadleaf pollen is present in the sample from the base of the Castelperronian (EJOP inferior), even though this level contains the highest proportions of arboreal pollen.

Second, the proportions of arboreal pollen decrease to 26 and then to 20%, only to increase once again to 30%. Along with pine, still in the majority, juniper is present in relatively unchanging amounts, as are some sporadic components of an oak forest. Herbaceous plants are heavily dominated by liguifloral, followed by graminates and tubuliflora.

The increase in arboreal pollen seen at the top of the Mousterian deposits in square C4 is therefore corroborated by this new diagram. No hiatus is apparent, however, because the proportions of arboreal pollen recorded in the Castelperronian level are clearly lower than those for the preceding column.

The Third Sequence

The palynological variation in the two columns from the Castelperronian deposits, which were taken quite close to each other, poses a new problem. In order to resolve this problem, a series of seven samples was collected in 1982 from throughout the Castelperronian levels (EJOP inferior and superior) in square G5 (Figure 6.6). The proportion of arboreal pollen oscillates from 13.6 to 5.3% in these new samples and then rises to 21%. Pine is predominant, accompanied by juniper in all but one sample and by very sporadic occurrences of broadleaf pollen. The pollen spectra are strongly dominated by liguifloral compositae.

Despite the uniformity of the sequence, two palynological subgroups can be distinguished. The first corresponds to EJOP inferior and to the base of EJOP

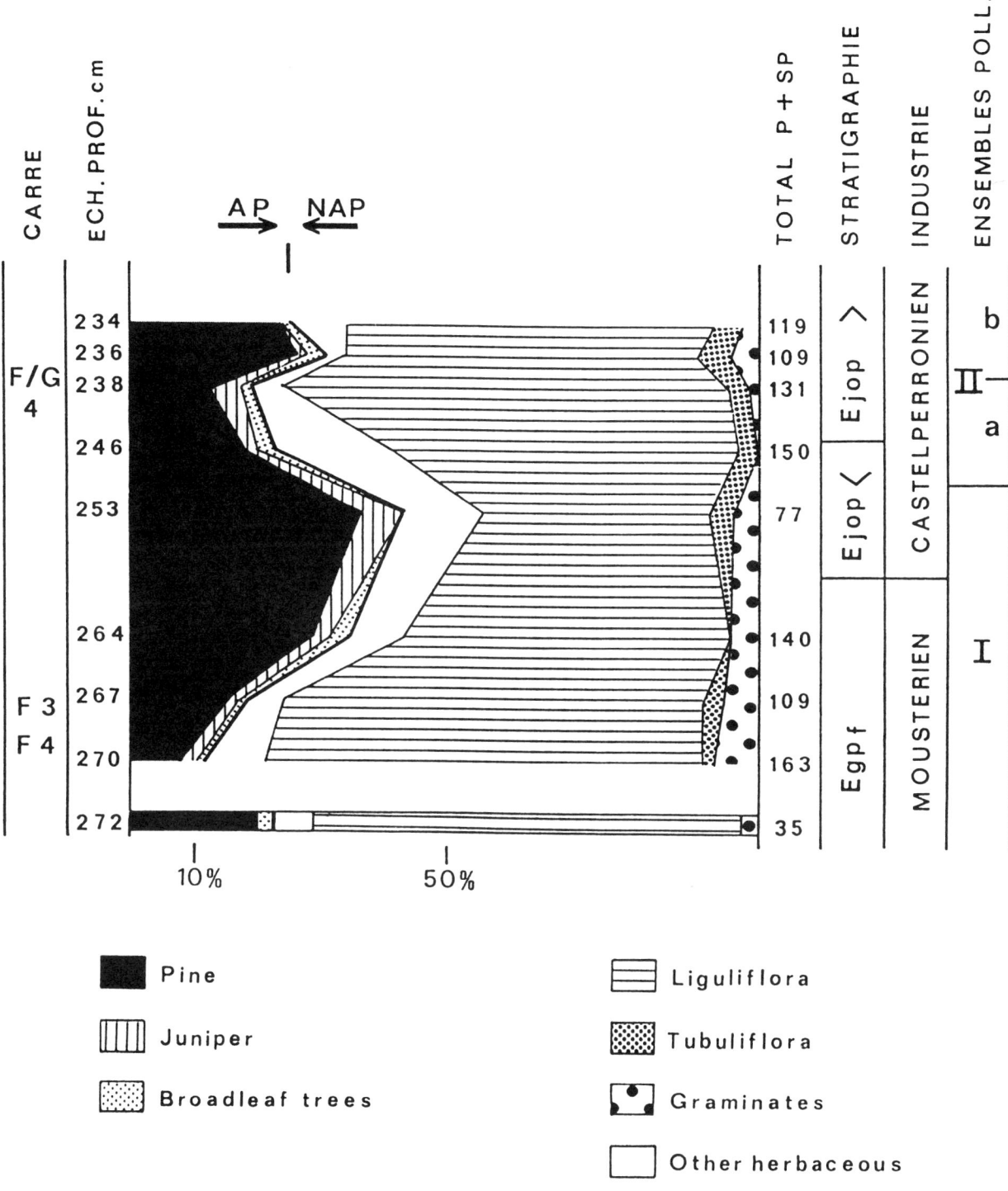

Figure 6.5. Simplified diagram of the second pollen sequence at Saint-Césaire, sampled in 1981 from squares F3/4 and F/G4.

Carré = square; Ech. prof. cm = sample depth (cm); stratigraphie = stratigrapy; industrie = industry; ensembles poll. = pollen assemblages.

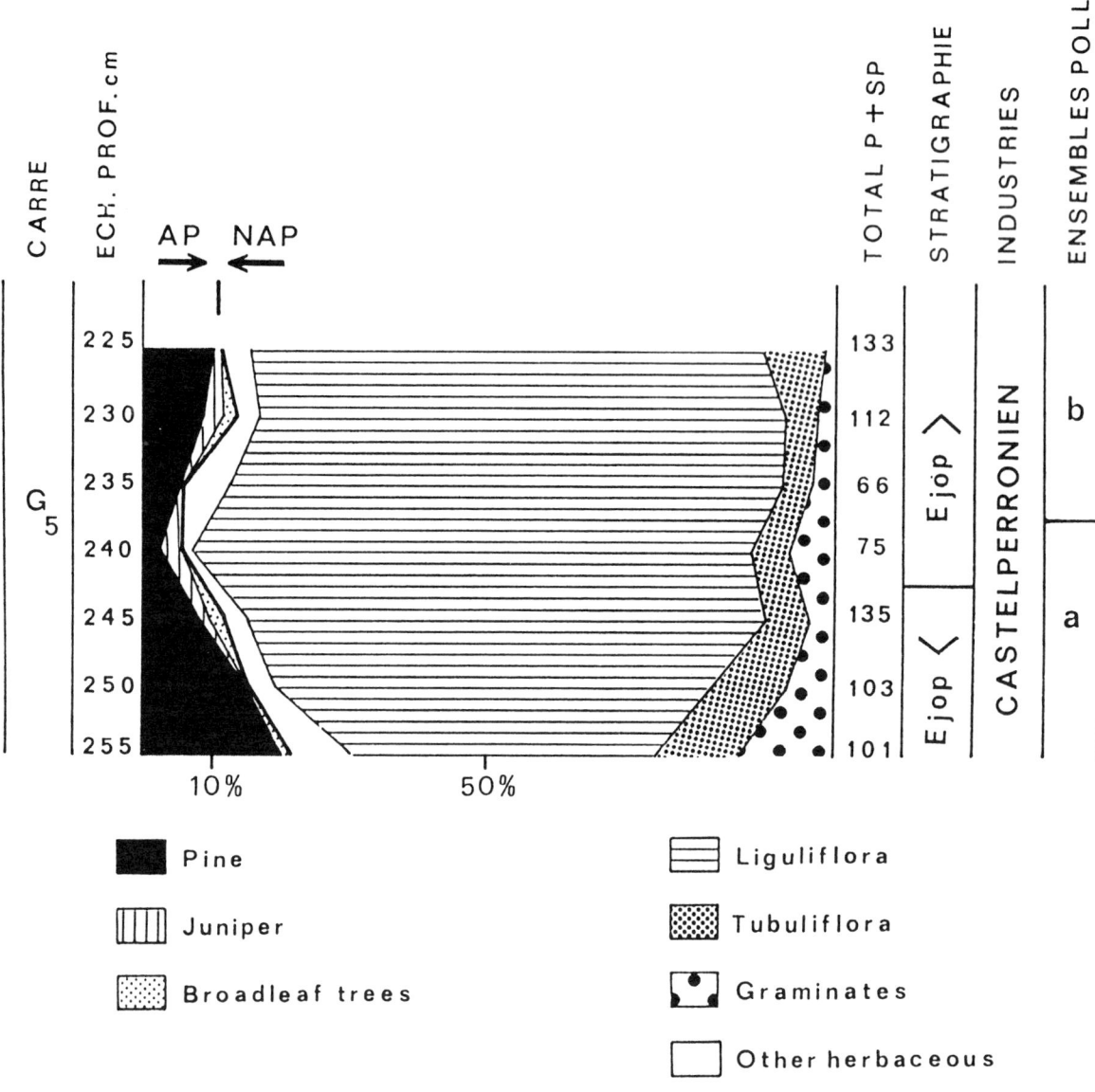

Figure 6.6. Simplified diagram of the third pollen sequence of Saint-Césaire sampled in 1982 from square G5.

Carré = grid square; Ech. prof. cm = sample depth (cm); stratigraphie = stratigraphy; ensembles poll. = pollen assemblages.

superior; it reveals a progressive decrease in arboreal pollen proportions. The second shows that pine, after being represented in the lowest proportion yet recorded, increases slightly, accompanied by some rare broadleaf trees.

Interpretation

We are therefore confronted with three different pollen sequences, all of which span the Castelperronian deposits. Although there is relatively little diversity in the floral list and in the internal organization of the pollen spectra (pine is always dominant, followed by juniper and sporadically a few mesophilous broadleaf trees; herbaceous plants are strongly dominated by liguliflora), the percentages are widely divergent. The highest proportions of arboreal pollen vary from 80% in the first diagram to 50% and then to 20% in the G5 profile. On the other hand, all three sequences show the same evolution in the arboreal pollen curve, which reaches its maximum with EJOP inferior and then diminishes.

These findings raise questions of interpretation regarding the variation between the different sample column locations. The variation may be explainable in terms of pollen dispersal: pine is an abundant pollen producer and could have been favored in certain zones of the site (squares F4/E4). We could perhaps even consider the inhabitants of the rockshelter at Saint-Césaire as factors in the concentration of pine pollen, involuntary or purposeful, by the transport of branches.

The difference in palynological representation can also be considered in sedimentary terms. The Castelperronian deposit may not be uniform: sedimentological variations not discernible during excavation could result in variation in pollen records because of analysis of different sediments.

The variation in proportional representation engenders a major problem of climatic and chronostratigraphic interpretation. The pollen sequence recorded in square F3 could be attributed to a warming trend based on the high proportions of arboreal pollen, which are rarely found in a pleniglacial context. The lack of continuity in the presence of broadleaf mesophilous trees, markers of a temperate oscillation, could be due to the development of a pine forest along the edge of the cliff. In the two most recently sampled columns, however, there was a much smaller proportion of pine. The lowest proportions of arboreal pollen (especially in G5), the near absence of broadleaf trees, and the predominance of liguliflora could even cast doubt on the interpretation of a warming trend.

Two solutions to this problem are available. On the one hand we can take all three columns into consideration and judge the first sequence to be unrepresentative. With regard to the profiles from F4 and especially G5, the Castelperronian levels would then be attributed to a cold, but not a harsh, episode. This solution in turn raises the problem of the chronostratigraphic placement of these deposits in the most recent third of isotope stage 3, characterized by a succession of oscillations (Duplessy 1978). Furthermore, it is generally acknowledged that the transition between the Middle and early Upper Paleolithic occurred during a temperate climatic episode (Leroyer 1988). If we consider the sequence as a continuous one, this interpretation sheds doubt on the existence of the Les Cottés oscillation, at least at Saint-Césaire. If we assume the existence of a hiatus in the sequence, the Castelperronian levels at Saint-Césaire could be situated in a period either preceding or following the Les Cottés oscillation.

On the other hand, we can consider the initial 1980 sequence (Figure 6.4) to be the most representative and the most complete, and maintain the interpretation proposed at the time, which ties in the Castelperronian levels to the Les Cottés oscillation but probably overestimates percentages of pine.

References Cited

Bastin, B., F. Lévêque, and L. Pradel
    1976 Mise en évidence de spectres polliniques interstadiaires entre le Moustérien et le Périgordien ancien de la grotte des Cottés (Vienne). *Compte Rendu de l'Académie des Sciences* 282:1261-1264. Paris.

Duplessy, J.-Cl.
    1978 Isotope Studies. In *Climatic Change*, edited by J. Griblin, pp. 46-67. Cambridge University Press, Cambridge.

Leroi-Gourhan, Arlette
    1968 Dénomination des oscillations würmiennes. *Bulletin de l'Association Française et Quaternaire* 17:281-288.
    1980 Les interstades du Würm supérieur. In *Problème de stratigraphie quaternaire en France et dans les pays limitrophes*. Supplément au Bulletin de l'Association Française et Quaternaire n.s. 1:192-194.
    1984 La place du Néandertalien de Saint-Césaire dans la chronologie würmienne. *Bulletin de la Société Préhistorique Française* 81(7):196-198.

Leroi-Gourhan, Arlette, and A. Leroi-Gourhan
    1965 Chronologie des grottes d'Arcy-sur-Cure. *Gallia Préhistoire* VII:1-64.

Leroyer, Ch.
    1987 Les gisements castelperroniens de Quinçay et de Saint-Césaire: Quelques comparaisons préliminaires des études palynologiques. In *Préhistoire de Poitou-Charentes, Problèmes Actuels*, Editions du Comité des Travaux Historiques et Scientifiques, Actes du 111ème Congrès des Sociétés Savantes (1986, Poitiers), pp. 992-102, Paris.
    1988 Des occupations castelperroniennes et aurignaciennes dans leur cadre climatique. In *L'homme de Néandertal*, vol. 8: La Mutation, edited by M. Otte, pp. 103-108. Etudes et Recherches Archéologiques de l'Université de Liège 34, Liège.
    1989 Les séquences polliniques de Saint-Césaire et de Quinçay: Essai de corrélation et implications. In *L'homme de Néandertal*, Vol. 7: L'extinction, edited by M. Otte, pp. 89-97. Etudes et Recherches Archéologiques de l'Université de Liège.

Lévêque, F., and B. Vandermeersch
    1980 Découverte de restes humains dans un niveau castelperronien à Saint-Césaire (Charente-Maritime). *Compte Rendu de l'Académie des Sciences* 291:187-189. Paris.

7

Macrofaune des Niveaux Castelperroniens de Saint-Césaire

Françoise Lavaud-Girard

Le gisement de Saint-Césaire, par sa séquence stratigraphique très complète, permet d'envisager la succession évolutive d'archéobiocénoses du Würm II au Würm IIIa. Le niveau médian (EJOP sup.) caractérisé par une industrie Castelperronienne associée à un squelette humain de type Néanderthalien, a livré un complexe faunique qui, bien qu'assez classique, présente des caractères particuliers rappelant les complexes Moustériens sous-jacents, mais annonçant déjà ceux du Paléolithique supérieur. Ceci nous conduit à accréditer l'hypothèse selon laquelle le Castelperronien pourrait constituer une véritable époque charnière entre le Paléolithique moyen et le Paléolithique supérieur.

La macrofaune est constituée des espèces suivantes: *Canis lupus, Vulpes vulpes, Martes sp., Crocuta spelaea, Sus scrofa, Bos et/ou Bison, Capreolus capreolus, Cervus elephus, Megaceros sp., Rangifer tarandus, Equus caballus cf. germanicus, Coelodonta antiquitatis* et *Mammuthus primigenius*. Certaines de ces formes présentent des variations anatomiques ou dimensionnelles notables, rarement signalées dans d'autres niveaux paléolithiques.

Cet ensemble faunique permet d'évoquer les contraintes écoclimatiques principales du paléoenvironnement de l'époque dans cette région du Poitou-Charentes. Une étude comparative des premiers résultats avec les quelques faunes castelperroniennes françaises connues à ce jour complète cette approche préliminaire.

Macrofauna from Castelperronian Levels at Saint-Césaire, Charente-Maritime

Françoise Lavaud-Girard

This paper presents preliminary research results on the macrofauna of the Castelperronian levels labeled EJOP at the site of La Roche à Pierrot, Saint-Césaire. This site has acquired international renown since the discovery in 1979 of a *Homo sapiens neandertalensis* skeleton (identified by B. Vandermeersch) in a Castelperronian level, a key level of transition from the point of view of both human evolution and archaeological change (Lévêque and Vandermeersch 1980). A crucial area of investigation concerns the verification of links between biocultural changes during this period and important changes in the paleoenvironment. These links provide the framework for this study.

The site has several exceptional characteristics: in particular, the quality of the stratigraphic sequence established over 11 years of excavation. From a paleontological perspective, every level of the deposit has yielded abundant osseous and dental remains, which have enabled the compilation of an initial faunal list; a more detailed study is currently being conducted.

Faunal elements recovered from these levels are highly fragmented, and therefore the number of precisely identifiable specimens is drastically reduced; nevertheless, we can propose a profile of the succession of fauna at La Roche à Pierrot. Their evolution can be traced with precision owing to the quality of chronostratigraphic information obtained through sedimentology (studied by Lévêque and Miskovsky, this volume) and F. Lévêque's study of lithic complexes (this volume), combined with the absolute dates provided by thermoluminescence (by H. Valladas and her colleagues; Mercier et al. 1991 and this volume).

Consideration of the results of the macrofaunal studies in parallel with those of palynological analysis (by Leroi-Gourhan and Leroyer, this volume) should help in the reconstruction of the paleobiological composition of the site in detail. Future refinements to this reconstruction will made from the study of microfauna and the identification of the rare specimens of birds, fish, and shellfish.

These paleontological studies are complemented by a taphonomic study (by Patou-Mathis, this volume), which will enable the evaluation of previous assumptions about the site. Spatial distribution studies of the different elements are the object of ongoing work in collaboration with Anna Backer (this volume).

Faunal Species from EJOP Superior, Saint-Césaire

Excavation and subsequent classification of field data in the laboratory by Lévêque, Backer, and Guilbaud have made it possible to distinguish three levels within the Castelperronian stratigraphic group: EJOP superior and inferior, and EJOP base. This paper concentrates on the material from EJOP superior.

Mammals

Carnivores (order Carnivora) are represented by only a few species. A few rare elements suggest the presence of wolves (*Canis lupus lupus*; Linnaeus 1758). Some of the few faunal remains that indicate the presence of red fox (*Vulpes vulpes*; Linnaeus 1758) might however be referable to arctic fox (*Alopex lagopus*; Linnaeus 1758). In 1986 a list of identified species included marten, but no new element has been found since that time to confirm the presence of *Martes* spp. The discovery in the EJOP superior level of a canine tooth, quite worn and partially broken, suggests the presence of a cave or spotted hyaena (*Crocuta spelaea spelaea*; Goldfuss 1832). Other carnivores may also be present.

A large number of artiodactyl remains (order Artiodactyla) have been identified. The presence of the forest-dwelling wild boar (*Sus scrofa*; Linnaeus 1758) is indicated by four isolated teeth. The presence of large bovines, *Bos* (Linnaeus 1758) and/or *Bison* (Smith 1827), is strongly marked in this level, although significantly reduced relative to the

Mousterian levels. The overlying Aurignacian levels witness a further reduction, but these animals occur in at least some quantity throughout the sequence.

Species attribution of fragments of bone and teeth is always delicate, since *Bos* and *Bison* remains are quite similar. Nevertheless, the morphology of the third lobe of the third lower molars—pinched, elongated, and vestibularly very offset—attests to the presence of *Bos*. The dimensions of the upper molars from level EJOP superior appear closer to the dimensions given for *Bison*, but I have already noted this same range of dimensions for Castelperronian *Bos* at Quinçay (Vienne) and at Gatzarra (Atlantic Pyrenees).

The presence of chamois (*Rupicapra* sp.; Linnaeus 1758), indicated by three isolated teeth, has not been confirmed by any new discovery during more recent analyses. A few elements have been ascribed to a small cervid that might be mountain sheep (*Capreolus capreolus*; Linnaeus 1758); other forms may be present as well. The presence of red deer (*Cervus elaphus*; Linnaeus 1758) is documented by quite a large number of elements. Giant or Irish elk (*Megaceros* sp.; Owen 1844) is rather rare, and it is represented here by several dental remains.

Reindeer (*Rangifer tarandus*; Linnaeus 1758) is the preponderant form in the level. Its importance becomes even more marked in the more recent levels, pointing to a climatic trend toward a more rugged environment of maximum cold conditions, especially for the Early Aurignacian (EJF) levels. Large numbers of reindeer antler were collected and have been studied by Patou-Mathis (this volume).

Numerous remains have been assigned to the order that includes both horses and rhinoceros (order Perissodactyla). Many, many fragments were identified as representing *Equus caballus* cf. *germanicus* (Nehring 1884). The teeth show clear attributes of horses—in particular the upper molars, which have a very long protocone with a corrugated lingual edge. This diagnostic enables classification to a particular subspecies without hesitation. Nevertheless, it should be noted that many pieces are small, a phenomenon previously described in other contemporary deposits. The possibility that a new form of equid developed during the Castelperronian should not be ruled out; this argument will be discussed in a subsequent work.

Many elements, usually lower molars at different stages of wear (from dental buds to teeth so badly worn that only the contours remain), enable positive identification of the presence of woolly rhinoceros (*Coelondonta antiquitatis*; Blumenbach 1803) in the Castelperronian. The great stability of this species is noteworthy, for it is found in the Mousterian levels (EGPF, EGP) as well as in the Aurignacian (EJF).

An upper first or second molar, moderately worn; numerous fragments of mammoth tooth plates from different age groups; and a second deciduous molar in the first state of wear have been assigned to the final mammal to be discussed here, mammoth (order Proboscidea, *Mammuthus primigenius*; Blumenbach 1803). This species is also present in the subjacent levels (EGC, EGF, EGPF) but apparently is not found higher than the EJOP levels.

Levels EJOP inferior and EJOP base have yielded at least the following elements: reindeer (*Rangifer tarandus*), the predominant form; horse (*Equus caballus* cf. *germanicus*); and abundant, large bovines.

In sum, in the upper Castelperronian level at Saint-Césaire, herbivores are very common and carnivores are rare. The dominant species are reindeer, large bovines, and horse, in that order. Next come other cervids (red deer, giant elk, and smaller forms). These data suggest a rather cold climate, which is confirmed by the presence of woolly rhinoceros and mammoth, though perhaps moderated slightly by the presence of temperate forms (red deer, for example). There is a juxtaposition of forest-dwelling species (e.g., boar and elk or red deer) and species adapted to open country.

The chronostratigraphic succession of faunal complexes from the site was presented by the author in 1986 at the Third Congress of the Sociétés Savantes in Poitiers (Table 7.1) (Lavaud-Girard 1987). More complete results will be furnished in an upcoming publication.

Discussion

The permanence of reindeer in this site is well-established, and the dominance of reindeer is sharply accentuated from the Castelperronian upwards, reaching a maximum in the Early Aurignacian. Large bovines are also ubiquitous, but the high proportions of these animals noted in the Mousterian levels begin to decrease from EJOP on.

Horses, remarkably constant throughout the deposits, increase very clearly in the Mousterian levels (EGPS-EGPF) and apparently begin to decrease with EJOP. This level is further characterized by the appearance of a form with marked horselike attributes but of small dimensions. Finally, the mammoth, represented by several finds in the lower levels, seems to be absent after the Castelperronian.

Taken together, these observations confirm the hypothesis that the Castelperronian was a turning point in the evolution of Paleolithic faunal complexes.

The data gathered from one site, no matter how complete, are hardly sufficient to build a paleoclimatic synthesis; for this reason, we have sought to evaluate these initial results using information from other

Time Period	Level	Fauna
Aurignacian	EJJ	*Vulpes vulpes; Bos/Bison*, small cervids, *Cervus elaphus, Rangifer tarandus; Equus caballus* cf. *germanicus*
	EJM	*V. vulpes; Bos/Bison*, small cervids, *R. Tarandus; E. caballus* cf. *germanicus*
Early Aurignacian	EJF	*V. vulpes, Crocuta spelaea spelaea*, indeterminate carnivores; *Bos/Bison*, small cervids, *Megaceros, R. Tarandus; E. caballus* cf. *germanicus, Coelodonta antiquitatis*
Proto-Aurignacian	EJO superior	Indeterminate carnivores; *Bos/Bison, C. elaphus, R. tarandus; E. caballus* cf. *germanicus*
Mousterian	EGPF	*C. spelaea spelaea*, indeterminate carnivores; *Bos/Bison*, small cervids, *Megaceros, C. elaphus, R. Tarandus; E. caballus* cf. *germanicus, C. antiquitatis*
	EGPS	*Bos/Bison, R. Tarandus; E. caballus* cf. *germanicus, Mammuthus primigenius*
	EGP	Indeterminate carnivores; *Bos/Bison*, indeterminate cervids; *E. caballus* cf. *germanicus, C. antiquitatis*
	EGF	Indeterminate carnivores; *Bos/Bison, Megaceros, R. tarandus; E. caballus* cf. *germanicus, M. primigenius*
	EGC	Indeterminate carnivores; *Bos/Bison*, indeterminate cervids; *E. caballus* cf. *germanicus, M. primigenius*
	EGB	*V. vulpes*, indeterminate carnivores; *Bos/Bison*, indeterminate cervids

Table 7.1. Chronostratigraphic succession of faunal complexes from other levels at Saint-Césaire

French Castelperronian sites. These data are limited.

Site density in the Poitou-Charentes region (Figure 1.2, Introduction, this volume) is relatively high: in particular, in the vicinity of La Roche à Pierrot are Le Gros Roc, which was the object of very early excavations, was subsequently plundered, and is currently being reinvestigated, and Le Bouil Bleu. These two sites have not yet furnished precise information on Castelperronian fauna, but it is hoped that the new excavations at Le Gros Roc will present opportunities for correlation with the basal Mousterian of Saint-Césaire.

In the Charente, the Castelperronian has been recorded at Abri du Chasseur, at Fontéchevade, at La Chaise, at La Quina, and at Le Trou du Cluzeau. Only the site of La Quina has yielded data on macrofauna: for Level 4, Henri-Martin reports that the fauna is rare, and includes reindeer, horse, rhinoceros, and indeterminate diaphyseal fragments. He points out that reindeer dominates (Henri-Martin 1961).

In Vienne, several sites are attributable to this period, including Les Cottés, the site famous for its pollen studies (by Bastin et al. 1976) that drew attention to major climatic variations. The macrofauna of Level G was published by Bouchud (1961): it includes reindeer, *Bos, Equus*, cave lion (*Felis leo spelaea*), spotted hyaena, cave bear (*Ursus spelaeus*), and woolly rhinoceros. The paleontology of the site of Belleroche has, as yet, not been published. La Grande Roche, Quinçay, which the author studied in 1980, displays an exceptional sequence of Castelperronian levels (Lavaud 1980). Fauna from the site are relatively complete (Table 7.2).

Comparison of initial results obtained at Saint-Césaire with the data set furnished by these deposits from the region enable us to envision more globally the importance of variability in the paleoenvironments of the last Neandertals of Poitou-Charentes during this transitional period; we should be extremely vigilant, however, in our attempts to distinguish the effects of widespread general variation and those due to local variation or to conditions limited to a particular lifezone.

Summary

At Saint-Césaire, as at the other Castelperronian sites of the region, reindeer is the dominant form, underlining the cold climate of this period. At each site are found horses with clear caballine attributes, closer from an evolutionary point of view to the Mousterian *Equus caballus germanicus* than to *Equus caballus gallicus* of Solutrean levels, but differing from it especially in their small dimensions. Large bovines are also noted in abundance. The presence of these two taxa argues in favor of milder climatic conditions during this period.

The equid/bovid ratio at Saint-Césaire is different from those recorded for the sites in the Vienne region, which is farther inland and presumably remained

Level	Fauna
Ens J	*Canis lupus lupus, Vulpes vulpes, Ursus spelaeus, Crocuta spelaea spelaea, Martes* sp., *Mustela nivalis; Bos/Bison, Rupicapra* sp., *Cervus elaphus, Rangifer tarandus; Equus caballus* cf. *germanicus, Coelodonta antiquitatis*
Ens M	*C. lupus lupus, V. vulpes, U. spelaeus, C. spelaea spelaea, Martes* sp., *Mustela nivalis; Bos/Bison, Rupicapra* sp., small cervids, *C. elaphus, R. tarandus; E. caballus* cf. *germanicus, E. hydruntinus, C. antiquitatis, Mammuthus primigenius*
Ens N	*Rupicapra* sp.; *E. caballus* cf. *germanicus*
Ens G	*C. elaphus, R. tarandus*

Table 7.2. Chronostratigraphic succession of faunal complexes from La Grande Roche de Quinçay

quite cold. For Saint-Césaire, the proximity of the Atlantic coast could explain a localized trend toward milder conditions, which seems to be confirmed by the presence of such temperate indicators as giant elk, wild boar, and the various forms of cervid.

The Castelperronian is not a period of drastic faunal change; nevertheless, it marks the end of the temperate biocenoses dominated by horses and large bovines of the Mousterian, and an increase in the Aurignacian tendency of reindeer-dominated faunas. The main species are morphologically very stable; only variation in size can set aside some forms with a typically Castelperronian cachet.

The exhaustive study of the material collected at Saint-Césaire, including intrasite comparison as well as contrasts with limitrophic deposits, and evaluation of these results with other work carried out at Saint-Césaire in other disciplines will refine these first impressions of Castelperronian sedimentation under rather cold and humid conditions in an environment with an important forested element and will inable us to detail the local or subspecific level of observed faunal variation.

References Cited

Bastin, B., Lévêque, F., and L. Pradel
  1976 Mise en évidence de spectres polliniques interstadiaires entre le Moustérien et le Périgordien ancien de la grotte des Cottés (Vienne). *Compte Rendu de l'Académie des Sciences de Paris* 282(D):1261-1264.

Bouchud, J.
  1961 Etude de la faune du gisement des Cottés (Vienne). *L'Anthropologie* 65(3-4):258-270.

Henri-Martin, G.
  1961 Le niveau de Châtelperron à La Quina (Charente). *Bulletin de la Société Préhistorique Française* 58(11-12):796-808.

Lavaud, F.
  1980 Les Faunes Paléolithiques du Würm II et III dans le Sud-ouest et le Centre-ouest de la France. Unpublished Ph.D. dissertation, Université de Poitiers.

Lavaud-Girard, F.
  1987 Les gisements Castelperroniens de Quinçay et de Saint-Césaire, quelques comparaisons préliminaires-les faunes. In *Préhistoire de Poitou-Charentes, Problèmes Actuels*, Editions du Comité des Travaux Historiques et Scientifiques, Actes du 111ème Congrès National des Sociétés Savantes (Poitiers, 1986) pp. 115-123, Paris.

Lévêque, F., and B. Vandermeersch
  1980 Découverte de restes humains dans un niveau castelperronien à Saint-Césaire (Charente-Maritime). *Compte Rendu de l'Académie des Sciences de Paris* 291:187-189.

Mercier, N., H. Valladas, J-L. Joron, J-L. Reyss, F. Lévêque, and B. Vandermeersch
  1991 Thermoluminescence Dating of the Late Neanderthal Remains from Saint-Césaire. *Nature* 351(6329):737-739.

8

Etude Taphonomique et Paléoethnographique de la Faune Associée au Néandertalien de Saint-Césaire

Marylène Patou-Mathis

L'assemblage osseux de la couche EJOP Sup. de Saint-Césaire est d'origine anthropique. Il n'a subi aucun bouleversement post-dépôt important. Il comporte une majorité d'ossements de grands Artiodactyles, principalement de Bovinés et de Renne, mais le Cheval est également abondant. La fragmentation est intense, elle est due à un piétinement important ou répété sur un matériel déjà fracturé par l'homme, soit directement, soit sur une couche sédimentaire de faible épaisseur. Si la pratique de la chasse, notamment aux Cervidés, est attestée, pour les autres espèces celle du charognage ne peut être exclue. Les animaux ont été dépecés, désarticulés et décharnés en dehors de la zone fouillée. Les ossements correspondent uniquement à des déchets domestiques. Ces déchets appartiennent, exceptés pour quelques restes de Renne, à des parties peu riches en viande. Ils attestent de la collecte de morceaux, soit sur des carcasses abandonnées par d'autres prédateurs, soit pour des commodités de transport sur leur gibier. Le traitement des ossements a été très important, tous les os longs (et mêmes les os courts) ont été fracturés pour en récupérer la moëlle et peut être même la graisse (bouillon?). D'après les bois de chute de Renne, les préhistoriques étaient présents dans le site au moins en hiver et au printemps. Ces bois ont été ramassés intentionnellement pour récupérer une partie de la perche. L'évaluation de la quantité de viande a permis d'éliminer les deux types extrêmes de campement : halte brève de chasse et base de très longue durée. Parmi les 26,838 esquilles, plus de 12% sont brulées, leur taille (< 2 cm) et leur composition (*spongiosa*) suggèrent l'utilisation des épiphyses d'os longs comme combustible. Leur présence hors de structure de foyer et leur dispersion relative avec quelques zones de concentration, permettent d'émettre l'hypothèse de vidanges de foyer. Aucune zone d'activités liées à la faune (de dépeçage, culinaire...) n'a été déterminée. L'ensemble correspond à une aire de déchets.

Tous ces résultats, obtenus uniquement à partir du matériel faunique, doivent être confrontés à ceux des autres disciplines : typologie, technologie, tracéologie, micromorphologie, paléoanthropologie.

Taphonomic and Paleoethnographic Study of the Fauna Associated with the Neandertal of Saint-Césaire

Marylène Patou-Mathis

The faunal material reported in this chapter consists of identifiable bone and bone fragments contained in the EJOP superior level at Saint-Césaire, where the remains of a Neandertal were discovered. A total of 27,591 bones was analyzed. Certain bone fragments from the EJOP level belong to EJOP superior but were not included in this study. The strictly paleontological aspects of this assemblage will not be dealt with here; we discuss taphonomic problems and formulate paleoethnographic hypotheses from faunal data alone.[1]

Cervids dominate (54% of the NISP and 31.6% of the MNI; Table 8.1).[2] Bovines (aurochs and bison) and equids are abundant (17% and 13.5% of the NISP, and 25% and 15% of the MNI, respectively). Carnivores are rare (only 5.5% of the NISP and 6.5% of the MNI), as are woolly rhinoceros, mammoth, and wild boar. Rabbit is represented by only three bones, the remains of an adult. Among the cervids, reindeer are in the majority (more than 63% of the MNI), and *Cervus elaphus*, roe deer, and megaloceros are present as well. Carnivores include remains of common fox, marten, wolf, and hyaena.[3]

Age profiles for identifiable species are as follows: For the cervids, bovines, and equids, the histograms are close to those for natural, living populations, with a slight deficit in juveniles, probably attributable to differential preservation biased against bones of younger animals, which are more fragile (Figure 8.1). The age profiles of these three families are similar, with slight peaks for animals between the ages of 5 and 10 years (Figure 8.2). Of the three woolly rhinos, two are young. The mammoth is mainly represented by fragments of tooth plates, except for a deciduous premolar of a young individual and a first or second molar of an adult.[4] All the carnivore and wild boar remains belong to adults (Table 8.1).

Sexual identification is always difficult, especially when the osteological sample is small and lacks anatomical elements that enable identification with certainty. Nonetheless, the robusticity of the bovine and reindeer bones indicates that they are likely those of females and subadults. One canine points to the presence of at least one male among the horses.

Origin and History of the Bone Assemblage

Bone concentrations can result from several factors: e.g., natural traps, water transport, transport by carnivores or burrowing animals, or human activities. These processes can sometimes be simultaneously operative. The bone materials then undergo the ordeal of time, burial, and fossilization processes. In an attempt to reconstruct the origin of the assemblage and understand its genesis, we have studied the preservation of the different anatomical elements of each species, their extrinsic characteristics, postmortem disorganization, and fragmentation.

Bone Preservation

Analysis of identifiable bone immediately shows a high percentage of cranial bones, especially teeth (66%). Analysis of the bone fragments, however, brings down this percentage abruptly to 1.8%. This finding underscores the highly fragmented condition of this material. As indicated by the teeth, preservation of the assemblage is, on average, 13%, a little higher among the cervids (15%), the bovines (17%), the equids (18.5%), and the rhinoceros (17.2%), and much less for the suids (3.5%) and the carnivores (8%). This calculation was done using the MNI for each species. Preservation is therefore relatively poor, but the discovery of 119 fragments of shed reindeer antler, mostly from animals less than 3 years old, shows a good potential for preservation, since antler deteriorates rapidly. Furthermore, the preservation profile for the various anatomical elements of reindeer is not the same as for the other herbivores. For reindeer, the postcrania are better represented (Figure

Species - Element	Number of Specimens			Minimum Number of Individuals	Age
	Cranial	Postcranial	Total		
Rangifer tarandus	188	48	236	12	2 <3 yrs / 10 adults
Cervus elaphus	4	4	8	2	2 adults
Capreolus capreolus	8	8	16	2	2 adults
Megaceros giganteus	7	0	7	2	2 adults
Indeterminate cervids	13	4	17	1	1 juvenile
Bovines	79	11	90	15	1 juvenile / 14 adults
Equus caballus	66	5	71	9	1 juvenile / 8 adults
Sus scrofa	3	0	3	2	2 adults
Coelodonta antiquitatis	15	9	24	3	2 juveniles / 1 adult
Mammuthus primigenius	14	0	14	2	1 juvenile / 1 adult
Subtotal, large herbivores	398	90	488	50	8 juveniles / 42 adults
Vulpes vulpes	7	7	14	1	1 adult
Martes martes	5	3	8	1	1 adult
Canis lupus	2	3	5	1	1 adult
Crocuta crocuta	1	0	1	1	1 adult
Subtotal, carnivores	15	13	28	4	4 adults
Oryctolagus cuniculus	1	2	3	1	1 adult
Talpa europaeus	0	6	6	5	5 adults
Batrachians (frogs)	0	3	3	2	2 adults
Birds	0	2	2	1	1 adult
Cranial fragments	27	-	27	-	-
Tooth fragments	55	-	55	-	-
Vertebral fragments	-	35	35	-	-
Rib fragments	-	85	85	-	-
Sternebra	-	1	1	-	-
Indeterminate bones	-	20	20	-	-
Indeterminate fragments	-	26,838	26,838	-	-
Total	496	27,095	27,591	63	8 juveniles / 55 adults

Table 8.1. Faunal Remains from Level EJOP Superior of Saint-Césaire (Charente-Maritime)

8.3). The profile corresponds more or less to the theoretical profile of differential preservation, favoring teeth and metapodia (Guthrie 1967). For the other species, human action, such as differential animal processing or a different mode of provisioning, may account for the deficit of certain bones in the profiles. In fact, the few carnivore remains and the high skull to postcrania ratio (Klein and Cruz-Uribe 1984) show that carnivores were not responsible for the formation of this assemblage. The near-absence of gnaw marks on the bones confirms this interpretation.

Extrinsic Characteristics
(not attributable to humans)

Climatic change and soil conditions modify the surface of bone, partially and sometimes completely destroying it, according to the mechanical resistance properties of the bones, their age, mass, and geometric structure (Bouchud 1975, 1977; Poplin 1977, 1983). In this assemblage, only 53 of the total of 27,591 bones, or 0.2%, exhibit evidence of nonbiological agents. Two elements have oxidation marks, 38 have exfoliation or desquammation marks accompanied by longitudinal cracks, and 7 have polished surfaces with

Taphonomic and Paleoethnographic Study of the Fauna 83

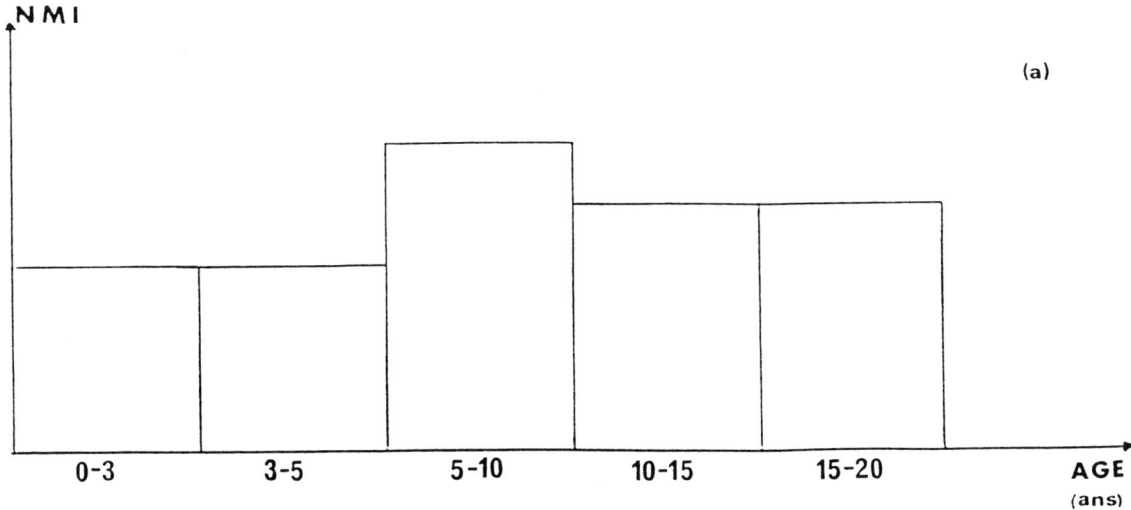

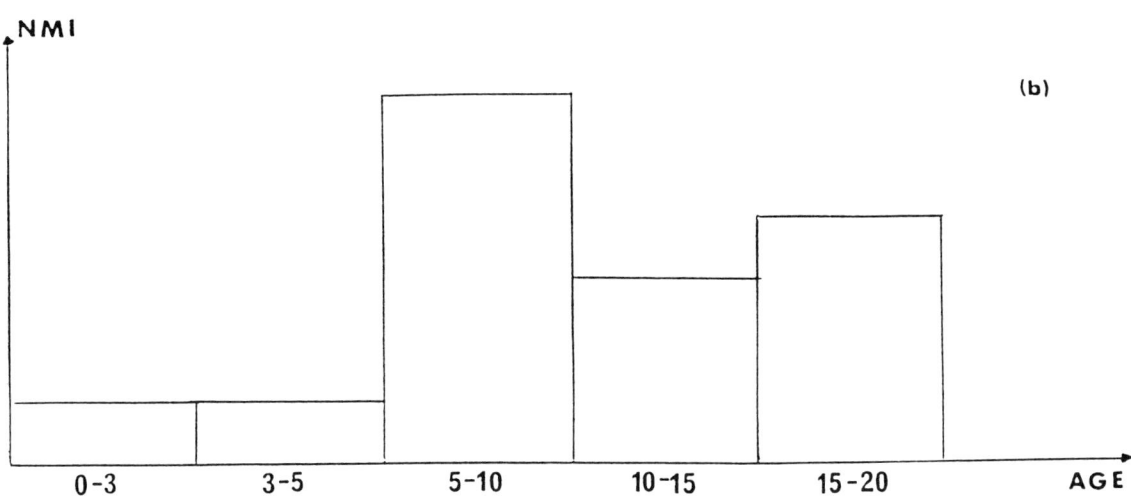

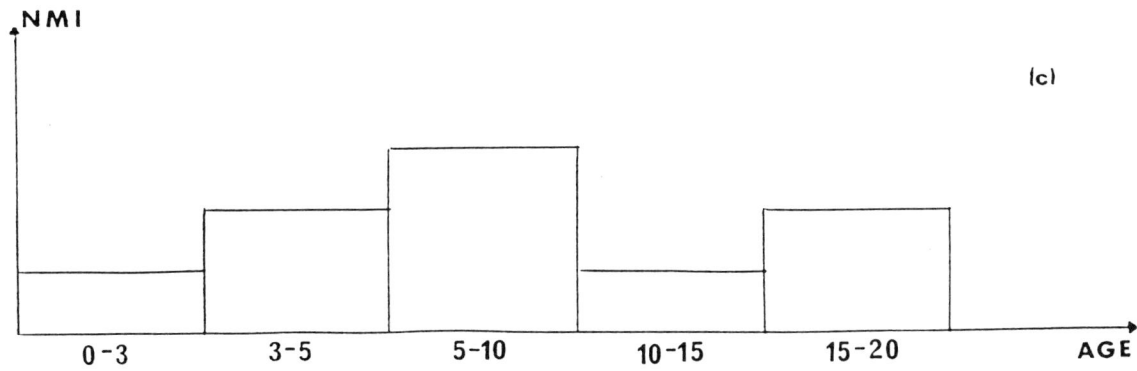

Figure 8.1. Age histograms for cervids (a), bovines (b), and equids (c) from level superior, Saint-Césaire.

NMI = MNI; age (ans) = age (years)

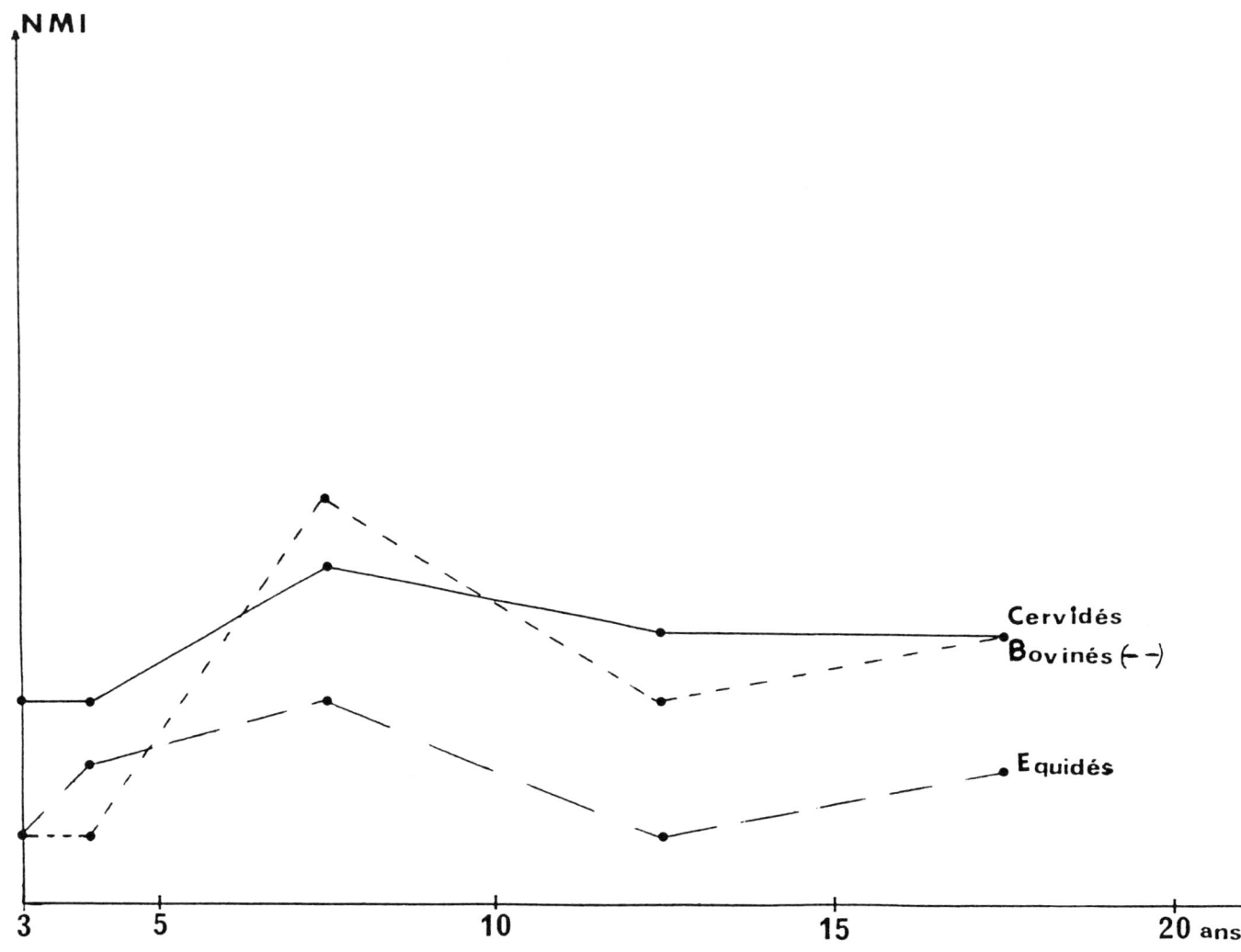

Figure 8.2. Comparison of age curves for cervids, bovines, and equids from level EJOP superior, Saint-Césaire.

NMI = MNI; cervidés = cervids; bovinés = bovines; équidés = equids; ans = years

rounding ("rolled bones"). These pieces were dispersed across the entire excavated area. They are generally characteristic of alternating dry/humid or freeze/thaw conditions, but are too few to be really significant. Similarly, only 3 bones exhibit marks made by carnivores: a long bone diaphysis of a lagomorph with a hole made by a fox canine, a distal extremity of rhinoceros metapodia that seems to have been gnawed by a hyaena (?), and a glenoid cavity of a reindeer scapula punctured by a wolf canine.

Postmortem Disorganization and Breakage

All the skeletal elements are dispersed; none was discovered in anatomical connection. They are extremely fragmented. Detailed study of the indeterminate fragments shows them to be distributed almost exclusively (99%) in two size classes: Class I, fragments smaller or equal to 2 cm, and Class II, with maximum dimensions between 2 and 5 cm (74 and 24%, respectively; Table 8.2).[5] Among the Class I fragments, 50% are pieces of spongy bone. The rest are mostly diaphyseal fragments of long bones of small or medium-sized herbivores (roe deer, reindeer, etc.). Observation of the fracture planes shows that most of this fragmentation is due to trampling, which is confirmed by the presence of three bone "buttons" indicative of sudden breakage via trampling of a hollow long bone with a small internal diameter (Giacobini 1982). The central detached fragment exhibits the typical *double bec de flute* aspect, once called "button." The small size of the fragments shows that this trampling intervened on bones already broken, speeding up the deterioration process and favoring their dispersal.

These data confirm an anthropic origin for almost all the bone material, which was buried without any major climatic, edaphic, or biological destruction or

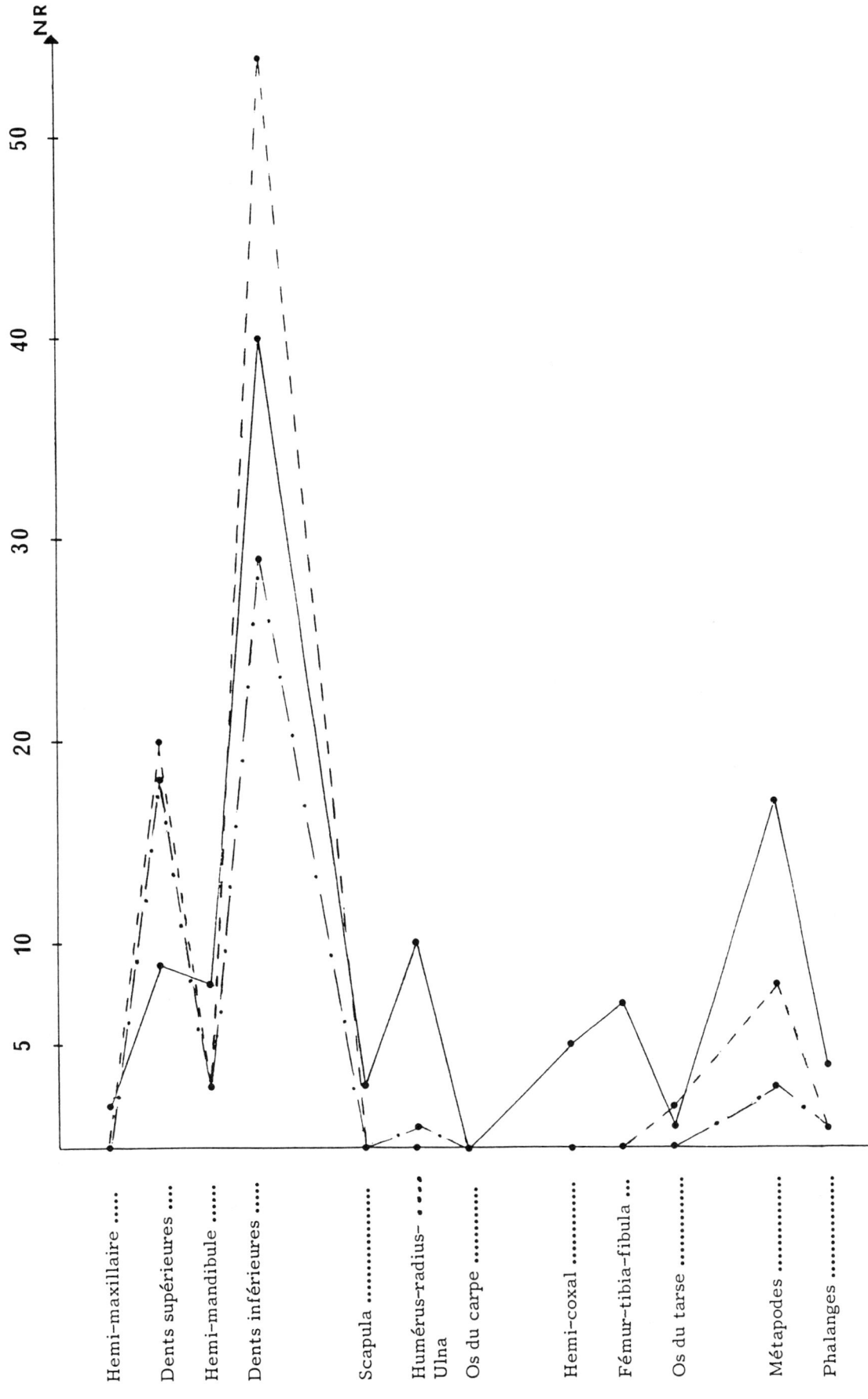

Figure 8.3. Preservation of different anatomical elements of reindeer (- -), bovines (———), and equids (- · -) from level EJOP superior, Saint-Césaire.

NR = NISP; hémi-maxillaire = half maxilla; dents supérieures = upper teeth; hémi-mandibule = half mandible; dents inférieures = lower teeth; os du carpe = carpal; hémi-coxal = half coxal; os du tarse = tarsal; métapodes = metapodials

	Size Class					
Square	Class I (≤ 2 cm)	Class I-II	Class II (>2 - 5 cm)	Class III (>5 - 10 cm)	Class IV (>10 cm)	Total
D 3 *	825	60	70	1	0	956
D 4	7	-	3	4	0	14
D 5	2	-	1	2	0	5
D 6	60	-	13	0	0	73
D 7 *	118	770	13	0	0	901
E 2	16	-	94	0	0	110
E 3	147	-	58	2	0	207
E 4	4	-	2	0	0	6
E 5	177	-	35	2	0	214
E 6	203	-	51	0	0	254
E 7	691	-	84	17	1	793
F 3	820	-	111	3	0	934
F 4	54	-	16	5	0	75
F 5	112	-	24	1	0	137
F 6	826	-	199	33	2	1,060
F 7	16	-	8	0	0	24
G 3	244	-	71	4	0	319
G 4 *	229	80	33	7	0	349
G 5 *	456	2,400	160	13	1	3,030
G 6 *	1,324	1,290	252	26	1	2,893
G 7	42	-	30	0	0	72
H 3	160	-	41	0	0	201
H 4 *	863	240	184	4	0	1,291
H 5 *	799	3,720	275	51	2	4,847
H 6 *	1,115	2,820	547	62	13	4,557
I 4	555	-	95	11	1	662
I 5 *	1,197	980	422	58	2	2,659
I 6	138	-	52	4	1	195
Total	11,200	12,360	2,944	310	24	26,838

* evaluated in part by weight

Table 8.2. Distribution of Bone Splinters at Saint-Césaire (Charente-Maritime) by Square and Size Class

upheaval (other than human). The heavy breakage resulting from trampling points to movements either directly on the material or on a very thin layer of sediment above the faunal material.

Paleoethnography

Qualitative and quantitative analysis of the bones produced counts by species from level EJOP superior at Saint-Césaire (Figure 8.4). Artiodactyls are dominant (Figure 8.5a), representing 60%. Bovines are the most abundant, aurochs and bison are represented by at least 15 individuals, just ahead of reindeer (12) and horses (9). Around 78% of the animals from EJOP superior have a body weight equal to or higher than 100 kg (Figure 8.5b). The occupants of Saint-Césaire consumed large-bodied animals by preference, primarily steppe-adapted forms (Figures 8.5c and 8.5d). The study of the ages of the principal herbivores (Figure 8.2) underlines the fact that no particular age group was targeted, confirming once again that humans rather than carnivores were responsible for the assemblage (Klein 1982). On the other hand, it appears that female herds with their young account for most of the bovines and reindeer. The small number of identifiable bone makes it impossible to delineate population structure with any precision.

Meat Acquisition Technique

Were these the bones of hunted animals, parts of collected carcasses, or both, depending on species? For all species, crania, axial skeletons, ribs and ver-

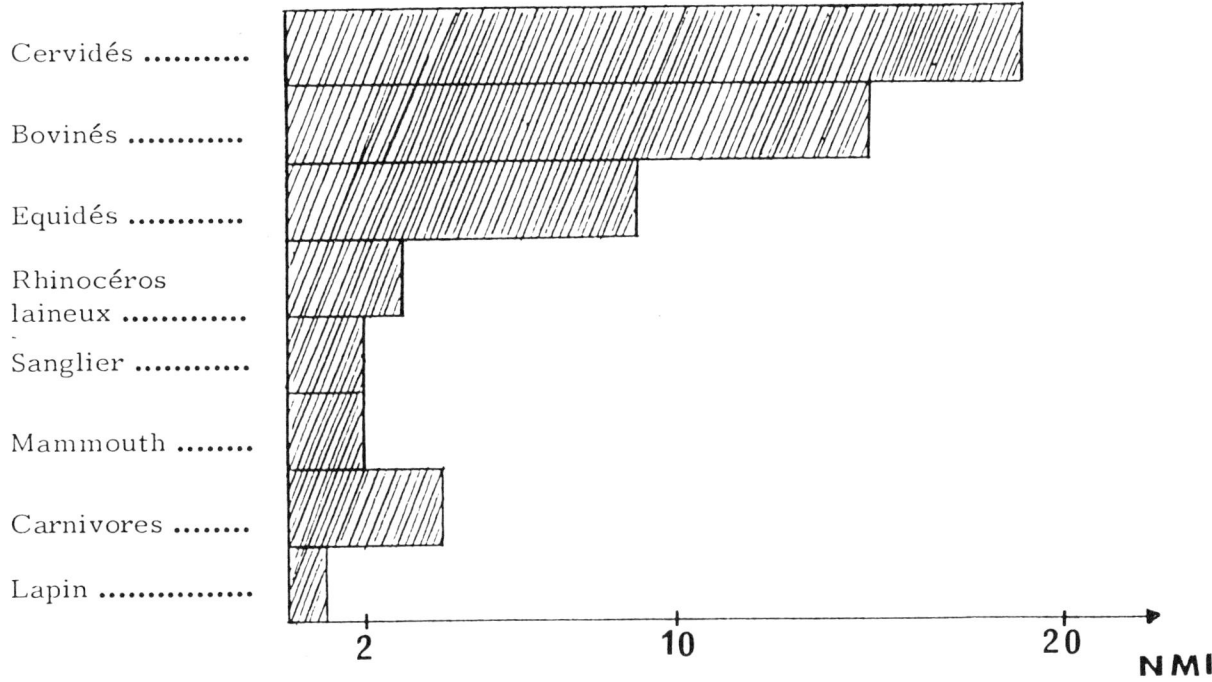

Figure 8.4. Large mammals from level EJOP superior, Saint-Césaire, by MNI.

NMI = MNI; cervidés = cervids; bovinés = bovines; équidés = equids; rhinocéros laineux = woolly rhinoceros; sanglier = wild boar; mammouth = mammoth; lapin = rabbit

tebrae are underrepresented or absent, but it should be kept in mind that some fragments were not identifiable as to species (Table 8.1). Differential preservation alone cannot explain this deficit, especially for the large herbivores. The same is true for the observed difference between the preservation curve for reindeer and those for bovines and equids (Figure 8.3). Only 2% of the bone fragments can be attributed to long bones of aurochs, bison, or horse. There is therefore a lack of postcranial elements, in particular from the pelvic and scapular girdles and upper limb bones (Figure 8.3). For bovines, only tarsals and metapodia are preserved (Figure 8.6). For horses, with the exception of a fragment of a radius, only broken metapodia and a partial phalanx (Figure 8.7) remain; of the rhinoceros, only rib and metapodial fragments and a distal humerus from a young animal are left. Boar and mammoth are represented only by teeth. For these animals as a whole, the preserved bones, with the exception of the young rhino humerus, are from parts yielding very little meat or fat.

The preservation profile for reindeer is quite different from those of bovids and equids (Figure 8.8). All the elements are present, but their number is clearly too low: from the postcranial data alone the number of individuals represented would be 5 at the most, but we know that at least 12 individuals are represented. Ribs, vertebrae, skull bones, carpals, and tarsals are rare. The presence of high meat- and fat-yielding parts is of note, however (calculated from the MGUI; Binford 1978). For the other cervids, megaloceros is represented only by teeth, and roe deer by seven teeth, one fragment of a mandible, the proximal end of a femur, the proximal end of a radius, two distal ends of the tibia, two metatarsal fragments, one proximal end of a metapodial, and the end of a first phalanx. Red deer is represented by four teeth, one glenoid cavity of the scapula, one proximal end of a radius, one malleolus, and one metatarsal fragment.

The presence of cutmarks from lithic tools on a reindeer second phalanx (D5IV266) resulting from skinning (Martin 1907-1910), and marks observed on the vestibular face of a reindeer's right mandibular condyle (H5III235) caused by head detachment indicate that at least one whole reindeer was brought into camp.

These results are inconclusive as to whether meat was acquired exclusively through hunting. In fact, for some of these animals (mostly the poorly represented ones) two hypotheses can be put forth. The first is that prehistoric humans collected parts of carcasses, after large predator and scavenger access,

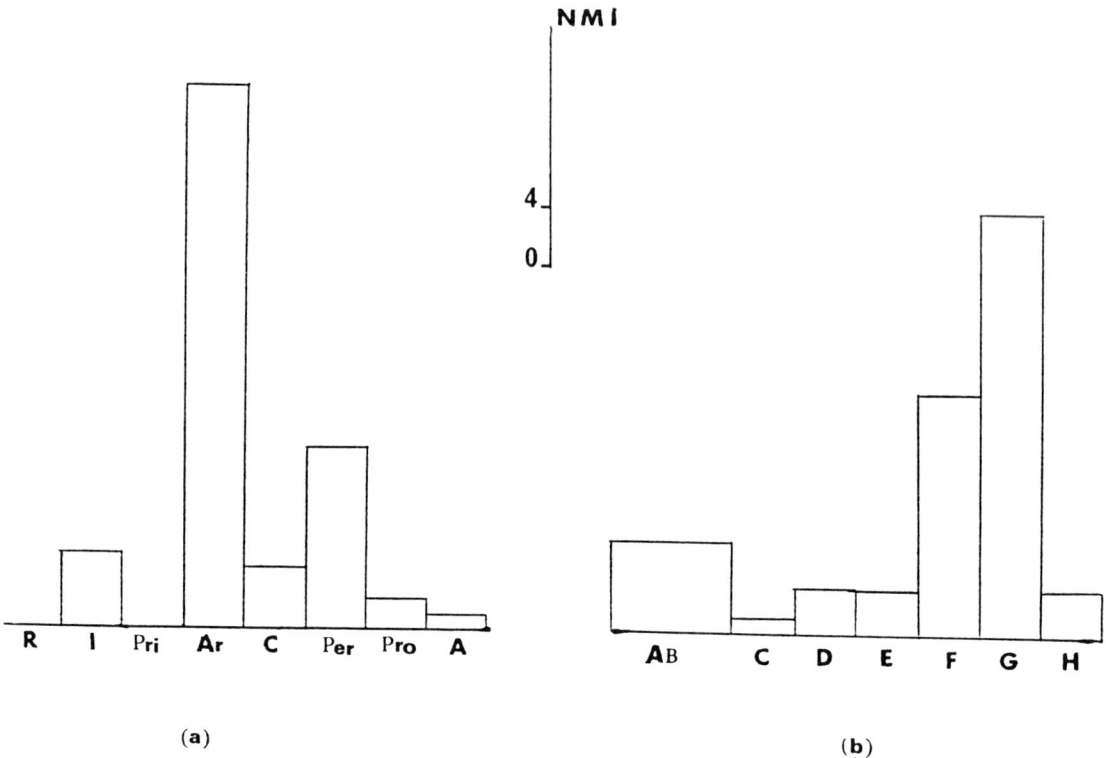
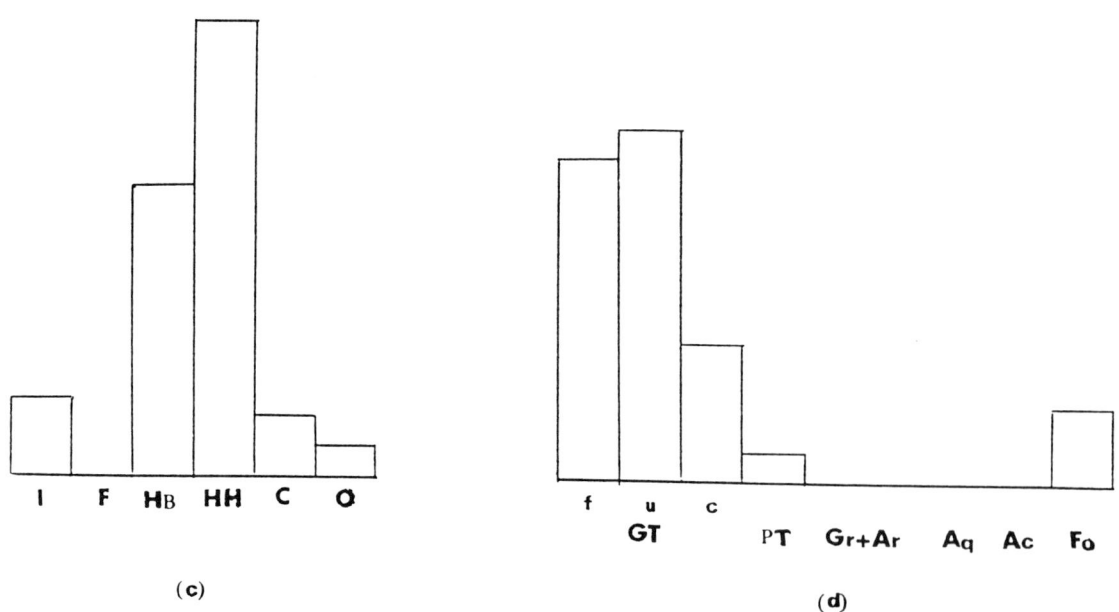

Figure 8.5. Ecological diagram (by MNI) of fauna from level EJOP superior, Saint-Césaire, following Guérin: (a) taxonomic histogram, (b) weight histogram, (c) subsistence histogram, and (d) locomotor histogram.

NMI = MNI

Taphonomic and Paleoethnographic Study of the Fauna

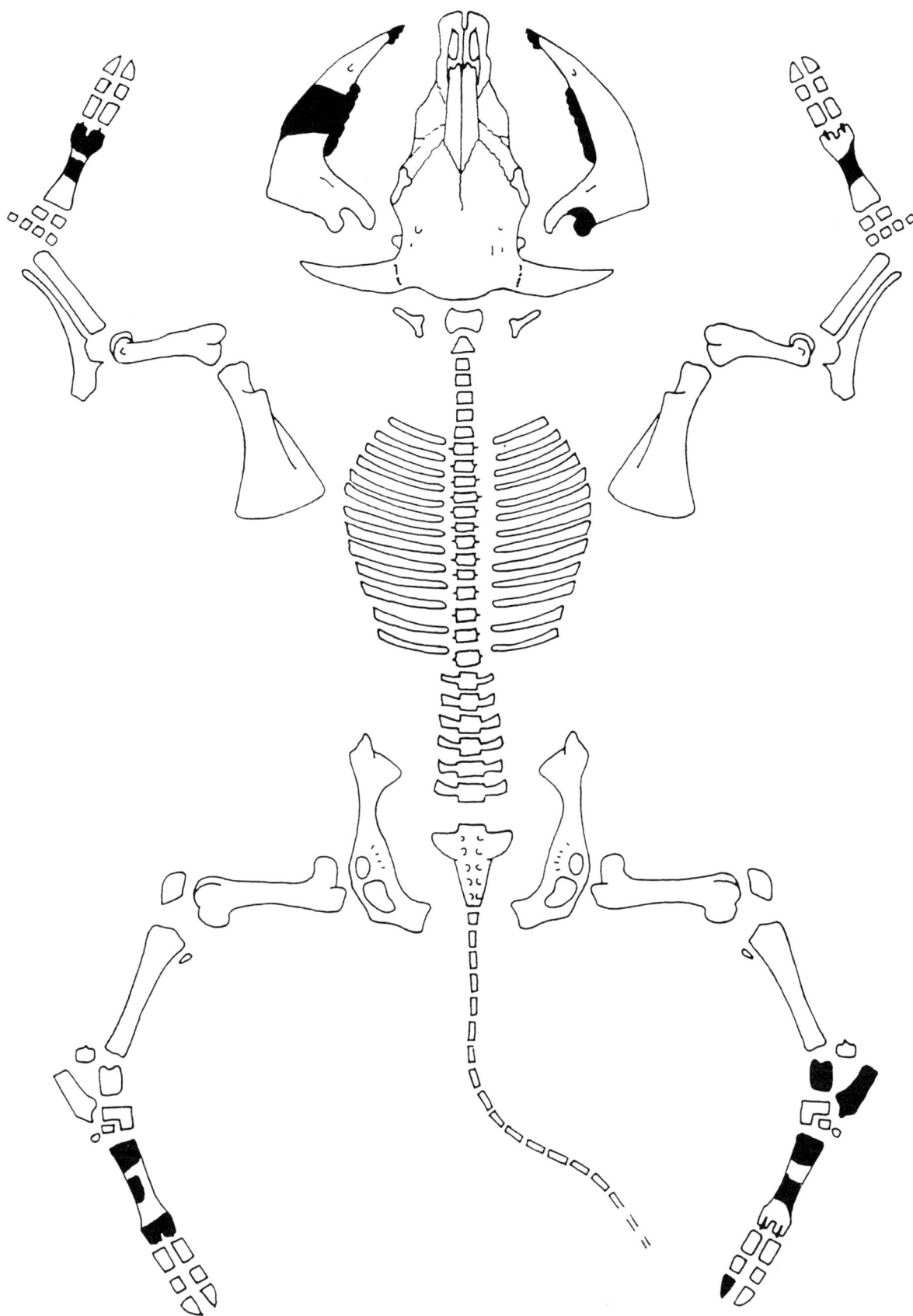

Figure 8.6. Preservation of bovine remains.

90 Context of a Late Neandertal

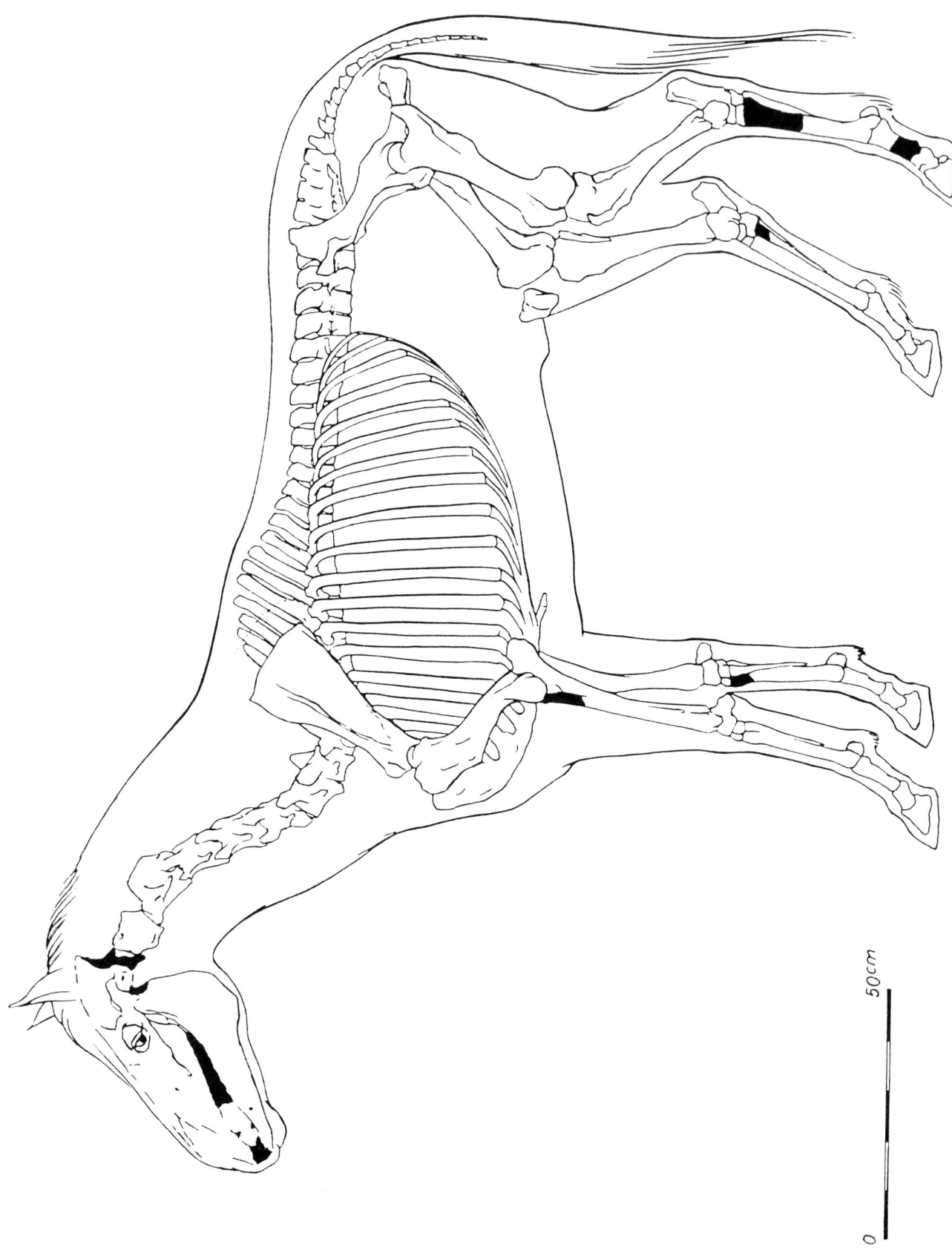

Figure 8.7. Preservation of horse remains.

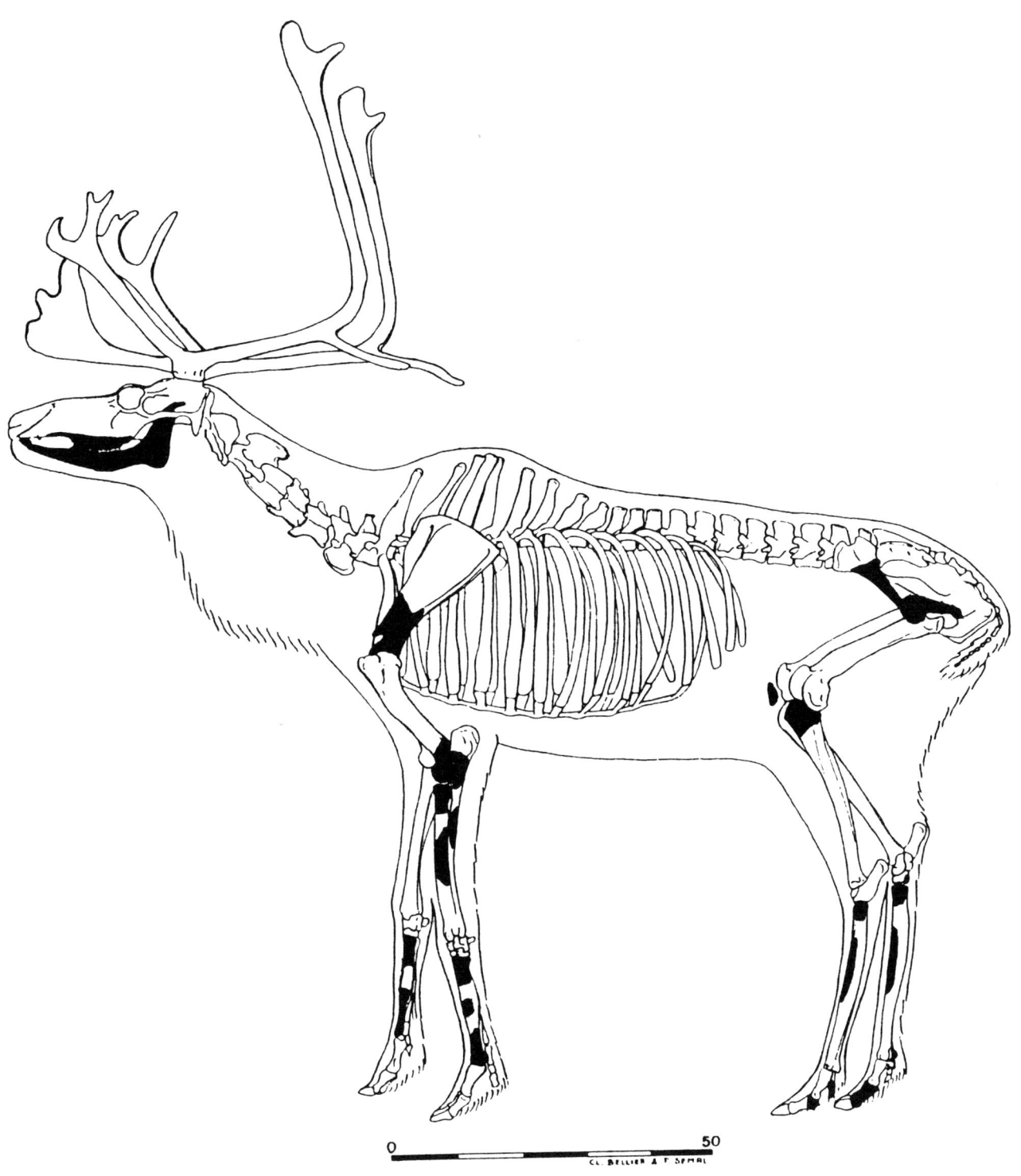

Figure 8.8. Preservation of reindeer remains.

indicated by the presence of bones mostly from less choice pieces. A second possibility is that they butchered, disarticulated, and defleshed their game (particularly the large herbivores) outside of the excavated site, enhancing its portability—the "schlepp effect" defined by Perkins and Daly (1968).

Seasonality and the Occupation of the Rockshelter

It is not possible to appraise seasonal frequencies with precision because complete mandibles and teeth of juveniles are scarce, and because the sample of reindeer and bovine molars is too small for crown height studies. Nevertheless, the presence of shed

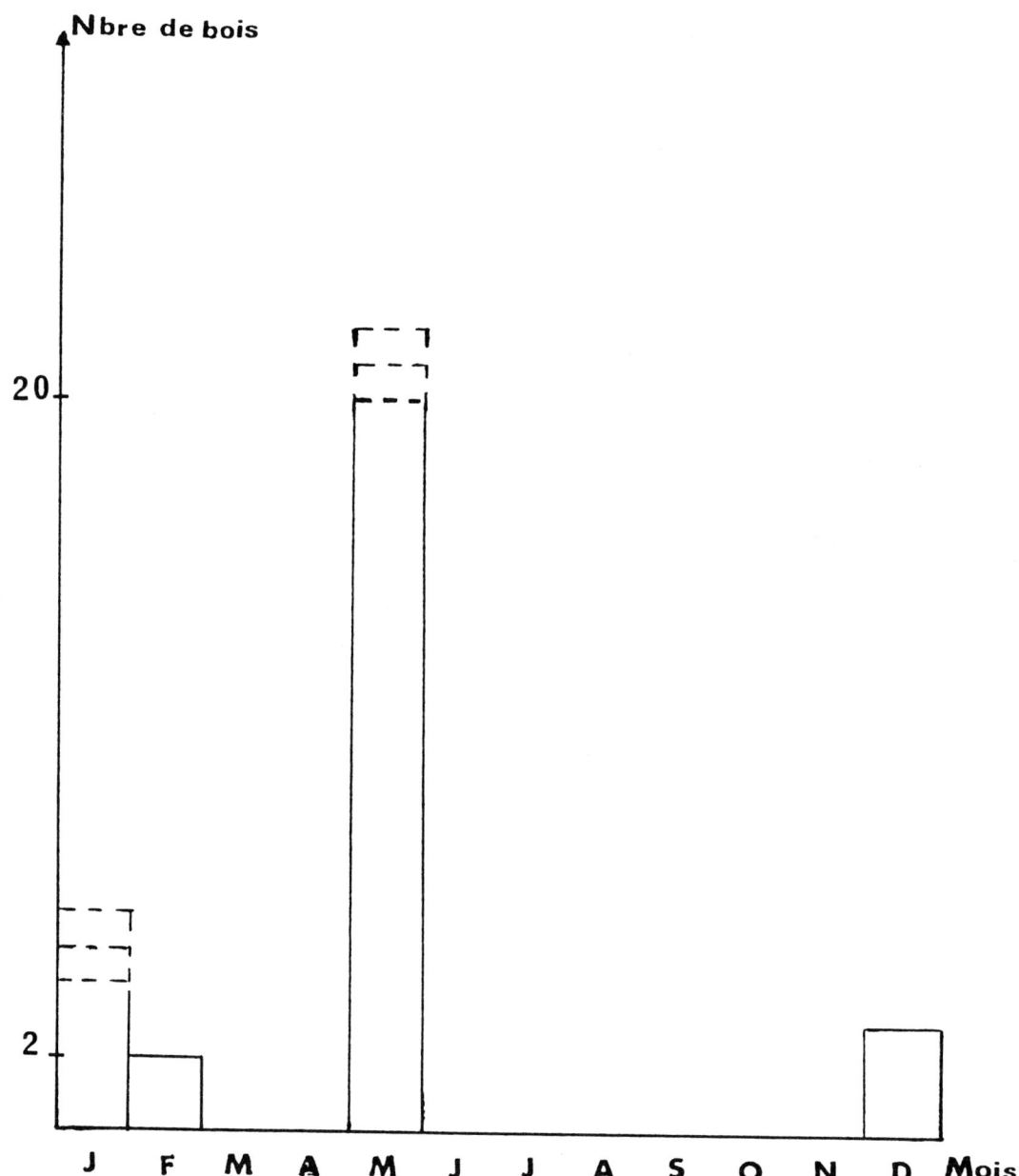

Figure 8.9. Period of antler shedding for reindeer present in level EJOP superior, Saint-Césaire.

Nbre de bois = number of antlers; mois = month

reindeer antler and the absence of stag antlers from these cervids show that the rockshelter was frequented by prehistoric humans at least during winter and spring (Figure 8.9).

In level EJOP superior at Saint-Césaire, all the reindeer antler is shed antler. A total of 119 remains have been identified: 32 bases, 10 shaft fragments, 39 shaft extremities (from juveniles in their third year), 9 pieces of palm tines, 6 tine fragments, and 23 tine points (Figure 8.10). Of these, only two belong to the *compressicornice* type, with a flattened cross-section; all the others are of the *cylindricornice* type. As indicated by the form of the bases, especially the detachment surface of the rack, the sex of individuals can be determined by distinguishing concave (for females) from convex (for males) medalions (Bouchud 1959). We have identified 18 females and 12 males (two were unidentifiable, because the preservation of the medalion was insufficient). The sex ratio of the herd (fawns, females, and young males) is one male for every three females, which corresponds to the theoretical sex ratio in a living wild population. Shaft diameter measurements taken just above the base allow evaluation of the ages of the individuals bear-

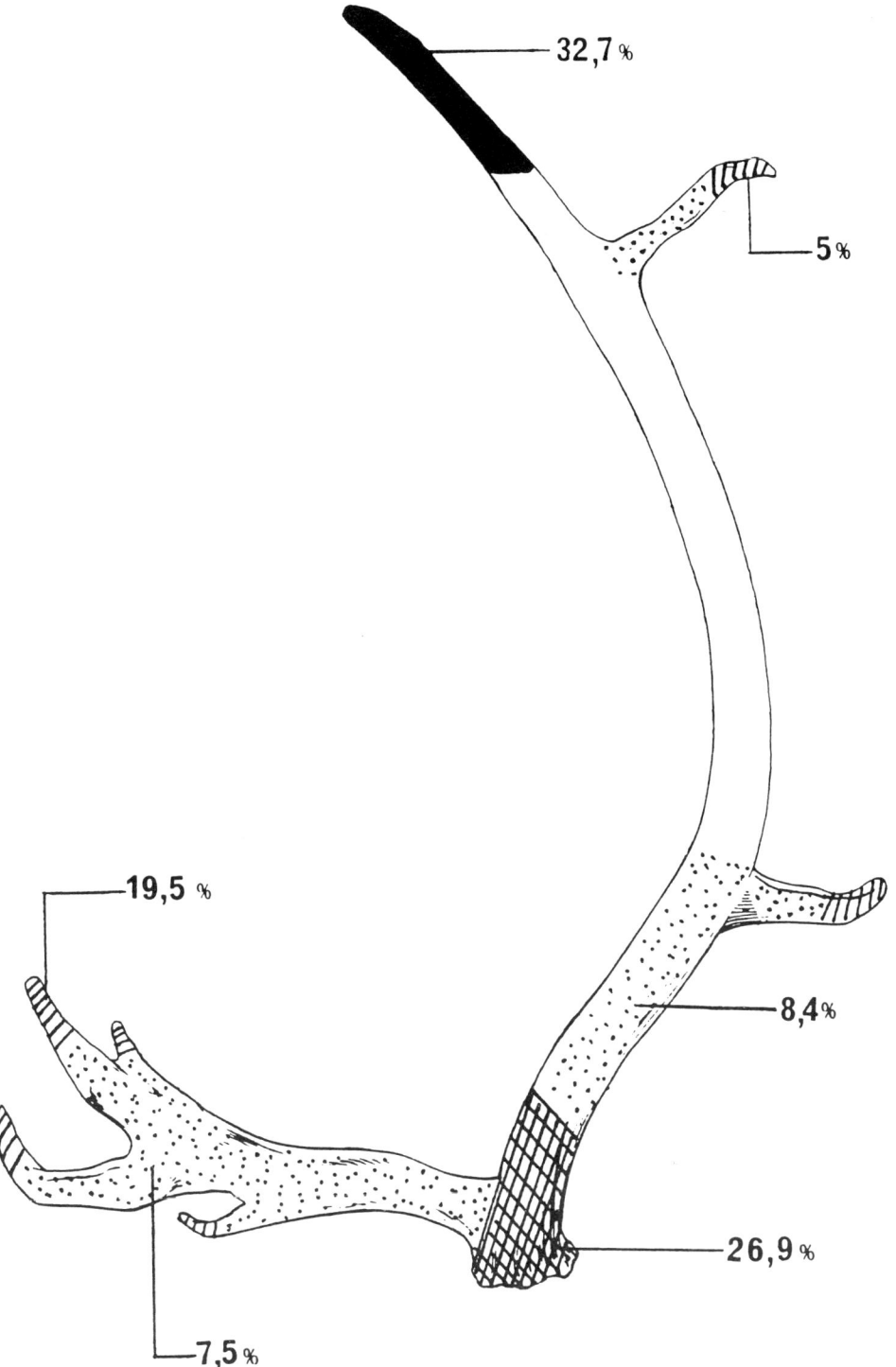

Figure 8.10. Preservation of shed reindeer antler.

ing these antlers, none of which were reconstituted as original pairs. We have recognized 4 fawns (first year), 4 young (second year), 15 juveniles (third year), and 9 adults (from 3 to 13 years old). Herd composition is therefore as follows: 12.5% fawns, 77% females, and 10.5% males. It is similar to the theoretical composition of wild reindeer herds, with a slight deficit in males (Banfield 1954; Bouchud 1959). The sex ratio and herd composition suggest the presence of a reindeer herd in the vicinity of the site.

These cervids do not all lose their antlers at the same time. Females and fawns lose them in May, two-year-old males in February, three-year-old males in January, and adult males in December (Figure 8.9).

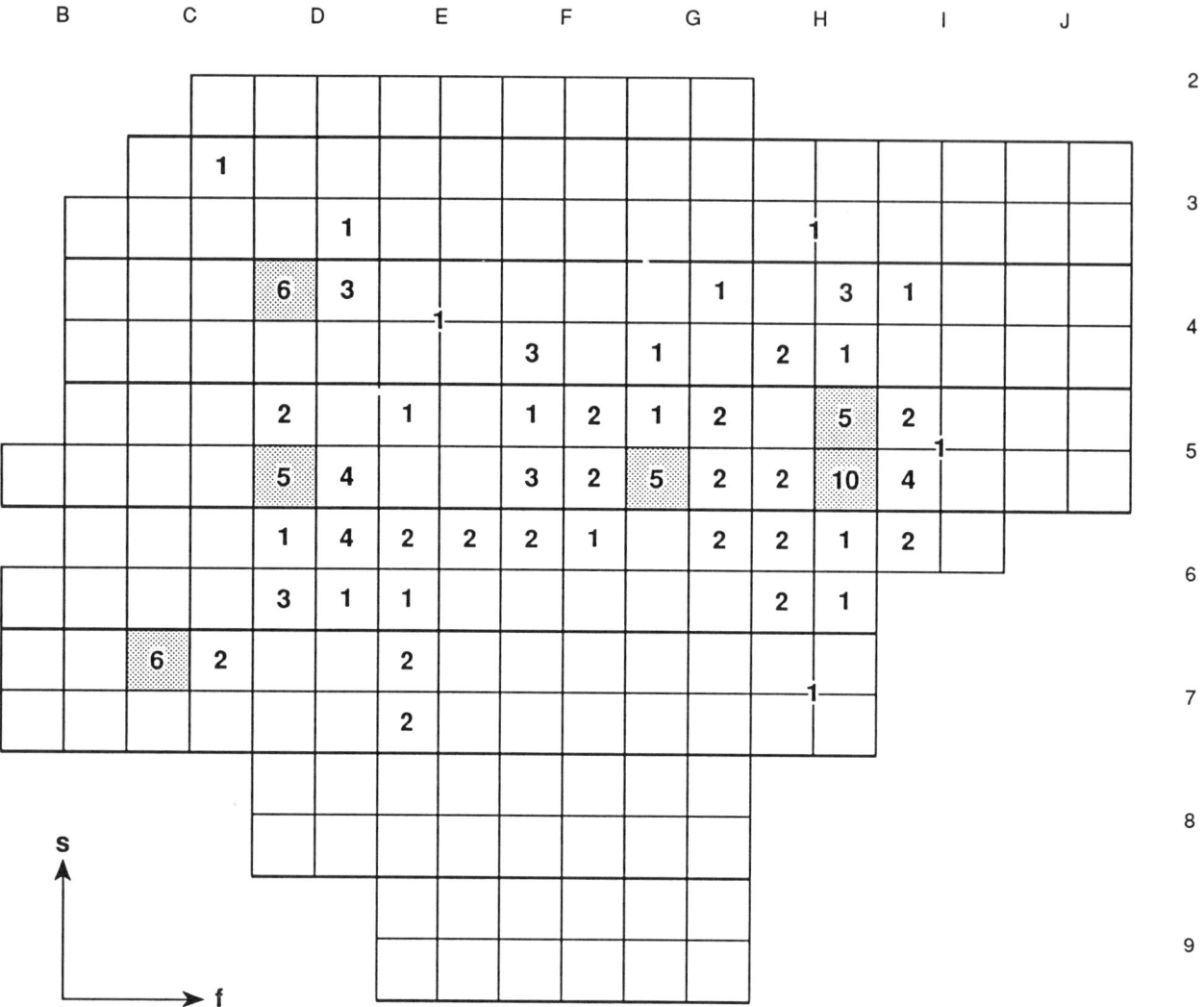

Figure 8.11. Distribution of shed reindeer antler.

s = south/southeast; f = west/northwest

Antlers are anatomical elements that preserve relatively poorly. They are irrigated by many blood vessels that create zones of lower tensile strength, with less resistance to pressure and climatic variation, and soon after they are shed, fracture lines appear that gradually lead to a crumbling away of the antler, accelerating their total disintegration. Furthermore, because antlers are equally very rich in mineral salts, they fall prey to rodents and sometimes even to calcium-deficient herbivores (Sutcliffe 1973). For all these reasons, it can be concluded that the reindeer antler was collected soon after it was shed. The people of Saint-Césaire gathered these antlers during winter and especially in spring (Figure 8.9). Their abundance relative to other bones cannot be explained by the probability of their preservation, which is low, indicating intentional action on the part of prehistoric humans. Preservation of different parts of the rack (Figure 8.10) is highly biased against shafts. This observation was confirmed by conjoins that have been performed. Here again, differential preservation cannot explain the observed pattern. The shaft does not disintegrate any faster than the tines. The hypothesis of human action is therefore proposed; large fragments of shaft were retrieved.

Saint-Césaire is not the only archaeological site

	MNI		Total weight by individual (kg)		Meat weight by individual (kg)		Total Meat Weight (kg)	Relative Meat Weight (%)
	Juvenile	Adult	Juvenile	Adult	Juvenile	Adult		
Reindeer (Spiess 1979)	2	10	60	120m 75 f	33	66m 41 f	≈550	≈3
Red deer (Spiess 1979)	0	2	200	340m 250 f	110	185m 137.5 f	≈310	≈2
Roe deer (Rozoy 1978)	0	2	-	22	-	13	26	≈0.1
Megaloceros (Guthrie 1967)	0	2	-	220	-	132	132	≈0.7
Bovids (Spiess 1979)	1	14	500	1400	275.0	770	11,055	≈59.6
Horse (Spiess 1979)	1	8	150	350	82.5	192.5	1,622	≈8.7
Wild boar (Jochim 1976)	0	2	-	135	-	81	162	≈0.8
Woolly rhinoceros (Pidoplichko 1969)	2	1	≈800	1200	≈480.0	720	≈1,680	≈9
Mammoth (Guthrie 1968)	1	1	≈2000	3000	≈1200.0	1800	≈3,000	≈16
Rabbit (Rozoy 1978)	0	1	-	1.8	-	1	1	-
Total	7	43	-	-	-	-	18,538	-

Table 8.3. Meat Weight Estimation for Herbivores from Level EJOP Superior at Saint-Césaire

where shed cervid antler has been found, and it is not the only site containing no evidence of this material having been worked. At Roc-en-Pail (Maine et Loire), for example, where Level 3 contained a Charentian Mousterian industry of the Quina type, about 3000 shed reindeer antler bases (Bouchud 1959; Gruet 1950) were found, on which no evidence of working was observed. Bone antler industries throughout the Upper Paleolithic show that, as in the Solutrean level (Bouchud 1959) at Badegoule (Dordogne), shed antlers of males were principally sought after. For intrinsic reasons, as more than two-thirds of the diameter is occupied by the hard outer layer when calcification is complete, these antlers are more resistant and more adapted to the manufacture of objects such as bone points, for example. Those of females and young have a much reduced hard outer layer. In the assemblage from Saint-Césaire, collection appears to have been random, based on an encounter strategy without any selection. Even during the Upper Paleolithic, selection does not appear to have been systematic. Magdalenian and Creswellian sites of the Meuse Basin in Belgium have yielded shed antler industries almost exclusively made on antler of females and juveniles. This finding can be explained by the absence, in that region, of prehistoric human occupations during cold seasons, especially winter, when shed antler of males could not be found (Patou, in press). The study of preserved parts and breakage patterns from these sites shows a similarity with the assemblages from Saint-Césaire. One of the bases (D6II270-77100) was sawed longitudinally and bears cutmarks from a stone tool a few centimeters above the articulation, showing that these shaft fragments were probably intentionally detached for subsequent use.

The people of Saint-Césaire therefore may have used these missing pieces, or in any case transported them away from the excavated area. They must have valued them. We can only get lost in conjecture as to the function of these pieces: percussion tools, "retouchers," "blade chasers," or perhaps bone points, like the ones discovered in the Chatelperronian level at Arcy-sur-Cure (Yonne).

The spatial distribution of these shed reindeer antler fragments (Figure 8.11), combined with the

Number	Anatomical Element	Species	Presumed Activity
I4 (IV) 23si	Cranial fragment	Medium herbivore	Skinning?
I4 (I) 22s	Rib shaft fragment	Bos or Equus	Defleshing
G4 (IV) 24i	Rib shaft fragment	Medium herbivore	Defleshing
I5 22i	Tibial diaphyseal fragment	Bos or Equus	Defleshing?
F5 (II) 228	Partial third right metacarpal without distal end	Rhinoceros	Carpometacarpal disarticulation
F4 (III) 231	Fourth left metacarpal	Rhinoceros	Carpometacarpal disarticulation
H4 (II) 218	Rib shaft fragment	Rhinoceros	Defleshing
D3 (I) 260	Metacarpal diaphyseal splinter	Bovid	Disarticulation?
F5	Femoral head	Roe deer	Coxial-femoral disarticulation
D5 (IV) 266	Second phalanx	Reindeer	Skinning
H5 (III) 235	Right mandibular condyle	Reindeer	Skinning
I5 (IV) 27s	Scapular wing fragment	Reindeer	Defleshing
D4 (I-IV)	Long bone diaphysis	Medium herbivore	Defleshing
F5 (IV)	Long bone diaphysis	Medium herbivore	Defleshing
F6 (II)	Long bone diaphysis	Medium herbivore	Defleshing
F6 (II)	Long bone diaphysis	Medium herbivore	Defleshing
G6 (I)	Long bone diaphysis	Bos or Equus	Defleshing
G6 (III)	Long bone diaphysis	Bos or Equus	Defleshing
H3 (III-IV)	Long bone diaphysis	Medium herbivore	Defleshing
H3 (III-IV)	Long bone diaphysis	Bos or Equus	Defleshing
H5 (III)	Long bone diaphysis	Bos or Equus	Defleshing
H5 (III-IV)	Long bone diaphysis	Medium herbivore	Defleshing
H5 (III-IV)	Long bone diaphysis	Medium herbivore	Defleshing
H5 (IV)	Long bone diaphysis	Bos or Equus	Defleshing
H5 (IV)	Long bone diaphysis	Bos or Equus	Defleshing
H6 (II)	Long bone diaphysis	Bos or Equus	Defleshing
H6 (II)	Long bone diaphysis	Bos or Equus	Defleshing
H6 (II)	Long bone diaphysis	Bos or Equus	Defleshing
H6 (III)	Long bone diaphysis	Bos or Equus	Defleshing
H6 (III)	Long bone diaphysis	Bos or Equus	Defleshing
H6 (IV)	Long bone diaphysis	Bos or Equus	Defleshing
H6 (IV)	Long bone diaphysis	Bos or Equus	Defleshing
H6 (IV)	Long bone diaphysis	Bos or Equus	Defleshing
H6 (IV)	Long bone diaphysis	Bos or Equus	Defleshing
H6 (IV)	Long bone diaphysis	Bos or Equus	Defleshing
H6 (IV)	Long bone diaphysis	Bos or Equus	Defleshing
I5 (II)	Long bone diaphysis	Medium herbivore	Defleshing

Table 8.4. Bones with Cutmarks from Butchering, Level EJOP Superior, Saint-Césaire

conjoins performed, points to three facts:

1) The antlers are relatively dispersed within five concentrations: H5 (II and III), C7 (I), D4(I), D5(IV) and G5(IV).

2) Bases with attached shafts, shaft extremities of young reindeer, and tines were broken in place. This breakage is due to pressure from trampling, either direct or through a thin layer of sediment. These observations were particularly noticeable in D4, D5, D6, G4, H4, H5, and I5. The fragments did not undergo much displacement, vertically (a maximum of 7 cm) or horizontally (a maximum of 68 cm), confirming the relative lack of upheaval in EJOP superior.

3) Once conjoined, the shafts with their bases never exceed 10 cm, showing once again that the shafts are underrepresented and were retrieved by prehistoric humans.

Meat Weight Estimates

Several problems impede a proper appraisal of quantities of meat consumed by prehistoric humans: weight estimates for fossil species, knowledge of the number of animals represented in the bone assemblage, and the extent of the occupied area relative to the excavated area. At Saint-Césaire, as at most sites, the mode of acquisition should be added to this list: whole animals or pieces scavenged from carcasses.

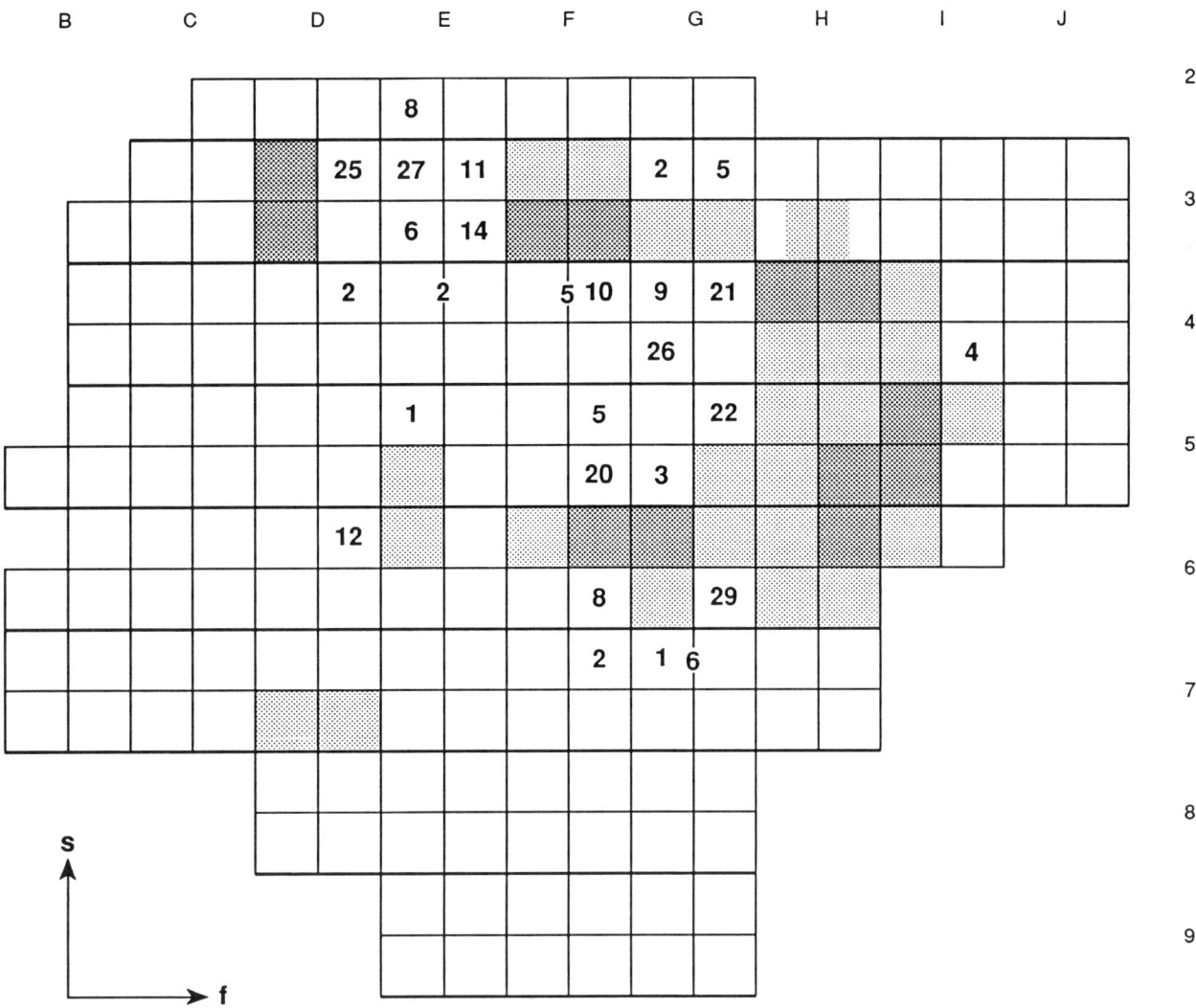

Figure 8.12. Distribution of burned bone fragments, dark gray: NISP ≥ 80; light gray: NISP ≥ 30.

s = south/southeast; f = west/northwest

Results presented in Table 8.3 are therefore only an estimate, but they allow us to discard the hypothesis that the site was only occupied during a brief hunting stopover. Similarly, the figures for total meat weight eliminate the possibility that this site was a base camp used over a long period of time, especially if only portions of the large species like rhinoceros, mammoth, horse, and bovines were brought back, as the preservation of their anatomical elements seems to indicate. Only with analysis of the archaeological data as a whole will we be able to determine with precision the nature of the camp at Saint-Césaire during this period.

Butchery and Culinary Processing

Cutmarks on bones attesting to the different stages of animal processing are too rare (Table 8.4); the postcrania are too underrepresented, even for reindeer; and the materials are too fragmented for a reconstruction of butchery techniques for each species. The absence of whole bones, the large number of fragments (Table 8.1), the stigmata from human percussion observed on at least 11 remains, and the 13 bone flakes show that all these bones were fractured

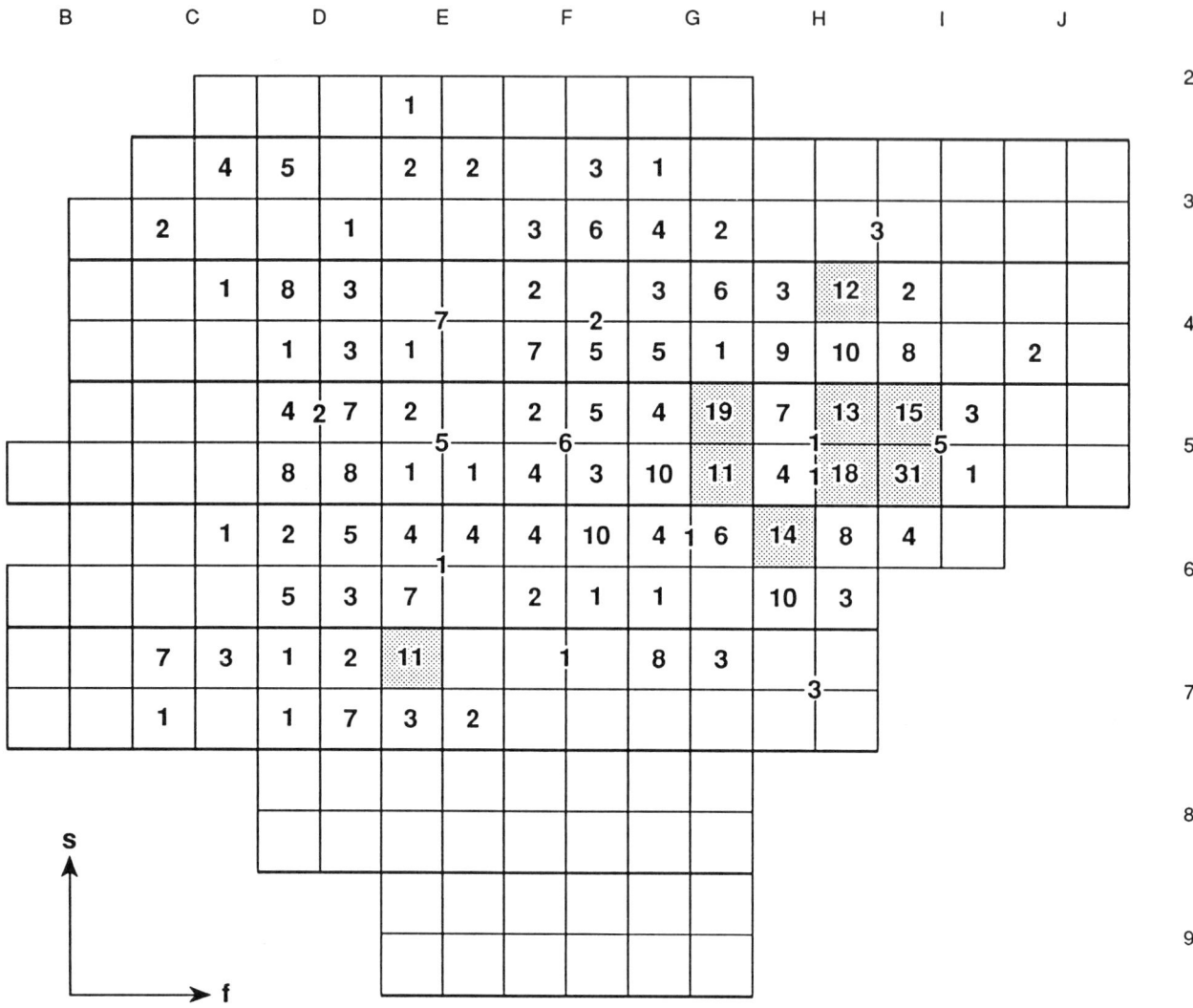

Figure 8.13. Distribution of identified bone (without shed reindeer antler).

s = south/southeast; f = west/northwest

by humans, even those of small dimensions like horse second phalanges. This finding suggests intensive domestic processing: meat, fat, and marrow retrieval, perhaps for making broth. On the other hand, no evidence for tendon retrieval or for the taking of furs of carnivores present in the assemblage was noted. It is difficult to ascertain whether meat was processed for storage (biltong), although defleshing marks are present on several rib fragments.

Herbivore hides, especially reindeer, were apparently retrieved, as shown by marks on a mandible and a reindeer second phalanx. Among the bone splinters are five diaphyseal fragments of long bones of large herbivores (between 5 and 15 cm long) that exhibit a grouped set of striations and pock marks resulting from loss of bone material on one end of their external surface. These work rests, active or passive, are commonly called "compressors."

As far as carnivores are concerned, there is no proof that they were eaten; they were hunted (opportunistically) or else they are intrusive (their contribution is limited to toothmarks present on three bones).

Of the 26,838 bone splinters, 3312 are completely or partly burned (12.34%) and 3209 (98% of these) are smaller than 2 cm. Most are spongy bone, except for a skull fragment, a tooth fragment, and a rib shaft frag-

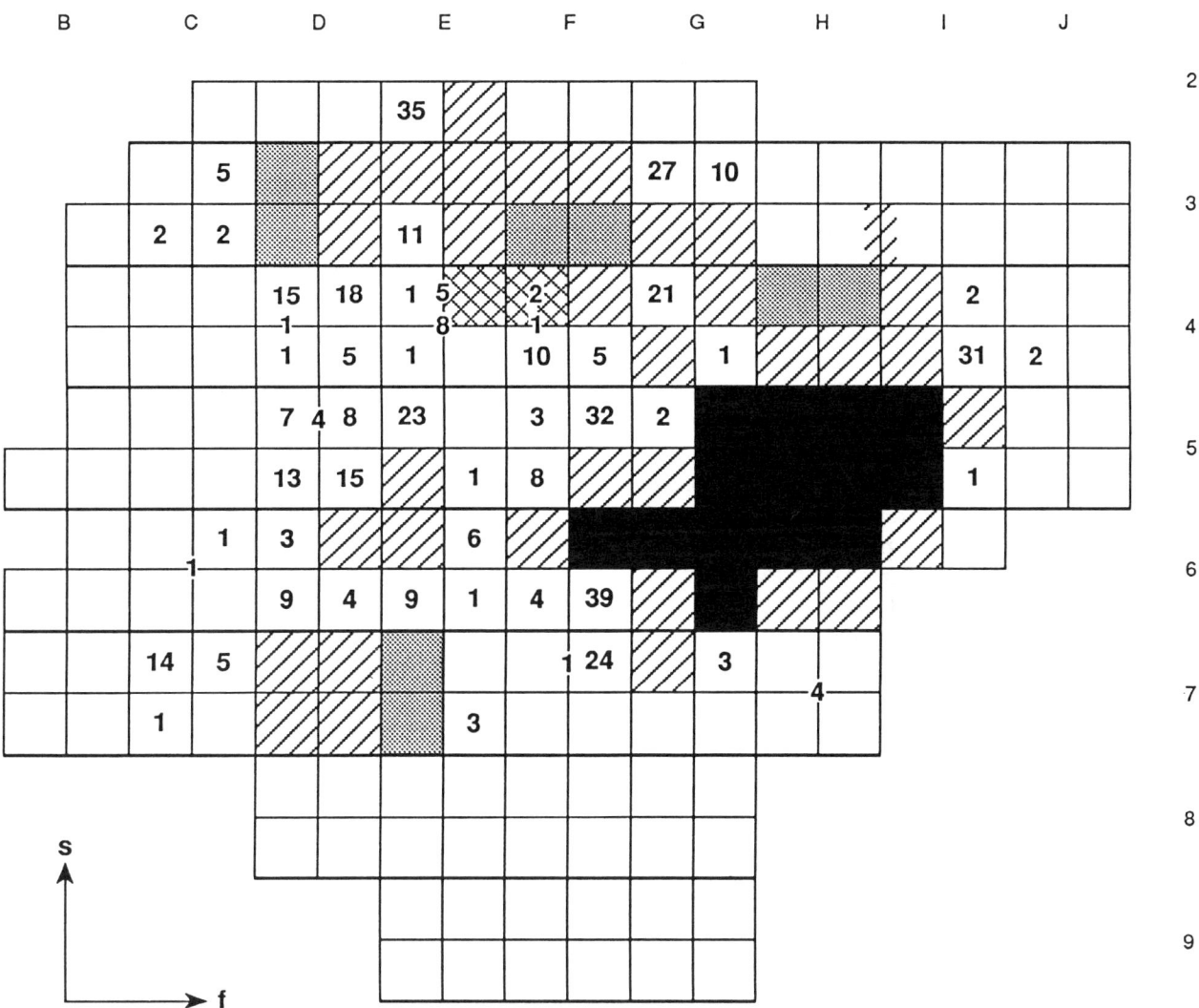

Figure 8.14. Distribution of all bones from level EJOP superior, Saint-Césaire, in black: NISP ≥ 500; hatched: NISP ≤ 40; in gray: concentration of burned fragments; crossed: schematized position of human remains.

s = south/southeast; f = west/northwest

ment (all three smaller than 2 cm). No identified bones are calcined. These remains (mostly spongy epiphyses rich in fat) are small, and their composition indicates that they were in a fire for a relatively long time. These bones probably served as fuel (Perlè 1977). The lack of hearth structures and the dispersal of these burned splinters with a few zones of concentration (Figure 8.12: F3 [II and IV], H4 [I and II], I5 [I and IV], F6[II] and G6 [II], E7 [I and IV], D3 [I and IV], H5 [III], and H5[II]) support the hypothesis that they result from the cleaning out of hearths. Fine particles of bone charcoal have been observed adhering to the surface of 15 nonburned fragments.

Activity Loci Involving Fauna

There is no concentration of bones that is a function either of species, of anatomical element, of fragment size, or of extrinsic characteristics (chemical or mechanical changes, striations, calcination, etc.). The bone materials are dispersed over almost the whole excavated area (Figures 8.13 and 8.14). No argument can be put forth describing any butchering areas or zones of cooking activity (Binford 1983). We are dealing here with domestic refuse. Processing and consumption activities were probably carried out outside. For the working of shed male reindeer antler, shaft fragments were possibly selected and brought back to the site (Figure 8.11). Associated with and in the immediate vicinity of the Neandertal skeleton were found a few teeth from horses, bovines, and cervids; a fragmentary reindeer maxilla;[6] a shed antler fragment; and about 30 bone splinters. Taphonomic studies of the Neandertal bones being carried out by Professor B. Vandermeersch will shed light on their presence in this context.

Conclusions

The bone assemblage of level EJOP superior, Saint-Césaire is the result of human action. It underwent no major postdepositional upheaval. A majority of bones are of large artiodactyls, mostly bovines and reindeer, but horses are also abundant. The bones are highly fragmented, resulting from a great deal of trampling or repeated trampling of material previously broken by humans, either directly or through a thin layer of sediment. Hunting is attested to, especially of cervids, but for other species scavenging cannot be ruled out. The animals were skinned, disarticulated, and defleshed away from the excavated area. The bones are all attributable to domestic refuse. This refuse belongs to low meat yielding parts, except for some of the reindeer remains. They indicate that parts were collected, either from carcasses abandoned by other predators, or for ease in transport of game. Bone processing was intensive; all of the long bones (and even the short bones) were fractured for marrow and perhaps bone grease (possibly for broth). As shown by the shed reindeer antler, the prehistoric people were present at the site at least in winter and spring. The antlers were intentionally collected for use of the shaft. Meat estimates indicate that the site does not resemble either of two extreme types of camp: brief stopovers while hunting and long-term base camps.

Among the 26,838 bone splinters, more than 12% are burned; their size (< 2 cm) and their composition (spongy bone) suggest the use of long bone epiphyses as fuel. Their presence with no prepared hearth structures and their relative dispersal within some concentrated zones have prompted us to investigate the hypothesis of the emptying out of hearths. No activity area linked to the processing of fauna (e.g., skinning, cooking) was noted. The whole corresponds to a refuse area.

All of these results, obtained solely from faunal material, must be combined with data from other disciplines—typology, technology, microwear studies, micromorphology, and physical anthropology, etc.—before ultimate conclusions can be drawn about the occupation at Saint-Césaire.

Acknowledgments

I would like to thank François Lévêque, Director of Excavations at Saint-Césaire, for allowing me to study this faunal material. I am also grateful to Anna Backer and Michel Guilbaud for facilitating access to the bone materials that they curated by level and nature, and also for helping me to study only the pieces belonging with certainty to EJOP superior. Finally, I would like to thank Anna Backer for the English translation.

Notes

[1] We performed only a brief identification of the materials. Data do not include any biometrics, which are being recorded by Françoise Lavaud-Girard.

[2] NISP = Number of identified specimens; MNI = Minimum number of individuals. The combined MNI is used here.

[3] The hyaena was identified by F. Lavaud-Girard.

[4] The M1 or M2 from a mammoth was pointed out by F. Lavaud-Girard (1987). It is currently in a museum case along with a reindeer metapodial, a carnivore tooth, and a calcaneum of a common fox.

[5] Only the fragments from level EJOP superior were studied. Those contained within the EJOP assemblage, which includes additional materials from EJOP superior as well as from EJOP inferior, were not taken into consideration because of time constraints. In my opinion, the sample of 26,838 bone fragments is sufficient to be significant. Also, in certain squares (* in Table 8.2) the number of very small splinters (< 2 cm) was too large, so I was obliged to evaluate them by weight.

[6] Professor B. Vandermeersch very kindly pointed out the presence of a reindeer maxilla and a few bone splinters associated with the human remains.

References Cited

Banfield, A. W.
    1954 Preliminary Investigation of the Barren-Ground Caribou. *Canadian Wildlife Service, Wildlife Management Bulletin.* Series 1.

Binford, L. R.
    1978 *Nunamiut Ethnoarchaeology.* Academic Press, New York.
    1983 *In Pursuit of the Past.* Thames and Hudson, London.

Bouchud, J.
    1959 *Essai sur le renne et la climatologie du Paléolithique moyen et supérieur.* Ph.D. dissertation, Université de Sciences, Paris.
    1975 La conservation différentielle des os et le problème des mesures biométriques. In *Problèmes actuels de Paléontologie: Evolution des vertébrés*, pp. 861-871. Colloque Internationale CNRS No. 218. Paris.
    1977 Etude de la conservation différentielle des os et des dents. In *Approche écologique de l'homme fossile*, pp. 69-73. Supplément au Bulletin de l'AFEQ No. 47, Paris.

Giacobini, G.
    1982 I boutons en os o "fibule musteriane" cenni di biomeccanica dell'osso edipotesi interpretativa. *Preistoria Alpina Revue*, pp. 243-256. Museo Tridentino di Scienze Naturali 18. Trento.

Gruet, M.
    1950 Restes d'un homme fossile en Maine et Loire: un Homo sapiens dans le gisement paléolithique de Roc en Pail. *Bulletin Société et Science d'Angers* 30:19.

Guthrie, R. D.
    1967 Differential Preservation and Recovery of Pleistocene Mammal Remains in Alaska. *Journal of Paleontology* 41:243-246.

Jochim, M.
    1976 *Hunter-Gatherer Subsistence and Settlement.* Academic Press, New York.

Klein, R. G.
    1982 Age (Mortality) Profiles as Means of Distinguishing Hunted Species from Scavenged Bones in the Stone Age Archaeological Sites. *Paleobiology* 8:151-158.

Klein, R. G., and K. Cruz-Uribe
    1984 *The Analysis of Animal Bones from Archaeological Sites.* University of Chicago Press, Chicago.

Lavaud-Girard, F.
    1987 Les gisements castelperroniens de Quinçay et de Saint-Césaire: Quelques comparaisons préliminaires - les faunes. In *Préhistoire de Poitou-Charentes, Problèmes Actuels.* Editions du Comité des Travaux Historiques et Scientifiques, Actes du 111ème Congrès des Sociétés Savantes (1986, Poitiers), pp. 115-123, Paris.

Martin, H.
    1907-1910 *Recherches sur l'évolution du Moustérien dans le gisement de La Quina: l'Industrie osseuse.* Ed. Schleider, Paris.

Patou, M.
 in press Apports de l'archéozoologie à la compréhension du peuplement magdalénien dans le Bassin Mosan (Belgique). In *Actes du colloque de Chancelade, Octobre 1988*. Editions du Comité des Travaux Historiques et Scientifiques, Périgueux.

Perkins, D., and P. Daly
 1968 A Hunters' Village in Neolithic Turkey. *Scientific American* 219(5):97-106.

Perles, C.
 1977 *Préhistoire du feu*. Masson, Paris.

Pidoplichko, I. G.
 1969 *Upper Paleolithic Mammoth Bone Dwellings in the Ukraine*. Naukova dumka, Kiev.

Poplin, F.
 1977 Problèmes d'ostéologie quantitative relatifs à l'étude de l'écologie des hommes fossiles. In *Approche écologique de l'homme fossile*, pp. 63-68. Supplément au Bulletin de l'AFEQ 47, Paris.
 1983 Essai d'ostéologie quantitative sur l'estimation du nombre d'individus, edited by Hermann Schwabedissen, *Jarbuch für Frühgeschichte* 16:153-164. Köln.

Rozoy, J. G.
 1978 *Les derniers chasseurs: l'épipaléolithique en France et en Belgique*. Charleville, France.

Spiess, A. E.
 1979 *Reindeer and Caribou Hunters: An Archaeological Study*. Academic Press, New York.

Sutcliffe, A.
 1973 Similarity of Bones and Antlers Gnawed by Deer to Human Artefacts. *Nature* 266(5433):428-430.

9

La Répartition Spatiale des Objets à La Roche à Pierrot, Saint-Césaire: L'utilisation Variée d'un Abri

Anna Mary Backer

L'analyse de la répartition spatiale des artefacts (sauf les esquilles osseuses non déterminables) du niveau EJOP supérieur de Saint-Césaire est présentée ici. Les outils retouchés (étudiés par F. Lévêque), les produits du débitage (étudiés par M. Guilbaud) et les fragments de faune déterminée (étudiés par Françoise Lavaud-Girard) sont repérés par rapport à un cadre spatial formé par l'abri naturel et par des structures culturelles possibles de foyer. La composante culturelle des foyers est examinée et evaluée grâce aux documents de fouille. En effet des foyers existaient dans ce niveau, des feux ont été construits par l'être humain plusieurs fois sur un même emplacement, et les artefacts sont concentrés autour de ces foyers, mais ceux-ci ont été déposés dans des contextes différents. Par ailleurs, la répartition des outils retouchés, des éclats entiers, et des éléments de faune révèlent deux secteurs très différenciés; l'un coïncide avec une zone découverte, l'autre avec une zone plus abritée.

Dans la zone arbritée (zone du squelette néandertalien), se trouvent, le plus souvent, le petit outillage et des outils de type Paléolithique supérieur (pointes à dos, becs) ainsi que des fragments de renne, alors que la zone découverte contient davantage de grands racloirs plats et de fragments de bovinés. Le squelette était recouvert et entouré de cassons de silex et d'éclats grignotés, modifiés par des enlèvements alternes et des fractures, peut-être d'origine cryoclastique. Bien que le bloc du squelette étudié par B. Vandermeersch contenait une très basse fréquence relative d'objets, la fosse de dégagement et les sédiments sus-jacents étaient remplis de ces cassons; ces derniers étaient beaucoup moins fréquents dans le reste du niveau.

Cet article explore l'importance du rôle des effets karstiques et celle du comportement humain dans l'origine de ces répartitions. Ni la différenciation des deux zones, ni l'emplacement des objets lithiques concentrés près des foyers, ni l'amas surprenant d'éclats rognés tout autour du squelette ne peuvent s'expliquer uniquement par des processus naturels. Je propose que les distinctions mises au jour par cette analyse reflètent en grande partie une différence de contexte de déposition de ces déchets par les humains. Bien entendu, cette étude préliminaire ne pourra prendre la forme d'une conclusion que lorsqu'elle sera soumise à une évaluation interdisciplinaire plus poussée des données, et à une comparaison plus détaillée entre la répartition spatiale à Saint-Césaire et d'autres sites occupés par des néandertaliens tardifs.

Spatial Distributions at La Roche à Pierrot, Saint-Césaire: Changing Uses of a Rockshelter

Anna Mary Backer

Recent dating of burned flints associated with the Saint-Césaire Neandertal (Mercier et al., this volume) shows that these late Neandertals could have been contemporary with the first anatomically modern humans in the area. With the advent of anatomically modern humans in western Europe, the Neandertals faced new situations. Adaptive changes during this transitional period may have carried with them changes in the organization of space use. Archaeological study of Castelperronian site structure has been limited to only a few sites described in detail in the literature. For these reasons, it is important to document as precisely as possible the depositional context of the Neandertal skeleton found in the upper Castelperronian level of Saint-Césaire.

The environmental context of this rockshelter and its position on the landscape are essentially oceanic. Occurring 37 km from the modern-day Atlantic coast, in a well-watered valley near an abundant source of good-quality stone on the plateau above, this north-facing shelter was used by Upper Pleistocene foragers over a long period of time. The excavated area (Figure 9.1) extends northwards from the cliff face. The *abri* curves around on the western side to form an alcove.

This study analyzes some of the spatial distributions of stone and bone artifacts in the level that contained a late Neandertal skeleton (level EJOP superior), whose discovery is amply described elsewhere in this volume. The placement of the human remains can be observed in Figure 9.1, and their stratigraphic position is described below.

Site Framework

Earlier deposits of Mousterian materials were capped by an episode of rockfall (Rockfall A), with large, round boulders coming to rest on top of a Mousterian occupation surface (level EGPF). Human use of the shelter continued, and artifacts were deposited between the boulders. At the same time, sedimentation filled these gaps (constituting level EJOP inferior) to form the surface on top of which the occupants who concern us here would have been standing. These people deposited what is known as EJOP superior, the upper Castelperronian level. Considerable rockfall occurred during the period of this artifact deposition, especially towards the end of the period: smallish, angular blocks (Rockfall B) form a cap on the level. The Neandertal skeleton and later the human phalanges were discovered at the base (incorporated within the lowest part) of Rockfall B (Lévêque, personal communication 1991; Lévêque and Vandermeersch 1980).

Figure 9.1 shows the excavated area with what remains of the rockshelter in the form of a cliff face. Columns B and C have been omitted from these preliminary plan views because of extensive damage to the levels by heavy machinery prior to the discovery of the site, and subsequent slumping. The windward squares G8, G9, E9, and H7 were also omitted because of difficulties with stratigraphic interpretation in the field: The Castelperronian level was indistinguishable from Aurignacian deposits in these squares and thus was lumped with them.

For the purposes of this analysis, contrasts are drawn between things found near the cliff face (sheltered space, to the lee of the dripline) and things found farther away (unsheltered, windward space). Artifacts found nearer the cliff had a higher probability of being covered by the rockshelter overhang or of being to the lee of the dripline at the time of their deposition. The Neandertal skeleton was located 1 m from the cliff face in an area likely to have been sheltered in the past (straddling squares E4/F4), but further removed from the alcove.

The organization of unsheltered and sheltered space can be expected to vary in different situations (Binford 1987). The remains of that organization, such as the placement and locations of hearth features, should be informative when compared with other

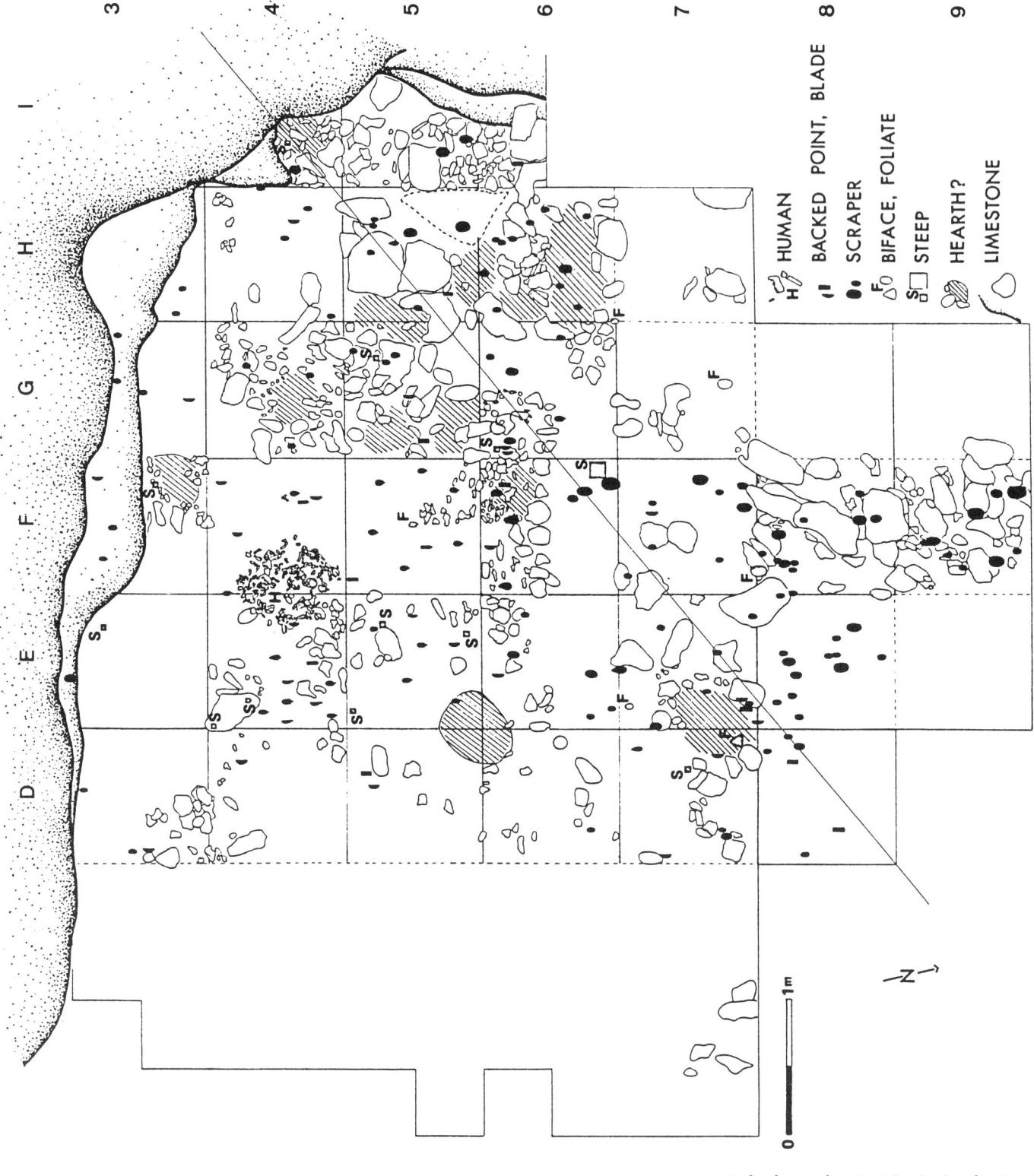

Figure 9.1.
Excavated area,
EJOP superior
(Upper
Castelperronian
level) showing the
rockshelter wall,
alcove and location
of the Neandertal
skeleton. Diagonal
line: theoretical
demarcation line
separating the two
areas.

Castelperronian intrasite organization. The distribution of artifacts around a hearth (and in relation to those features that can be distinguished as the remains of fire-building or fire-related activities, such as dumping behavior) can inform us about spatial organization in the past, not by the mere fact of being burned, but by their special associations and contextual aspects.

Most prehistorians would probably agree that identification of hearths requires an argument based on structural association. What kinds of remains appear diagnostic of burning episodes in the past, hearth construction techniques, and hearth maintenance? That the Neandertals used fire is an accepted fact—that they arranged stones into circles for the purpose of building a fire between these stones is a matter of debate (see Straus 1989; Bar-Yosef 1992). We have remarkably few parameters for understanding Neandertals' use of fire, and therefore, we experience difficulty in interpreting the remains of their fire-related activities. In this study I present arguments for and against the identification of hearth-building episodes in the Castelperronian at Saint-Césaire, based on evidence documented in the field. The following descriptions of burned archaeological remains were translated from field notes and summarized in an attempt to evaluate the grain of hearth-building remains from this level. Artifact distributions are then examined in relation to these possible hearths and to the rockshelter wall, alcove, and skeleton. Possible hearth locations can be seen in Figure 9.1.

Sheltered Space

The sheltered space can be divided into three areas: a zone abutting the shelter wall (with two possible hearths, one in F3 to the east and one in I4, in the alcove), the area under the shelter overhang (where the skeleton was discovered, to the east, and with a group of hearths to the west in alcove squares G4, G5, and H5), and the dripline vicinity in the center of the excavated area (featuring two hearths on the east side, F6II and D5/6/E5/E6 and with possible hearth H6 in front of the alcove).

The rockshelter wall yielded evidence of intense heat and burning (in F3 and I4), and large stones (Rockfall A) in the alcove form circles around burned bone and flints (G5/6 and H5/6) (see Figure 9.1).

The Shelter Wall: F3 and I4

Hearths in F3 and I4 were described as heavily indurated, fire-reddened sediments (therefore probably not dumped materials). High frequencies of tiny fragments of burned bone were found everywhere in F3III (Leroyer, field notes 1985), and traces of ochre with burned materials were found in F3IV (Lavaud-Girard, field notes 1985). This hearth was flanked by a few large, unretouched flakes and a dense concentration of tiny flakes. A small, subcircular burned patch of approximately 6 cm in diameter was described, with a fire-hardened, indurated lower zone. This possible hearth was located just at the base of the shelter wall on a bed of large stones belonging to EJOP inferior (Rockfall A). The Neandertal skeleton was found less than a meter from this accumulation of burned remains, resting on the sandy clay at the base of Rockfall B.

Evidence of burning from square I4IV (abutting the shelter wall in the corner of the alcove) was noted as pinkish, indurated sediments, "perhaps the base of a hearth" (Court, field notes 1985) — presumably not dumped materials. The two hearths directly abutting the shelter wall, therefore, were both small, one behind the skeleton and one in the sheltered part of the alcove.

Alcove Hearths: G4, G5, H5

In squares G5I and G5IV, burning is reported as a concentration within EJOP, just below the angular blocks (Rockfall B), with burned bone, reindeer antler, traces of red ochre, backed points and a possible bone point, all found in a 5 to 8 cm thick lens of burned material (Girard, field notes 1980; Lavaud, field notes 1980). In G5II the lens was dense, tapering to 2 cm (Girard, field notes 1982). H5 contained evidence of burning, and a high diversity of artifacts (e.g., Upper Paleolithic core, sawed-off rhinoceros molar). Excavators concurred in noting the presence of burned remains here, with the EJOP materials distributed within and around the large Rockfall A blocks (Lévêque, field notes 1983; Petit, field notes 1983; Girard, field notes 1983; Bourgueuil, field notes 1983). Materials in G4 and G5 were very dense and diverse, and burned bone was recorded beneath an upper layer of small blocks (Rockfall B) and within and around the lower, larger Rockfall A (Girard, field notes 1983; Joulian, field notes 1983).

Judging whether or not the use of natural features such as boulders for hearth building constitutes structuring is a question of interpretation. It appears that the alcove was used more than once for the purpose of building a fire. I suggest that natural combustion need not be invoked to explain the orange, indurated beds of these hearths. Reuse of an alcove for fire-building is not a particularly revolutionary concept.

Hearths near the Dripline: F6II, D5/6/E5/6, and H6

In the center of the excavated area, the 50 by 50 cm unit called F6II contained large proportions of burned bone, and next to it lay a concentration of large tools, mostly scrapers of green chert (an unusual patina for

108   *Context of a Late Neandertal*

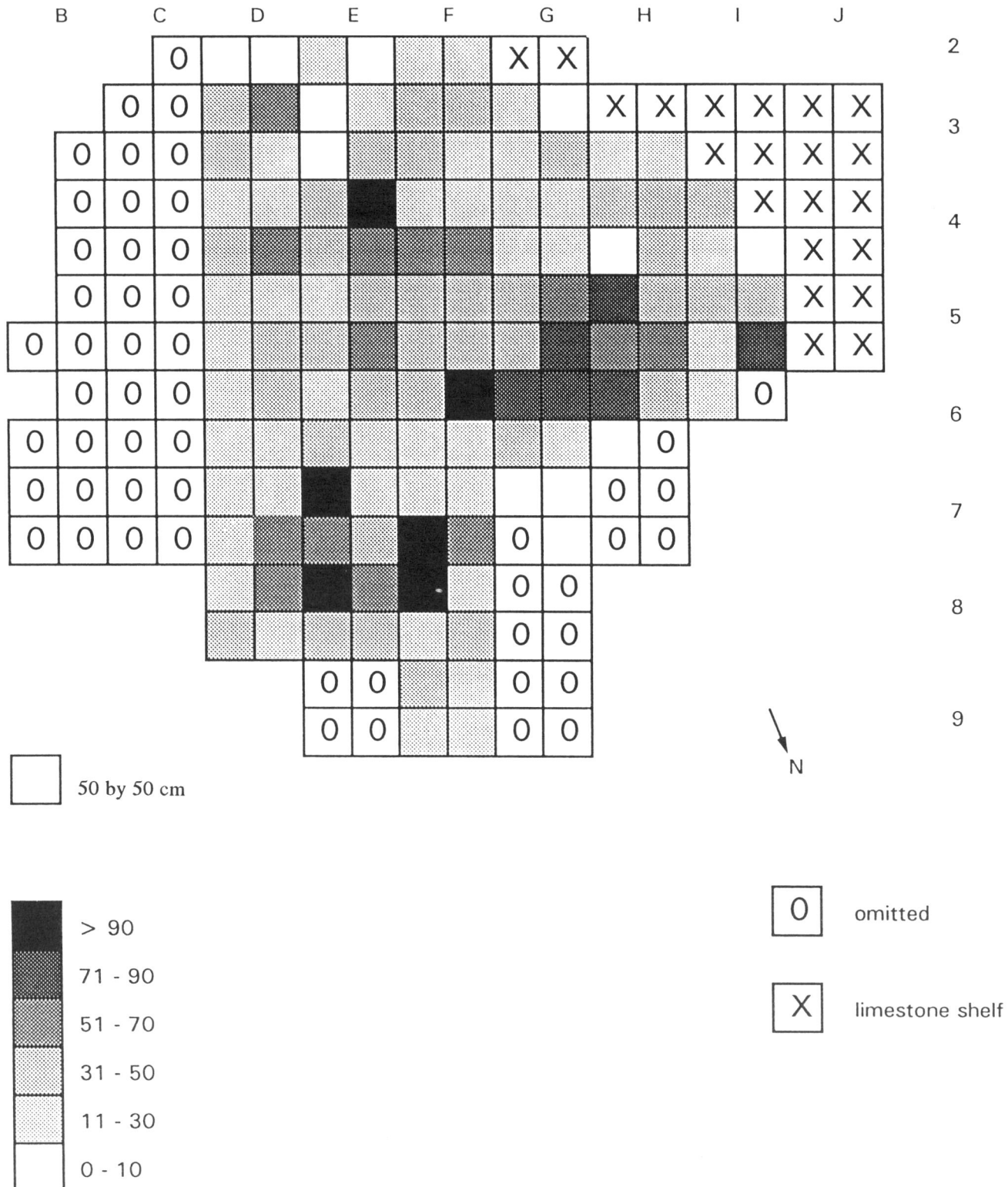

Figure 9.2. Distribution of unretouched flakes greater than 2 cm in maximum length.

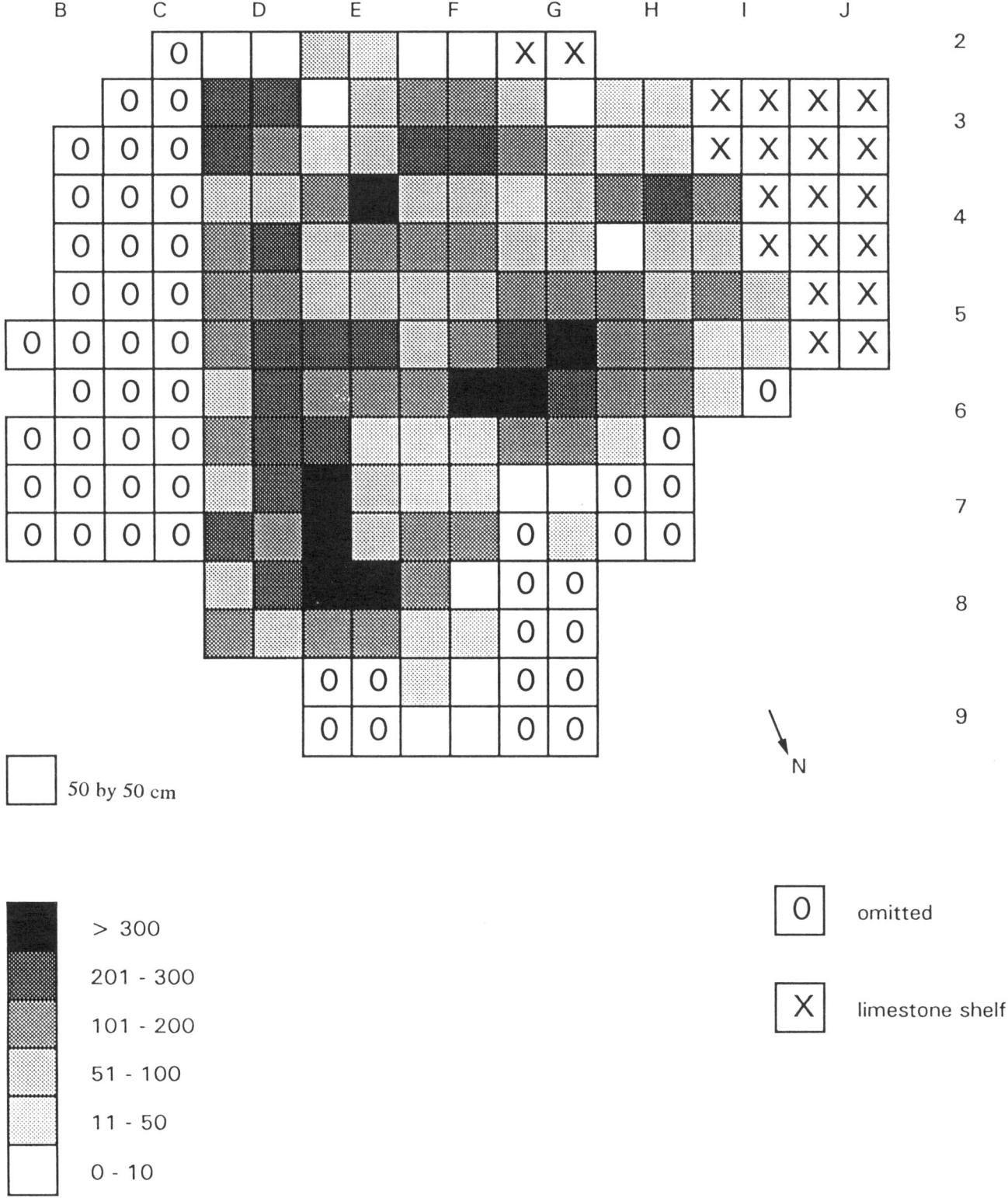

Figure 9.3. Distribution of unretouched flakes less than or equal to 2 cm in maximum length.

the site). Unretouched flakes of all dimensions are clustered here (Figures 9.2 and 9.3). A stone alignment, perhaps the result of natural roof fall (Rockfall B), was deposited after the Castelperronian artifacts. The stones rested on top of the artifacts, and one long bone is even reported to exhibit smashing and crushing, possibly because the stones fell on top of it (Pecout-Restou, field notes 1982). On the other hand, some of the burned items may have amassed after the blocks fell. Perhaps the blocks played a part in the subsequent accumulation of some of this debris, acting as an artifact trap. An incline begins here, with the larger blocks appearing to delimit the archaeological materials, probably preventing subsequent downslope movements of artifacts. Significantly, however, the field notes describe two discrete, superimposed lenses of burned materials beneath Rockfall B. Referred to in the field notes as a hearth, this square yielded "excessive amounts" of burned bone (Bourgueuil, field notes 1981). Furthermore, when possible hearth locations in Figure 9.1 are compared to unretouched flake distributions (Figures 9.2 and 9.3), it becomes clear that the high density of chipped stone in and around this hearth is probably not fortuitous, because other squares located to the lee of the stone alignment did not contain such concentrations, nor a unique set of artifacts.

If prehistorians are leery of recognizing a prepared, structured hearth in F6II, they might have even more trouble entertaining the possibility that these piles represent the cleaning out of hearths. If the concentration is a dump, it implicates cleanup or sweeping behavior, about which we know very little if anything for this ancient period. In any event, the cleaning out of hearths implies that fires were built elsewhere.

Another concentration of burned objects was noted in D5/6/E5/6. This possible hearth would have been at or near the dripline. It was located at the same distance from the shelter wall as the possible hearth in F6II. This concentration of burned artifacts was also the same distance from the skeleton as F6II. The burned area in D5/6/E5/6 was not accompanied by any large blocks or boulders.

H6I yielded ochre, burned items, and possible worked bone; the sediment was stained orange (Petit, field notes 1983), so it is unlikely to be the result of dumping. In H6III and H6IV, ochre was noted, as was the presence of burned bone (Babin, field notes 1984).

Unsheltered Space

A hearth surrounded by Rockfall A boulders and partly covered by Rockfall B limestone was recorded in E7. This feature was accompanied by very high densities of stone chipping debris, both large and small. Backed points and a foliate biface are clustered here with red ochre in what was called in the field a "small hearth?" — an accumulation of small pieces of charcoal, burned bone splinters, and lithics within a 20 cm zone (Lavaud-Girard, field notes 1982). Here again, as in F6II, there appeared to be a superpositioning of circumscribed hearths in E7IV.

In sum, at the time of recovery, the skeleton was, in a certain sense, surrounded by possible hearths: two separating the human remains from the open air, and one directly between the body and the back of the rockshelter. Towards the alcove was another area with high proportions of burned materials; as will be shown below, this area differs significantly from the area of the skeleton in terms of artifact association. Finally, another concentration described in the field as a hearth was found in front of the shelter. The windwardmost, northerly squares contain no mention of any hearth. With this site framework in hand, it is now possible to place into context certain quantified observations from EJOP superior (lithic and faunal data) and examine rudimentary patterns.

Level EJOP, like all Paleolithic levels, represents a palimpsest of debris superimposed after an unknown number of depositional episodes, an unknown number of visits to this sheltered area by humans. Therefore, all artifacts found together were not necessarily deposited together. Rather, piles of debris generated at different times by a stable system or by different systems can be seen as overlapping. Concentrations of artifacts inform us about the repetitive aspect of discard in a particular location, or intersecting zones of discard (see Camilli 1983; Ebert 1992; Wandsnider 1989). The shelter could have been reused in what may have been unrelated contexts or situations. During this transitional period, with either or perhaps both Neandertals and modern humans present on the landscape, we may be dealing with more than one system of human adaptation in this region, and it follows that more than just one kind of structured disposal context could be implicated by the artifact distributions. Spatial relationships between artifacts record not only a superpositioning of items discarded in the context of this biocultural change, but also the natural transformations and patterns imprinted over patterns that reflect repetitive human behavior. Rather than espousing the concept of activity area, I examine artifact concentrations for repetitive patterns in an attempt to gauge the contribution from an amalgamation of discarded objects, on the one hand, and natural processes on the other. By examining associations and combinations in artifact relationships, and by regarding them in relation to natural features (such as the rockshelter topography) and cultural features (such as hearths), the spatial tendency of discard emerges as clusters representing the repeti-

Square	x	y	Tools	Bones	Flakes > 2 cm	Flakes < 2 cm	Cores	Manuports	Modified Flakes	Angular Debris
D2	2	7	0	0	5	2	0	0	2	3
D3	2	6	6	11	171	834	1	0	41	54
D4	2	5	3	23	131	456	6	0	39	19
D5	2	4	6	39	96	642	4	1	62	26
D6	2	3	4	21	105	687	2	0	28	26
D7	2	2	12	10	135	712	8	3	34	50
D8	2	1	11	5	137	484	1	2	25	25
E2	3	7	1	1	31	100	2	0	4	15
E3	3	6	5	6	70	175	1	0	21	21
E4	3	5	19	24	267	792	9	4	124	60
E5	3	4	17	12	138	614	9	1	119	29
E6	3	3	9	23	117	574	9	0	57	34
E7	3	2	14	20	236	854	9	1	33	84
E8	3	1	21	24	246	262	6	3	24	14
F2	4	7	1	2	55	0	0	0	0	0
F3	4	6	6	15	135	847	4	0	26	65
F4	4	5	11	14	147	592	5	0	101	38
F5	4	4	14	26	161	385	12	1	81	81
F6	4	3	11	25	193	654	9	0	15	61
F7	4	2	11	30	189	393	3	1	31	37
F8	4	1	15	19	157	213	13	2	14	27
F9	4	0	10	16	106	43	5	3	5	10
G3	5	6	7	7	87	226	2	0	16	45
G4	5	5	6	27	56	286	11	4	77	34
G5	5	4	6	67	232	963	13	0	52	112
G6	5	3	11	18	212	879	6	2	7	77
G7	5	2	4	12	20	45	2	0	0	9
H3	6	6	2	4	48	93	2	2	7	4
H4	6	5	9	38	108	486	19	5	46	28
H5	6	4	15	48	241	478	10	0	13	23
H6	6	3	17	56	138	353	9	1	8	13
I4	7	5	7	8	74	298	2	0	32	19
I5	7	4	4	60	170	297	8	0	10	26
I6	7	3	3	13	21	48	0	1	1	2
Total			298	724	4435	14767	202	37	1155	1171

Additional flakes 335
Total flakes 19537

Grand total = 23124 artifacts

Note: Tool counts are slightly lower than Lévêque's owing to the omission in this study of the artifacts from the B and C columns.

Table 9.1. Artifact Inventory, EJOP Superior

112   Context of a Late Neandertal

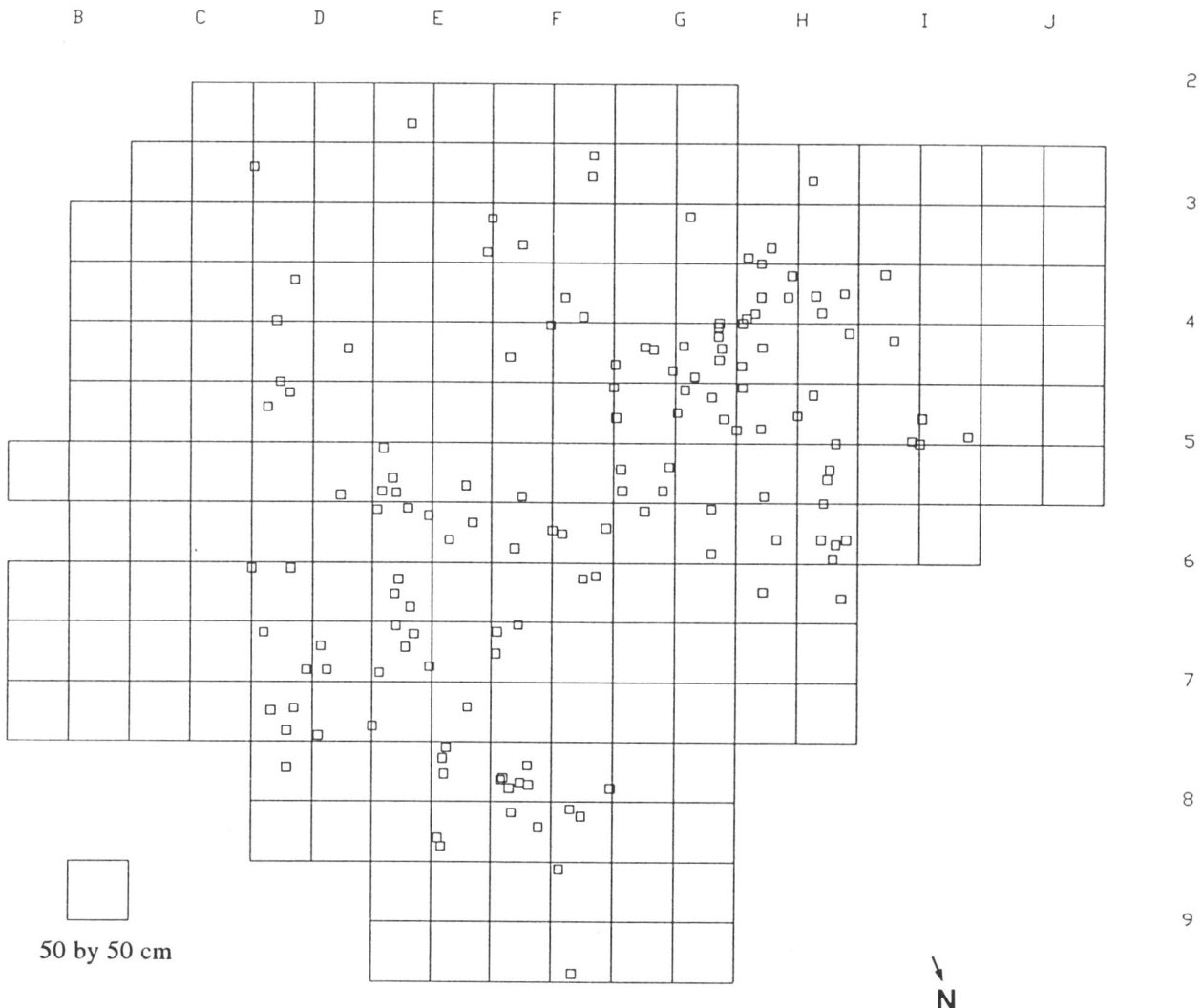

Figure 9.4. Distribution of cores.

tive placement of discarded items or systematic effects of natural processes.

The following analysis of lithic and faunal distributions suggests that contextual relationships differ between the unsheltered space on the one hand and the sheltered space containing the skeleton on the other; a line can be drawn bisecting the alcove (see Figure 9.1), separating the two major tool classes, the size classes, and the faunal groups into two zones that do not strictly follow natural features, such as the rockshelter wall.

Artifact Distributions

Spatial distributions of chipped stone artifacts and faunal remains are presented here (see Lévêque, Guilbaud, and Lavaud-Girard, this volume). A total of 23,124 lithic pieces was plotted (Table 9.1), namely flakes larger than 2 cm in maximum length (Figure 9.2), flakes equal to or smaller than 2 cm (Figure 9.3), cores (Figure 9.4), tools (Figure 9.5), and naturally modified pieces (flakes modified by alternate, sinuous, steep retouch, some of which may be the result of cryoturbation; Figure 9.6). A total of 724 bones was plotted, representing only the identified material (Lavaud-Girard 1987).

Distribution of Stone Tools

Of the 305 tools studied by François Lévêque, the scrapers, foliates, and backed points and blades were selected to be illustrated and drawn to scale in Figure 9.1, since they describe a distinct spatial pattern about the theoretical demarcation line mentioned above.

Spatial Distributions at La Roche à Pierrot 113

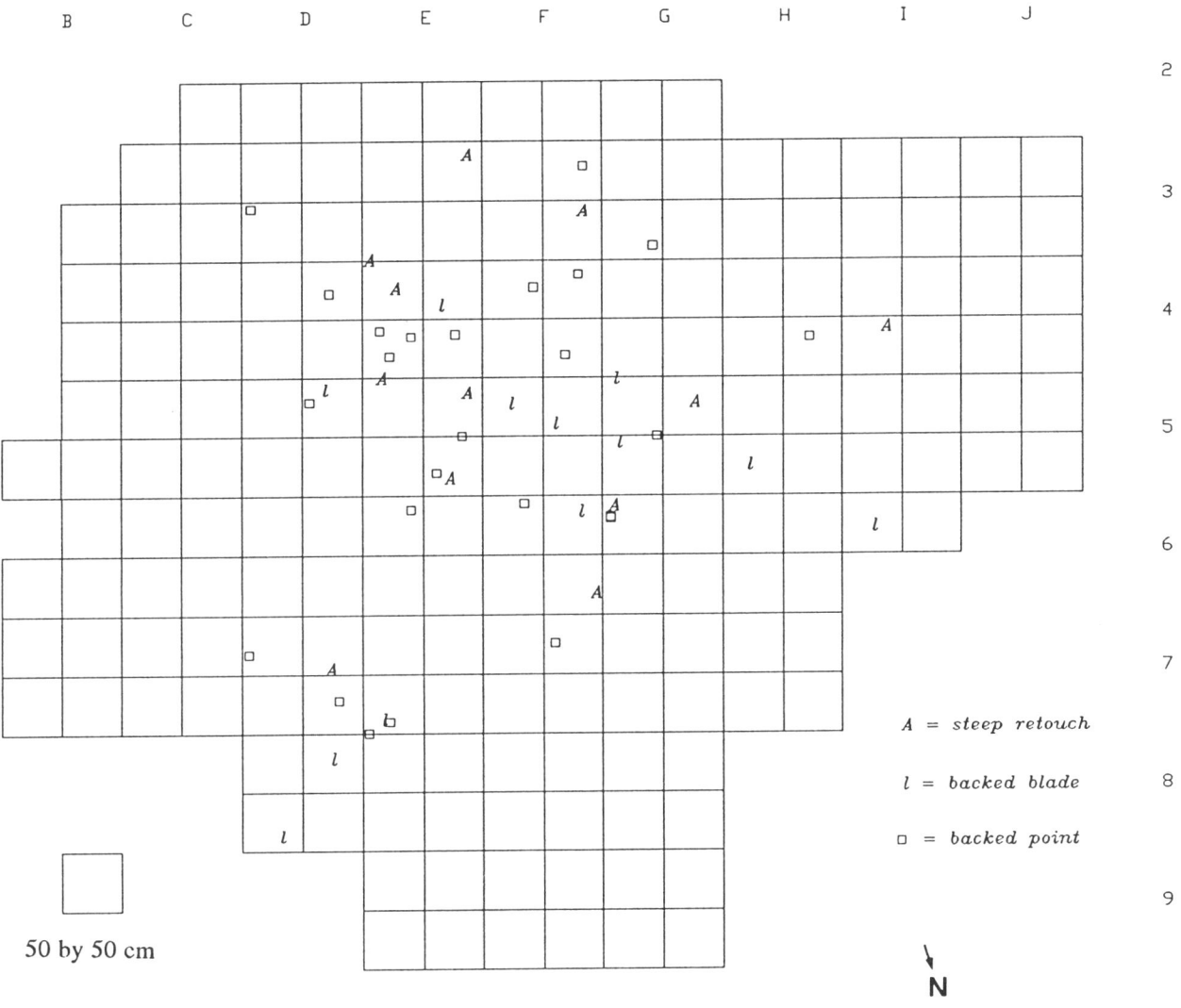

Figure 9.5a. Distribution of tools: steep retouch, backed blades, and backed points.

Tool Size

The area downslope, that is the windward, unsheltered space in front of the shelter, towards the north and the river, contained Rockfall A boulders. A dense accumulation of retouched items (mainly large, flat scrapers — see Figure 9.5) was found on these stones. In the sheltered area, conversely, mostly small tools (backed knives and points, small scrapers) were found. Bone fragments from the unsheltered zone also tend to be larger than bone fragments inside the shelter. Analysis of variance of mean unbroken tool length between this open area, the sheltered zone, and the alcove shows significant spatial variation in tool length. Generally, tools found outside are significantly bigger than those found inside. Sample squares were selected for comparison from the alcove, the shelter wall, around the skeleton, and from the open-air squares. The sheltered sample and the skeleton sample contain significantly smaller tools than the unsheltered space, whereas mean tool length in the alcove sample falls in between, bisected by the theoretical demarcation line mentioned above. These size differences could be seen as the result of size sorting from natural processes, such as runoff. The pattern is not just restricted to tool size, however, but is also reflected in the distribution of tool types, as shown below.

Tool Type

Scrapers cluster systematically in the open air and in the alcove, whereas backed knives and backed points (*couteaux de Châtelperron*) are much more numerous within the shelter than outside it. There are no backed items at all windward of the theoretical demarcation line. The occurrence of both major tool groups in concentrations around the hearths in F6II,

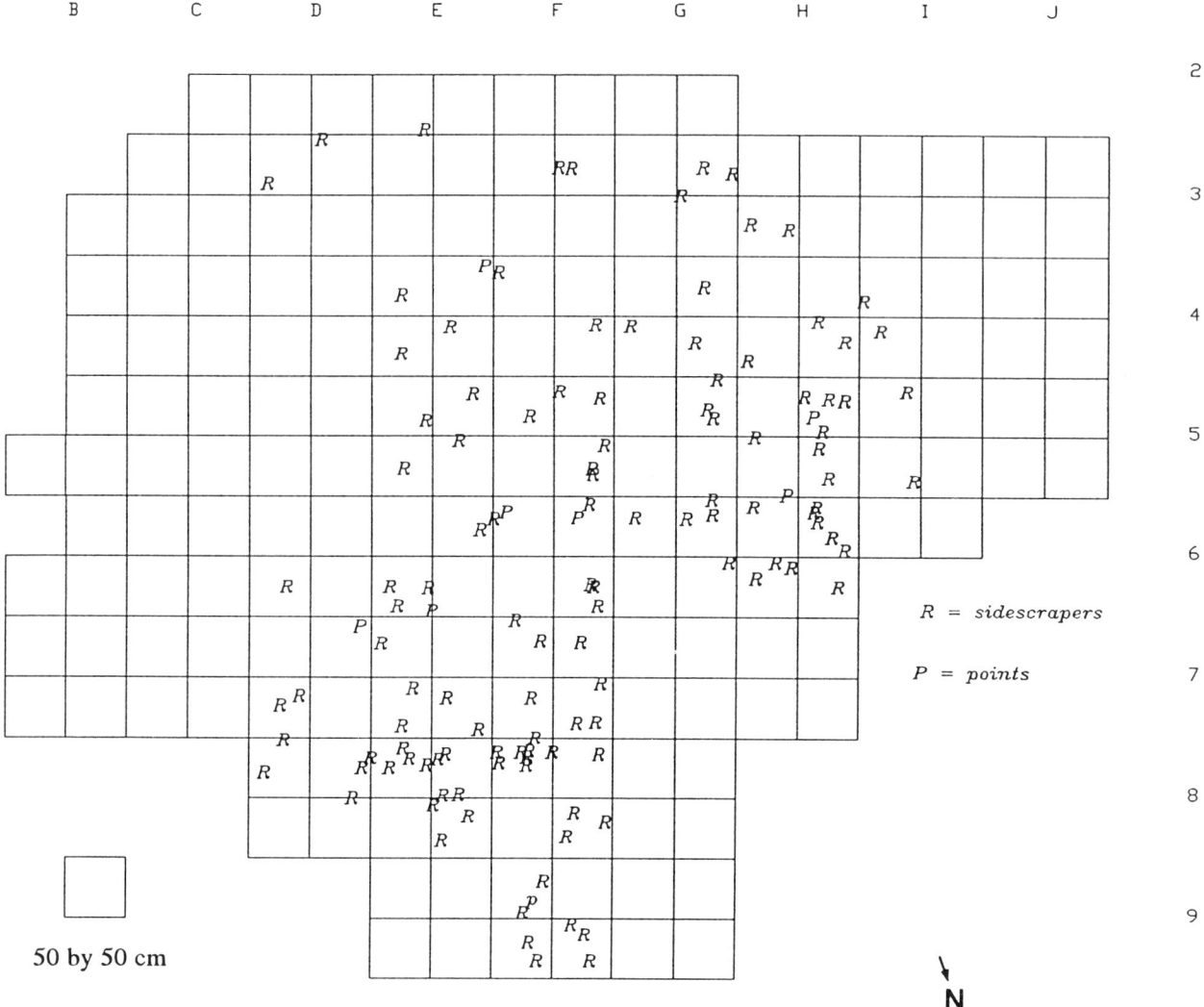

Figure 9.5b. Distribution of tools: sidescrapers and points.

G5/6, and E7 is provocative, especially since they were not found together in the more windward alcove squares or in windward squares F8 and F9. Hearths F6II and E7 are both bordered by clusters of tools on their windward side. This north-facing shelter would have been exposed to north by northwesterly winds and, therefore, hearths built at or near the dripline would have enclosed a sheltered, leeward area. The tool clusters windward of these two hearths are diverse in composition and include both backed knives and large, flat, foliate scrapers as well as a foliate biface.

Many more backed items were found in the sheltered zone, whereas scrapers, foliates, and the biface tend to be distributed farther away from it and in the alcove. Larger proportions of backed tools are concentrated close to the Neandertal skeleton, but very few large tools accompanied the skeleton. The two major tool classes (backed knives and large scrapers) are roughly distributed on either side of the theoretical demarcation line, which, as I have pointed out, does not follow the natural topography of the rockshelter wall.

The other principal tool types (see Lévêque, this volume) are evenly distributed across the excavated area, with the exception of *becs*, which were recovered only from the sheltered zone (see Figure 9.5c).

In sum, the stone tool distribution in level EJOP superior at Saint-Césaire shows distinct patterning when the two main tool classes and tool size are arrayed about a theoretical demarcation line that crosscuts the natural site framework. Small scrapers and backed items cluster around the Neandertal skeleton but are also found associated with two hearths, one of which was at or near the dripline, the other just in front of the shelter. Large scrapers are found windward of the dripline, and in the windward

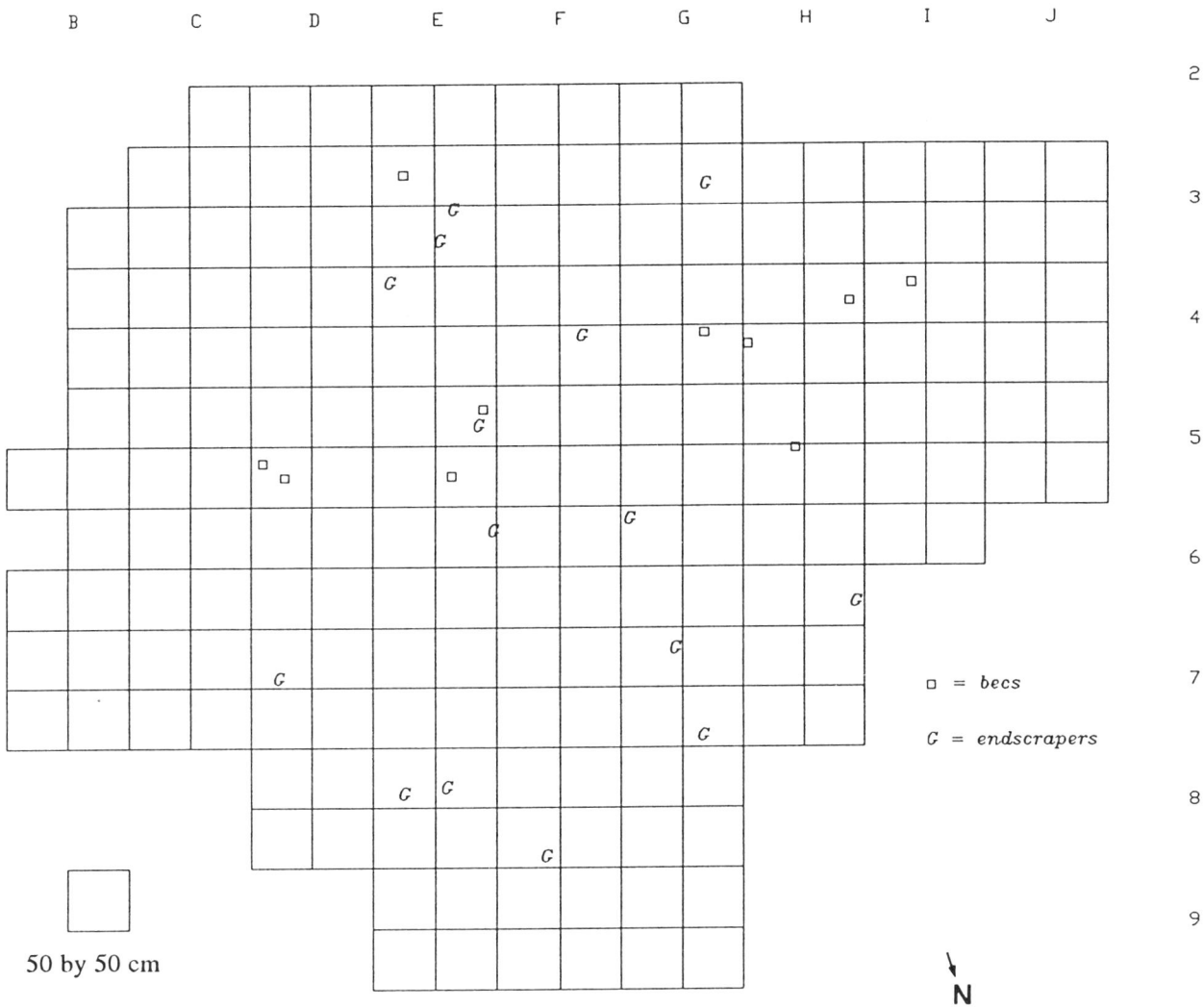

Figure 9.5c. Distribution of tools: endscrapers and becs.

alcove hearth squares. No backed points were found in this zone.

Unretouched Flake Distribution

Analysis of spatial distributions of unmodified flakes of different sizes also shows definite patterns. The aim here is to judge whether we can distinguish between patterns resulting from repetitive behavior or differential discard contexts, given the site framework described above, and those resulting from natural processes, and to attempt to gauge the relative contribution of noncultural and behavioral transformations. Figures 9.2 and 9.3 show the spatial distributions of flakes smaller and larger than 2 cm, in 50 by 50 cm units. The concentrations in F6II, G5-H6, and E7 are clearly visible. A large number of objects can also be seen in E4, where the Neandertal skeleton was found.

Few flakes were found within the plastered block removed and studied in the laboratory by B. Vandermeersch, however (20 flakes >2 cm, 26 flakes < 2 cm), especially flakes smaller than 2 cm.

The whole, large flakes (> 6 cm; Figure 9.7) are obviously clustered in front of the alcove and windward of the theoretical demarcation line, except for a few large flakes deposited in a small concentration beside the hearth in F3. Most of the large, whole flakes are windward of the alcove hearths, associated with the large, flat scrapers. The patterns in tool size distributions among the unretouched pieces are mimicked by patterns in the distributions of tool types. The differences in flake length and tool length define a theoretical demarcation line and do not follow the natural topography of the rockshelter wall or the slope. I therefore argue that the size distributions are not sole-

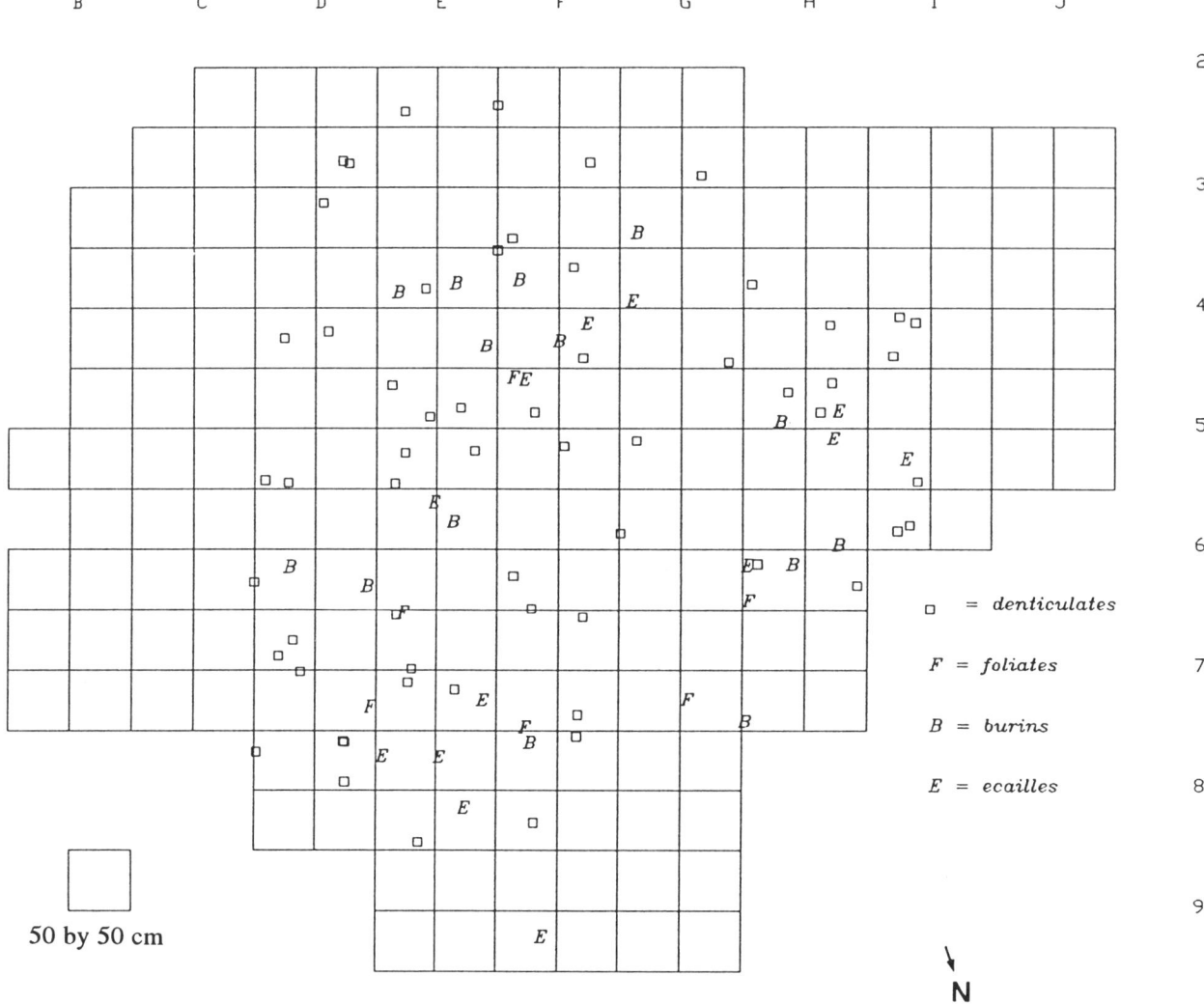

Figure 9.5d. Distribution of tools: denticulates, foliates, and burins.

ly due to natural size-sorting processes. I also suggest that these artifacts had variable use-lives and were discarded in differing contexts. The unretouched flakes cluster distinctly in and around the possible hearths, revealing significant site structure in level EJOP superior, and I argue that given this structure, these unretouched items were deposited in the context of repetitive hearth-related disposal. Two hearths (E7 and F6II) have been described as superimposed lenses and appear to have been reused; these hearths are associated with clusters of tools, whereas other hearths (F3, G5, G6, H5, H6, and D5/6) have a different configuration of unretouched and retouched pieces. Very few tools, for example, are associated with F3, but large, unretouched flakes cluster there, suggesting a different context of disposal from hearths surrounded by concentrations of retouched tools.

Small-Flake Surplus

In order to evaluate the relative importance of unmodified flakes smaller than 2 cm, the ratio of small to large flakes was calculated. Figure 9.8 shows concentrations of small things no longer swamped by absolute frequencies of lithics. Small-flake surpluses are expected to result from stone modification activities, because tiny retouch flakes and debris are likely to remain embedded in the substrate once they fall to the ground, whereas larger flakes might be taken away for use. The tiny flakes are not expected to be further modified. Figure 9.9 shows that concentrations of surplus small flakes are located adjacent to larger artifact concentrations. The concentrations (darkest squares) in this ratio map are certainly associated with hearths, but they tend to avoid the concentrations (darkest squares) in the distributions of

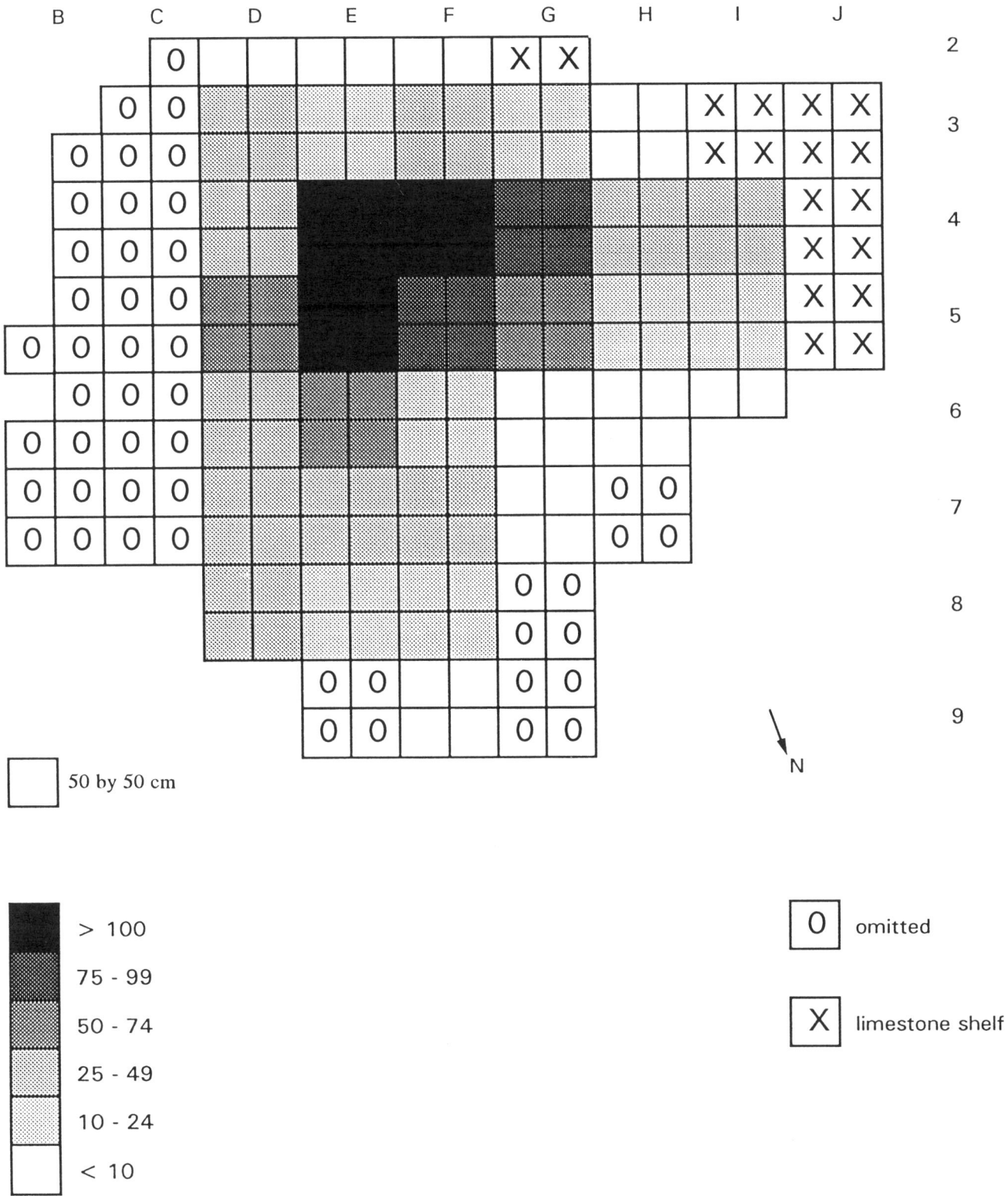

Figure 9.6. Distribution of "naturally" modified pieces.

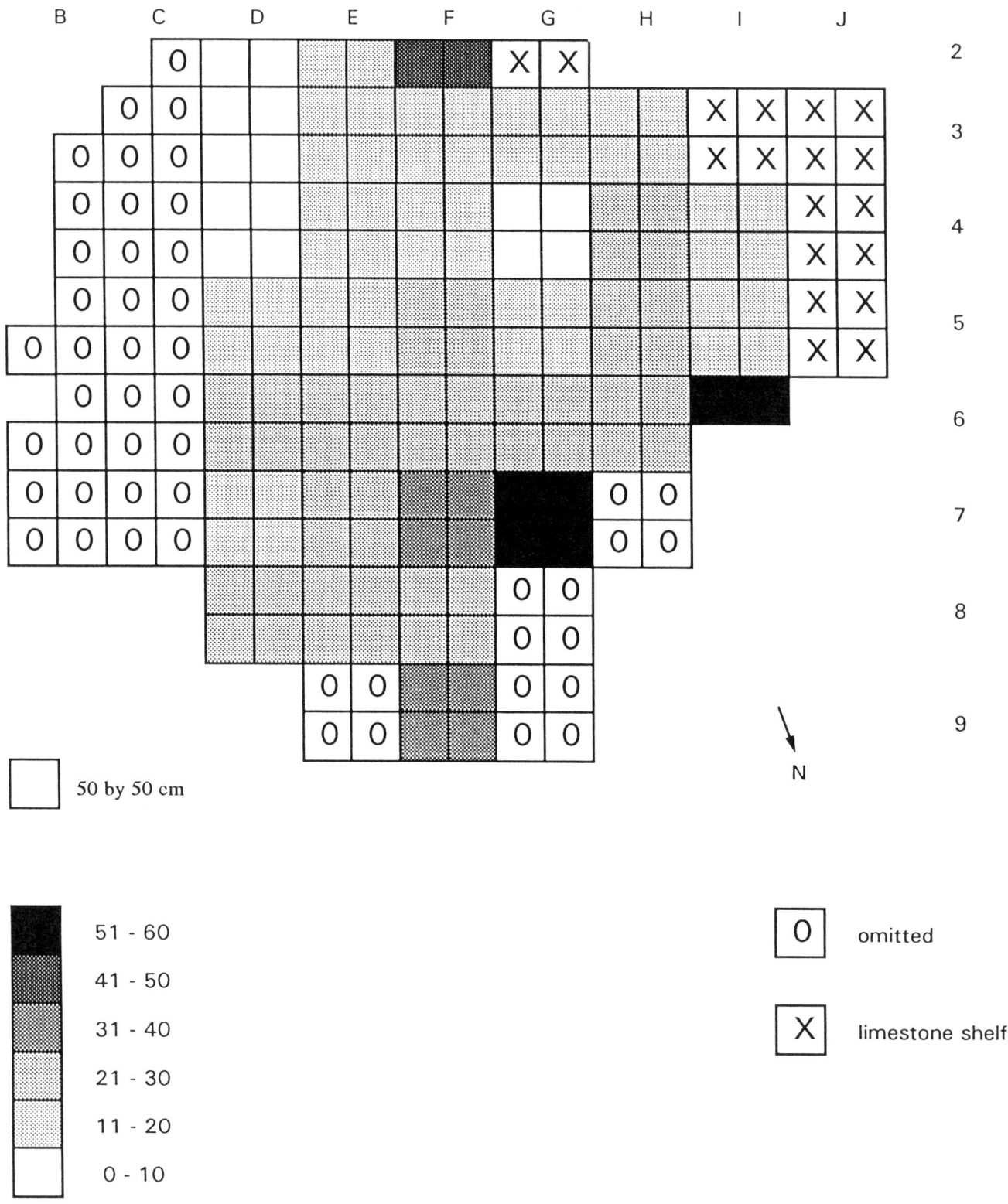

Figure 9.7. Whole, large flakes (greater than 6 cm in maximum length)

Spatial Distributions at La Roche à Pierrot 119

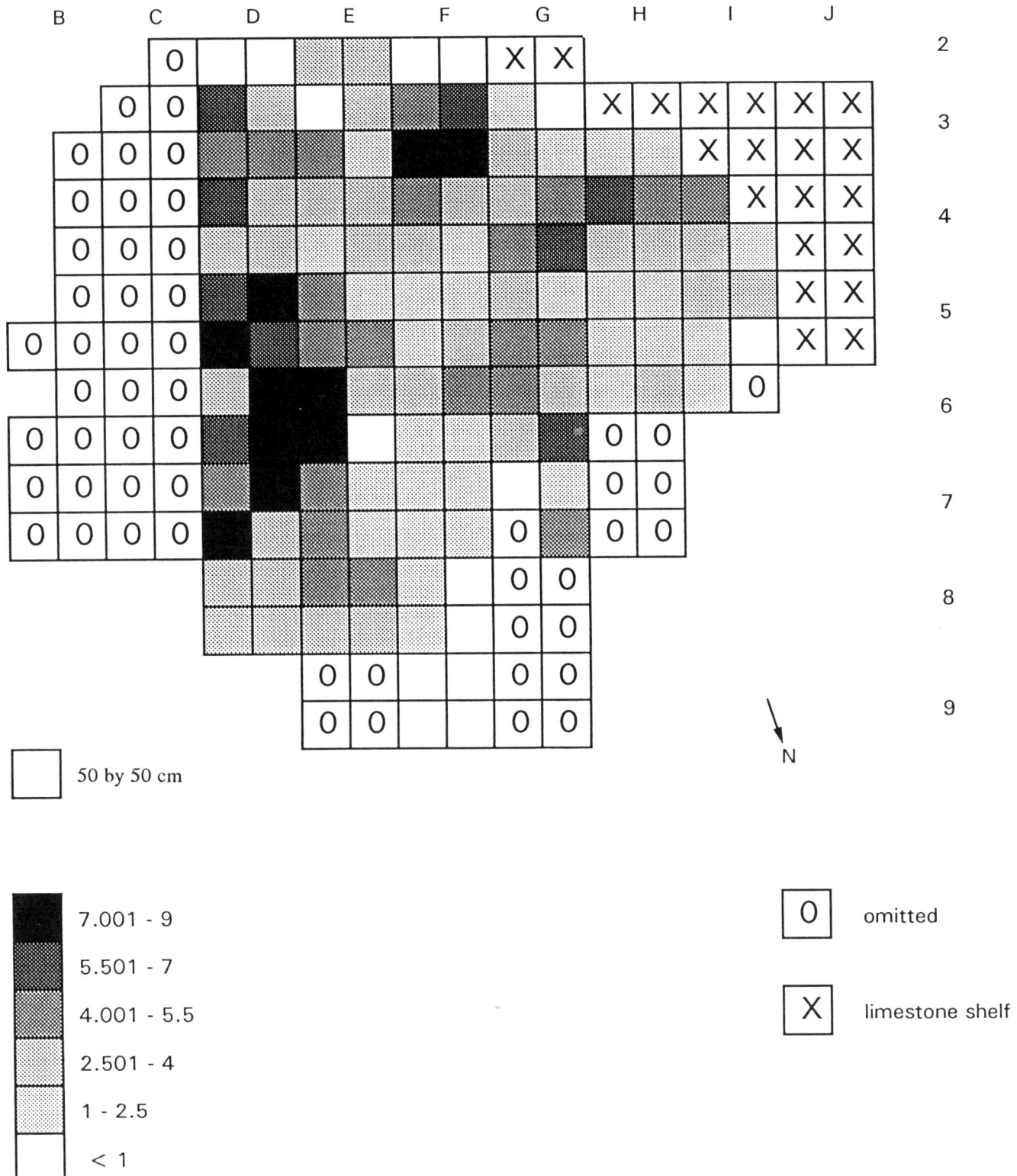

Figure 9.8. Small-flake surplus.

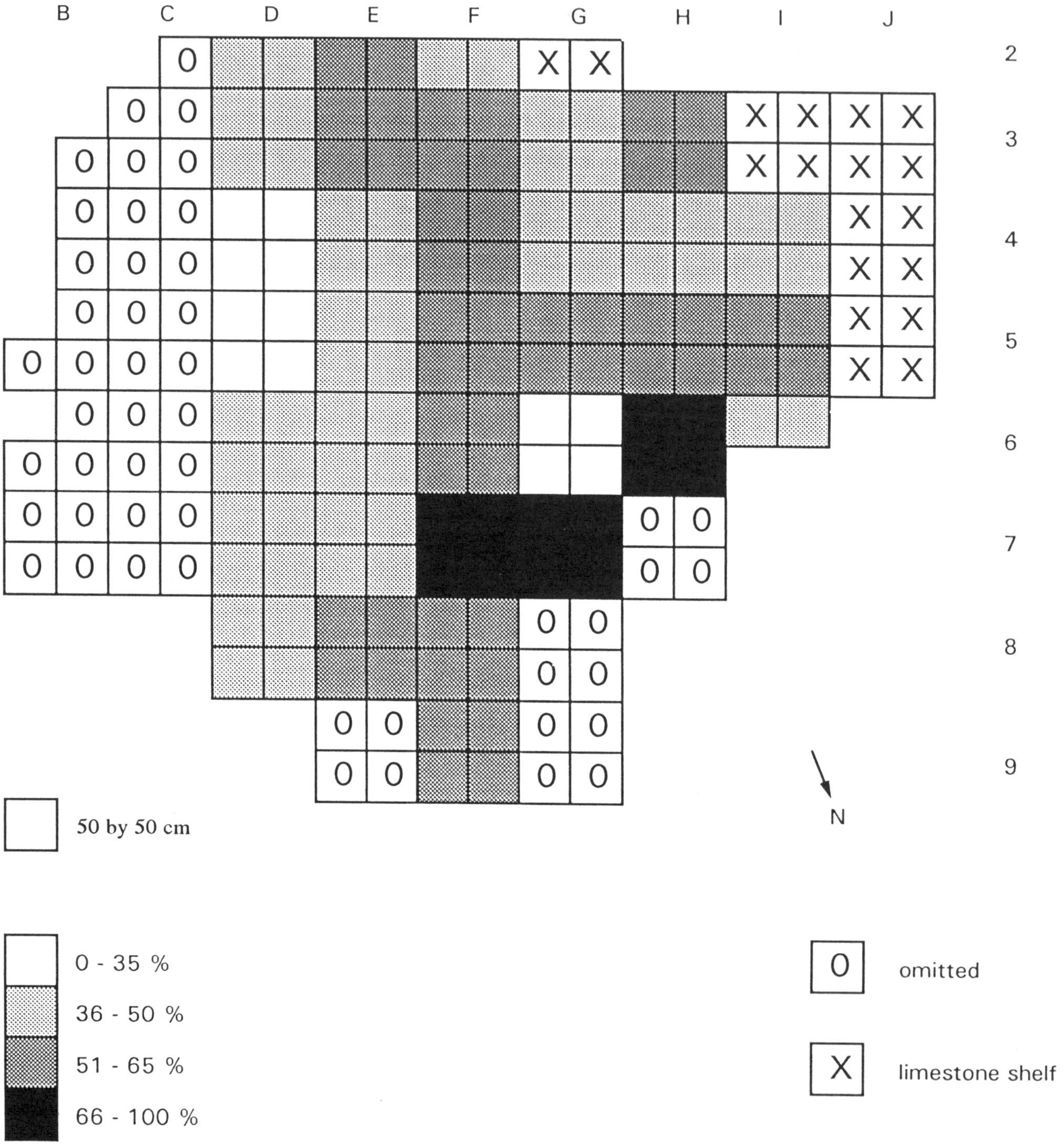

120 Context of a Late Neandertal

Figure 9.9. Distribution of whole flakes.

absolutely large quantities of flakes (Figures 9.2 and 9.3). They form a very dense cluster in one area, between the hearths in D5/6 and E7. Small-flake surpluses are also associated with the hearth abutting the shelter wall (F3). It is likely that these small flakes remained in place after repeated knapping activities occurred in this zone. No systematic relationships exist between the rockshelter's natural features and the small-flake clusters. Although flakes smaller than 2 cm are present on the windward side of the theoretical demarcation line, few small-flake surpluses were found there.

Naturally Modified Pieces

Figure 9.6 shows flakes with edge modification that may be due to natural processes and were not featured in the other frequency distributions. The modifications include alternate retouch, sinuous edges, isolated retouch removals, steep retouch, and breaks caused by pressure, which could have been the result of these objects being crushed against each other from trampling, rock fall, or cryoturbation, or a combination thereof. Interestingly, these objects are concentrated on and around the human remains and do not coincide with the areas of concentrations of surplus small flakes and debris. If in fact these objects had been modified by postdepositional, noncultural processes and remained in place, one would expect to find them associated with the retouch flakes, notch flakes, and other small debris that could have resulted from their modification or to find them systematically distributed in relation to rockshelter topography. But this is not the case; rather, the possibly naturally modified flakes tend to avoid these areas and are concentrated in the squares where the Neandertal skeleton was found.

Alternatively, these objects could represent discarded pieces that had been reworked by human-induced breakage, truncations, or rejuvenation flakes (see Dibble 1987). Unfortunately, it is difficult at present to distinguish unequivocally between human modification and non-human action on every single lithic piece. This sort of modification has been noted at many sites dating to this period, and it is generally believed to be the result of cryoturbation. At Saint-Césaire, these pieces (whether intentionally reworked or naturally modified) were found concentrated in the area where the human remains were deposited. They are relatively close to the cliff face but are not arrayed systematically alongside it. Although it is difficult, perhaps impossible, to determine the origin of their modification, the place they finally ended up is probably not the result of any fortuitous sequence of events. Their distribution lends credence to the possibility that the Saint-Césaire Neandertal was purposefully buried (Vandermeersch, this volume).

Differential Breakage

Whole flakes (Figure 9.9) tend to be concentrated in the alcove area towards the unsheltered zone, windward of the alcove hearths. Unbroken, large unretouched flakes (Figure 9.7) are more often farther away from the cliff but closer to the alcove, mimicking the tools. The converse is also true (more breakage occurs in the sheltered area). Most of the unretouched, broken flakes are to be found in or around hearths.

The absence of whole, large flakes close to the shelter wall could be interpreted as resulting from breakage of large items close to the cliff face because of rock fall or other karstic processes, such as increased effects of cryoturbation in the vicinity of the shelter wall. Broken items cluster mainly on and around the skeleton, however, and do not coincide with high frequencies of small debris surplus, nor do they coincide with all squares adjacent to the shelter wall (in particular the F3 hearth, which contained larger and more whole flakes on average than any sheltered square), as might be expected if all of this breakage were postdepositional.

In sum, significant site structural patterns can be discerned from initial comparisons of distributions of lithic artifacts in this level. Large, flat scrapers and whole, large unretouched flakes are more numerous as one goes farther from the skeleton, but rather than following the natural rockshelter features, they are arrayed about a theoretical demarcation line that crosscuts the natural topography. Breakage is more frequent on items in the sheltered area, but the placement of broken items cannot be explained purely by accidental breakage resulting from natural processes, although preconception tells us this must account for some of the highly modified pieces with alternate retouch, sinuous edges, and steep retouch. An argument for a behavioral component to the structure reflected in the spatial arrangement of unmodified flakes, retouched tools, and battered items is made with reference to the repetitive placement of stone tool manufacture and discard of unwanted items around hearths, using a site framework evaluating detailed information from the field notes and a site map (Figure 9.1) pieced together from plan views and sketches.

I suggest that aspects of these provocative spatial distributions reflect different contexts of repeated disposal in the vicinity of the different hearths. The repetitive use of the alcove for hearths was not accompanied by disposal of any backed points on the windward side of the hearths. The hearth at or near the dripline, however, and the hearth just in front of the shelter were also used more than once, judging from the superpositioning of hearth lenses in both cases, but these hearths were accompanied by both backed

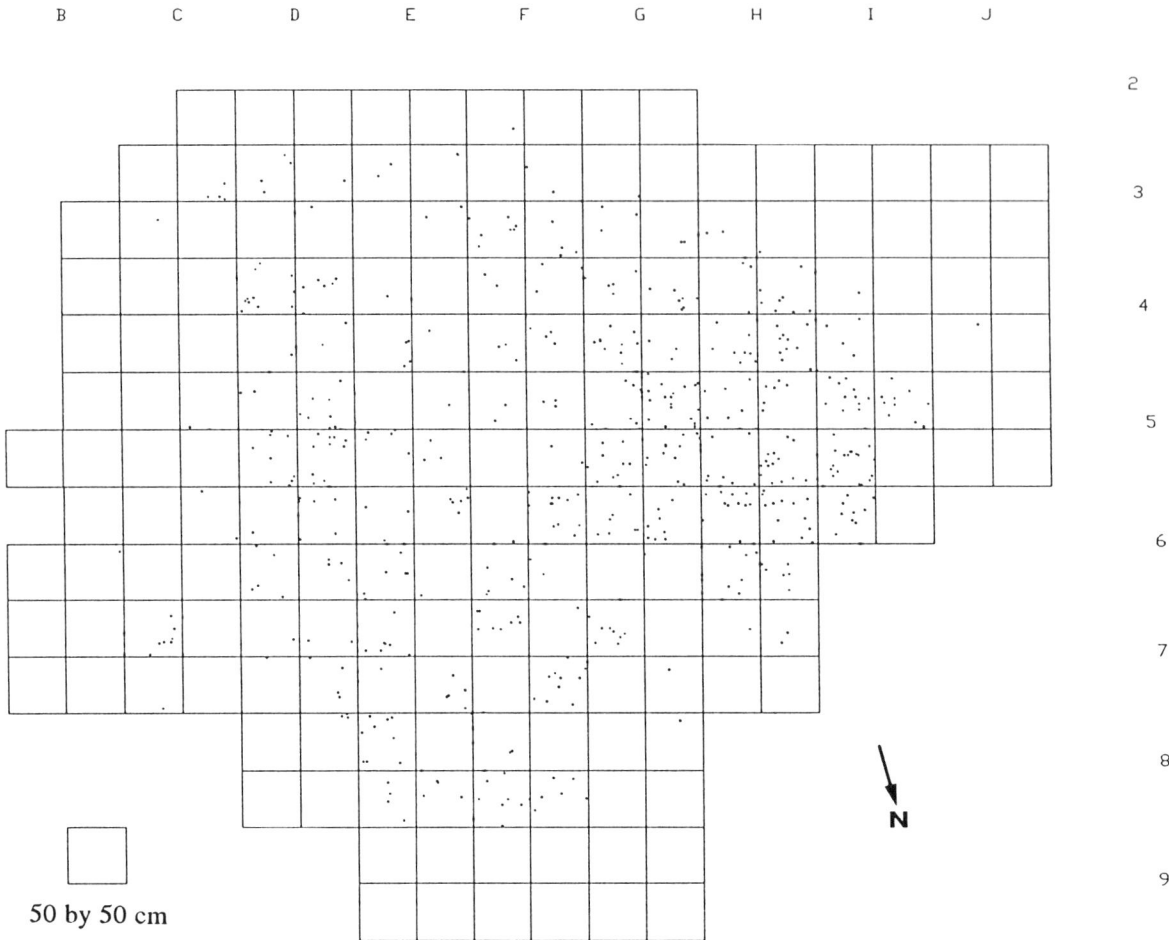

Figure 9.10. Distribution of faunal remains (identified material only, data provided by F. Lavaud-Girard).

points and large, flat scrapers. On the other hand, the hearth at the base of the cliff face contained almost no tools at all but was flanked by concentrations of very large flakes.

The small-flake surpluses, reflecting a context of *in situ* tool manufacture or the reworking and rejuvenation of tools, with large proportions of tiny flakes being deposited where they fell, are concentrated to the lee of an outside hearth and in the vicinity of a hearth at or near the dripline.

Thus it can be seen that the unmodified flakes and tools were deposited in varying hearth (activity and/or disposal) contexts whereas the highly modified pieces were treated differently, perhaps kicked out of the way or intentionally amassed on and around the Neandertal skeleton.

Faunal Distributions

A plot of 724 identified faunal remains (Figure 9.10) shows higher frequencies of bone remains within the alcove area than in the other parts of the rockshelter. The theoretical demarcation line mentioned above is immediately noticeable when the distributions of bovines (Figure 9.11) and reindeer remains (Figure 9.12), and especially reindeer antler (Figure 9.13), are compared: the two faunal classes have a tendency to "avoid" each other, and it is quite clear that the bovines are associated with the outside hearths in the unsheltered area and in front of the alcove, where the large, flat scrapers were found, while the reindeer remains are more often found under the shelter, with the backed points and the skeleton.

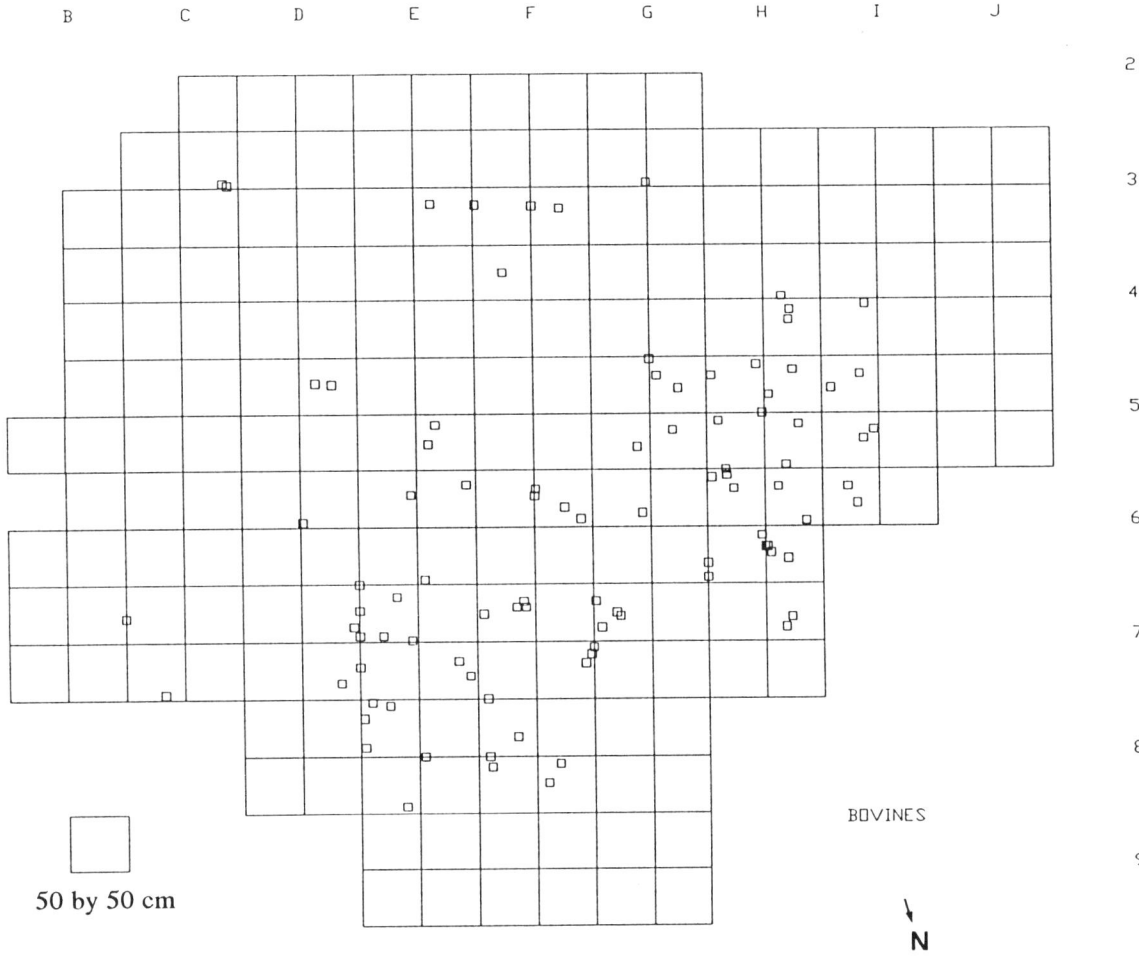

Figure 9.11. Distribution of bovine remains.

Discussion

Size sorting from natural processes is apparently not the dominant agent responsible for the artifact distributions, because differences in size distributions cannot be tied in a systematic fashion to any of the natural features of this site (dripline, shelter wall vicinity, alcove) and also because the patterns in the spatial distributions of artifacts by size are also visible when tool types and faunal species are plotted. Rather than being arrayed in relation to karstic features, a theoretical demarcation line separating two zones of very different artifact composition can be seen to crosscut the natural site framework. Differential breakage is a factor separating the two zones, but the fact that the faunal species are also distributed according to the two zones indicates that there is indeed a contextual difference in disposal that doesn't follow natural site topography. Contexts with site structural integrity are dominated by a) hearth-related disposal, which is quite variable; b) manufacturing disposal; and c) disposal in the vicinity of the skeleton, which appears to have been covered over by heavily modified and broken pieces with no remaining functional value. All three of these contexts occur only to the lee of the theoretical demarcation line. I suggest that a systemic difference stands behind the differentiation of these two areas.

That the Castelperronian level at Saint-Césaire contains significant site structural patterns of the sort alluded to in this paper may come as a surprise to some prehistorians. I was not expecting to find such clearcut patterning when I first embarked on this research. Perhaps I was prejudiced against Neandertals; I expected their organization of space to

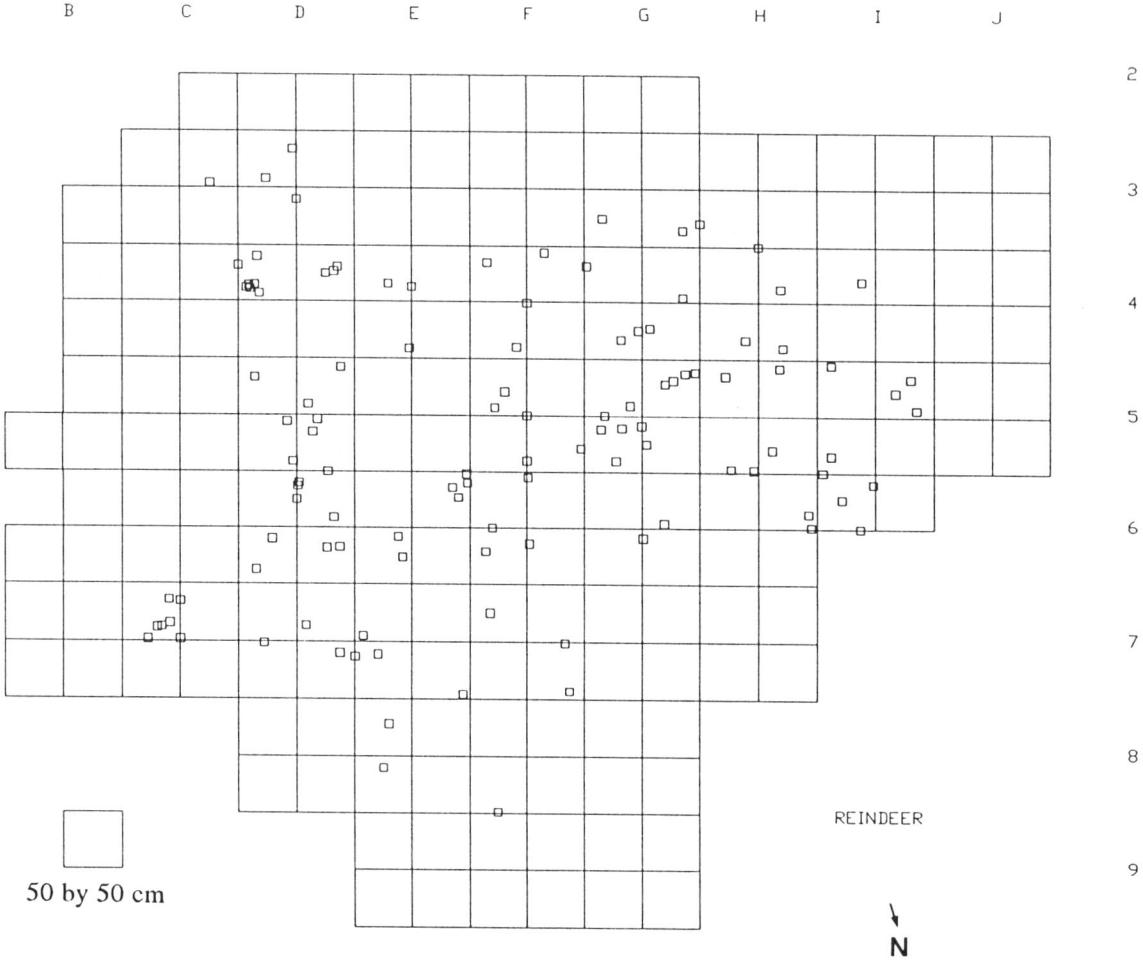

Figure 9.12. Distribution of reindeer remains.

differ dramatically from that of anatomically modern humans, whose activities are clearly segmented into different zones and whose sites clearly evidence sweeping behavior and complex, stone-lined hearths (see Enloe and David 1989). Nevertheless, detailed scrutiny of the records that I have presented here has brought me to the conclusion that this preconception was unwarranted. On the other hand, the organization of space use suggested by the spatial distribution patterns described here may in fact not have been laid down by Neandertals at all, but by modern humans: as suggested in this volume and elsewhere (Mercier et al. 1991), Neandertals and anatomically modern humans appear to have been contemporary in the region during this transitional period, and therefore, modern humans may be responsible for some, if not all, of the artifact distributions. This is not necessarily the most parsimonious explanation, however, since a Neandertal is actually present in level EJOP superior.

Conclusion

A certain degree of integrity characterizes the grain of spatial distributions in this assemblage. Tools and modified pieces were deposited in different contexts. A theoretical demarcation line distinguishes two areas that may correspond to a systemic difference in disposal context. Repetition of hearth placement, stone tool manufacture, and refuse disposal has produced concentrations and overlapping distributions that are significantly different between the two areas. The context of the Neandertal skeleton differs from the windward context in every aspect studied here: tool type, tool size, breakage, faunal associations, and flake size.

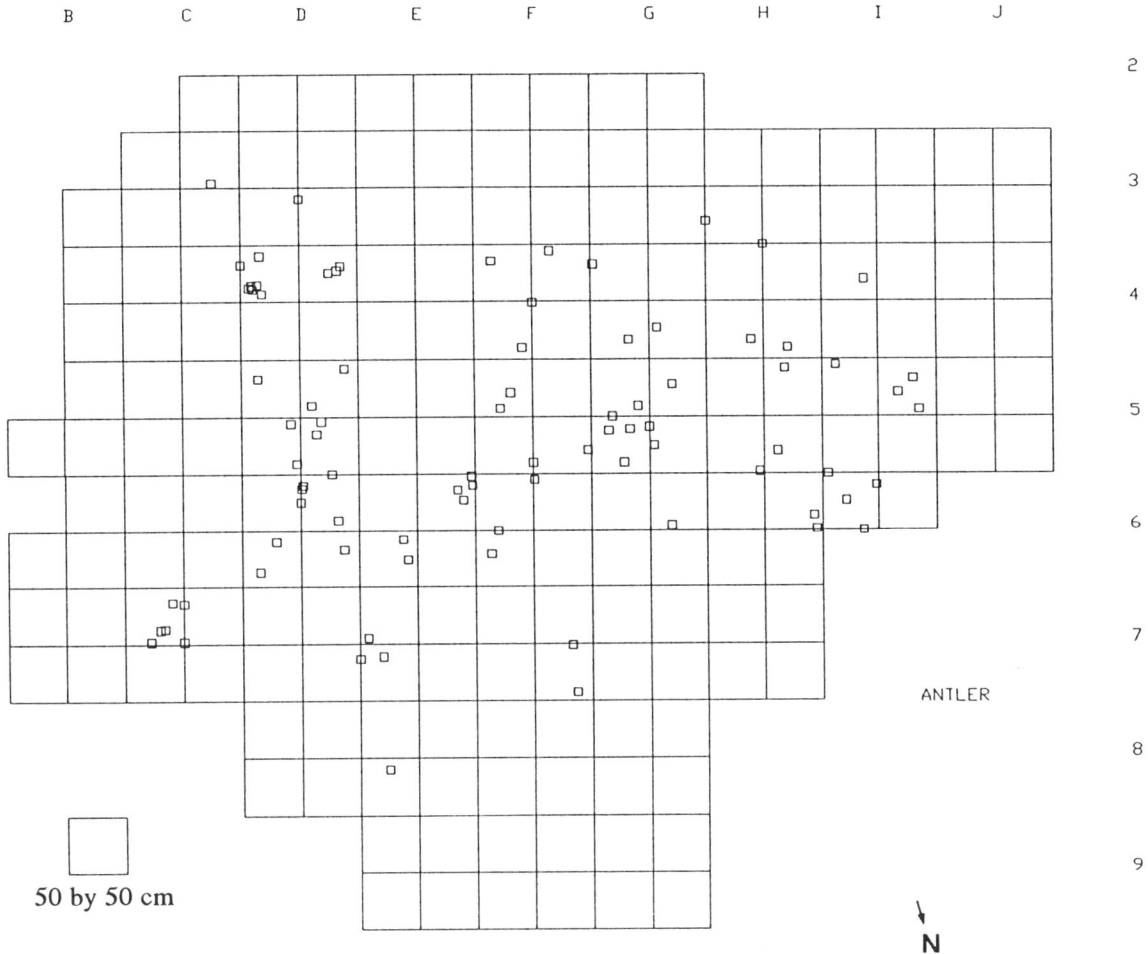

Figure 9.14. Distribution of reindeer antler.

Oddly enough, it is the context of the Neandertal skeleton that exhibits differentiation in spatial organization.

Questions of changing patterns in space use by late Neandertals cannot be answered by studying the site structure of only one site. This paper contributes to knowledge of this sort heretofore available from only two sites: Arcy-sur-Cure (Leroi-Gourhan 1976) and Cueva Morín (González-Echegaray and Freeman 1971). It is hoped that further site structural research and comparative work on Castelperronian contexts like La Grande Roche at Quinçay (Lévêque 1989) and other sites will aid in the explanation of cultural changes that occurred in the transition to Upper Paleolithic adaptations.

Acknowledgments

This research was funded by a L.S.B. Leakey Foundation grant and by the Department of Anthropology and the Student Research Allocations Committee of the University of New Mexico, for which I am very grateful. I would like to thank François Lévêque of the Direction des Antiquités in Poitiers for granting me permission to study spatial distributions at Saint-Césaire, and for his encouragement and support. I am grateful to Françoise Lavaud-Girard for graciously sharing with me her data on faunal element and species, and to Michel Guilbaud for spending a great deal of time working with me. I am also grateful to my professors, Lewis R. Binford, Erik Trinkaus, and Lawrence G. Straus for helping to launch this research.

References Cited

Bar-Yosef, O.
    1992 The Role of Western Asia in Modern Human Origins. Paper presented at the meeting on The Origins of Modern Humans and the Impact of Science-Based Dating, The Royal Society, London, 26-27 February 1992, organized by M.J. Aitken, P.A. Mellars and C.B. Stringer.

Binford, L.R.
    1987 Researching Ambiguity: Frames of Reference and Site Structure. In *Method and Theory for Activity Area Research*, edited by S. Kent, pp. 449-512, Columbia University Press, New York.

Camilli, E.
    1983 Site Occupational History and Lithic Assemblage Structure: An Example from Southeastern Utah. Unpublished Ph.D. dissertation, University of New Mexico.

Dibble, H.L.
    1987 The Interpretation of Middle Paleolithic Scraper Morphology. *American Antiquity* 52(1):109-117.

Ebert, J.
    1992 *Distributional Archaeology*. University of New Mexico Press, Albuquerque.

Enloe, J.G. and F. David
    1992 Food Sharing in the Paleolithic: Carcass Refitting at Pincevent. In *Piecing Together the Past: Applications of Refitting Studies in Archaeology*. Edited by J.L. Hofman and J.G. Enloe, pp. 296-315. BAR International Series 578.

Field notes (excavation crew)
    n.d. Notes from 1978-1987 Excavations of La Roche à Pierrot, Saint-Césaire, Charente-Maritime. In the possession of F. Lévêque, Principal Investigator, Centre d'Archéologie, 13, rue de l'Hôtel Dieu, 86000 Poitiers.

Gonzalez-Echegaray, J., and L. Freeman
    1971 *Cueva Morin: Excavaciones* 1966-1968. Patronato de las Cuevas Prehistoricas, Santander.

Lavaud-Girard, F.
    1987 Les gisements Castelperroniens de Quinçay et de Saint-Césaire, quelques comparaisons préliminaires: les faunes. In *Préhistoire de Poitou-Charentes, Problèmes Actuels*, Editions du Comité des Travaux Historiques et Scientifiques, Actes du 111ème Congrès National des Sociétés Savantes (Poitiers 1986):115-123, Paris.

Leroi-Gourhan, A.
    1976 Les structures d'habitat au Paléolithique supérieur. In *La Préhistoire Française*, edited by H. de Lumley, CNRS, Paris:656-663.

Lévêque, F.
    1989 The Stratigraphy of Saint-Césaire: Preliminary Results. Paper presented at the 54th Annual Meeting of the Society for American Archaeology, Symposium on the Upper Paleolithic Culture Change, Organized by R. White, H. Knecht and A. Pike-Tay. Atlanta, Georgia.

Lévêque, F., and B. Vandermeersch
    1980 Découverte de restes humains dans un niveau Castelperronien è Saint-Césaire, Charente-Maritime. *Compte-Rendu de l'Académie des Sciences* (Paris) 291(D):187-189.

Mercier, N., H. Valladas, J-L. Joron, J-L. Reyss, F. Lévêque, and B. Vandermeersch
   1991 Thermoluminescence Dating of the Late Neanderthal Remains from Saint-Césaire. *Nature* 351:737-739.

Straus, L.G.
   1989 On Early Hominid Use of Fire. *Current Anthropology* 30(4):488-490.

Wandsnider, L.
   1989 Long term Land Use, Formation Processes, and the Structure of the Archaeological Landscape: A Case Study from Southwestern Wyoming. Ph.D. dissertation, University of New Mexico.

Appendix

Was the Saint-Césaire Discovery a Burial?

Bernard Vandermeersch

The first human bones from Saint-Césaire were found by F. Lévêque in July 1979, but it was only in September, after excavating a part of the uppermost layers, that it was possible to have access to the whole skeleton. We were lucky because the earth-moving equipment that had accidentally discovered the archaeological deposits stopped very close to the human remains.

The bones were crushed, soft, and fragile, and it was impossible to clean them in the field, even with a fine brush. We decided only to search for the limits of the human bone distribution, and to take the whole skeleton in a block of sediment to the laboratory. This block was 20 cm thick, to ensure that all the bones were included. Before removing the sediment, a mold was made by M. Chech. At that time only some human fragments were visible, and we did not know what kind of hominid was there. It was only in the laboratory after a part of the skull was cleaned that it became obvious we were dealing with a Neandertal.

All parts of the skeleton are preserved, except the feet, but the majority of elements are very fragmented and crushed. Almost all the epiphyses disappeared, and the diaphyses are in small fragments. We recorded more than 500 pieces of bone, some of them possibly non-human, in the upper part of the block, where the skeleton was located. They are very small and smooth, and if we cannot connect them to more complete bones holding more information we shall never know if they are human, except by microanalysis which is destructive and not always convincing.

We have possible fragments of the sternum, fragments of the clavicle, scapula, and humerus; an almost complete radius; many hand fragments; one fragment of an innominate; and fragments of the femur, patella, tibia and fibula. This short list will probably be enlarged in the future.

The Skull and Mandible

This skeleton is a Neandertal. The right half of the skull, with the exception of the occipital region, and the right half of the mandible are preserved, but we also have a lot of teeth from the left side. The front of the cranium has a thick supraorbital torus, which is separated from the frontal bone by a depression. Seen from the front this torus is massive, continuous, and very elongated. The cranial vault is low with a receding frontal bone. This outline is entirely comparable to those of the La Chapelle-aux-Saints or La Ferrassie skulls. On the temporal bone we can see many classic Neandertal features such as a thick, high, and very flattened posterior zygomatic tubercle.

We have enough fragments of the face to say that the maxillary bone is of the extension type, without depression under the orbits. The malar bone is flat and oblique posteriorly and externally.

Postcranial Characteristics

On the axillary border of the scapula there is only a large dorsal groove, as on other Neandertal scapulae, and not a dorsal and ventral one as on modern scapulae. The radius is very curved and the position of the tuberosity is also characteristic of Neandertals.

Therefore, even in the details of its characteristics the Saint-Césaire skeleton is similar to the classic Mousterian Neandertals. According to F. Lévêque, the disappearance of the left part of the skull and of many postcranial bones may be the result of climatic change at the end of the Saint-Césaire Castelperronian period, that included a renewal of strong water activity. This water activity could also be responsible for the displacement of many pieces of bone.

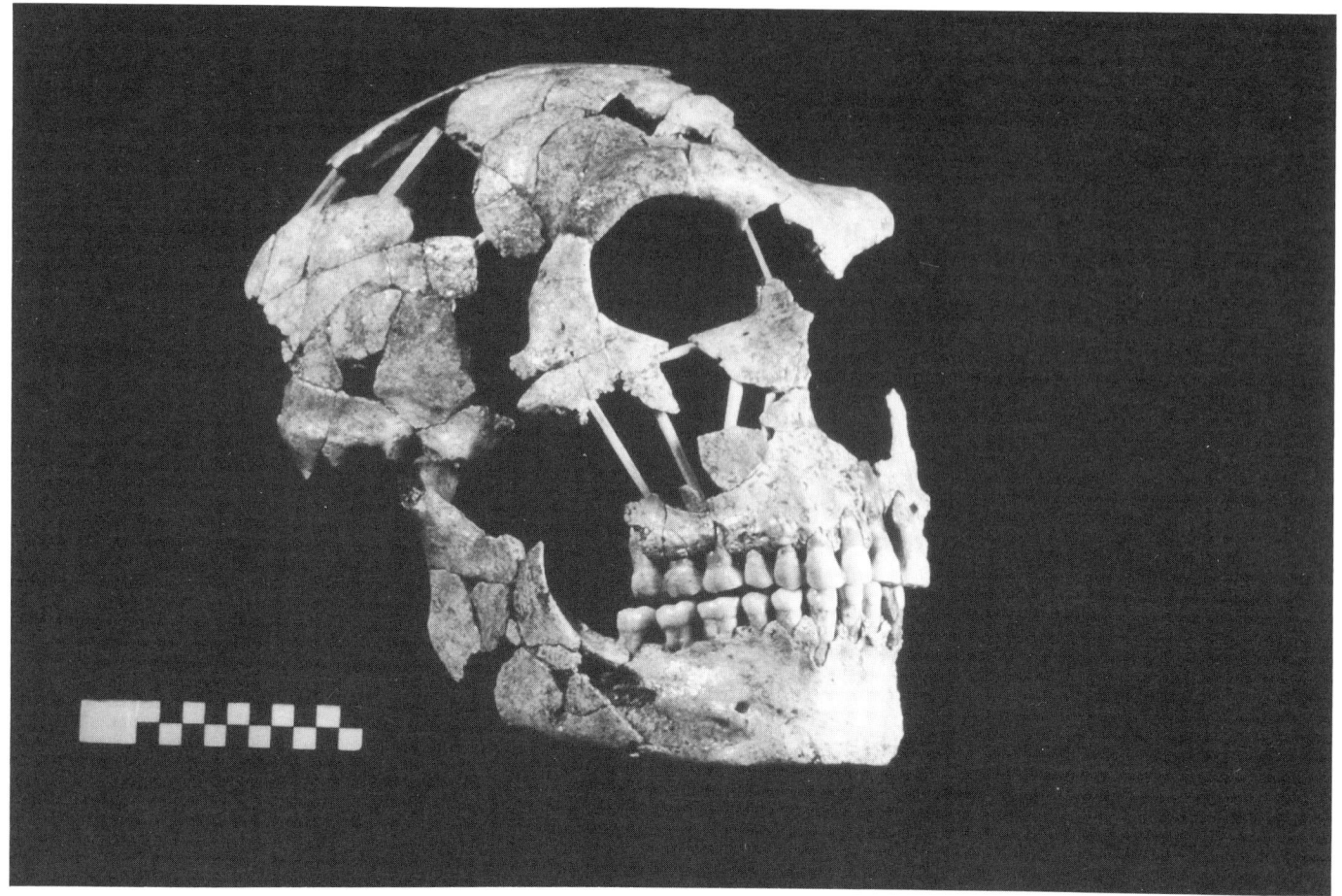

Figure A.1. Neandertal skull found at Saint-Césaire (photo B. Vandermeersch).

Discussion

One of the questions we need to ask is whether the human bone deposit was the result of natural or human activity. In other words, was this a burial?

I do not have a definitive answer but I can present here some arguments which are important in this debate:

1. We observed no differences between the skeletal deposition area and the other parts of the layer. There was no apparent pit.

2. The archaeological layer contained many limestone blocks, but these blocks were absent from the skeletal area. They were very close to the skeleton, but not between the human bones.

3. There was also a very low frequency of lithic artifacts directly associated with the skeletal block.

4. All the human bones were found within a small area, almost circular, measuring about 70 cm in diameter.

5. All the bones were at the same level and the human bone deposit was only a few centimeters thick.

6. Some elements, but not all, were articulated. For instance, the maxillary and the mandible were almost in occlusion and articulated. Some fragments of the tibia and fibula diaphyses were side by side. Many of the hand bones were only slightly disturbed from their relative anatomical position. Unfortunately, we have not been able to fully reconstitute the skeleton in place; too many bones are fragmented and the fragments displaced.

7. By comparison we must remark that no articulated animal skeleton or even any part of any animal skeleton in anatomical position has been found in this layer.

8. Finally, no cut marks have been observed so far on the preserved human bones.

If we consider all these arguments it seems to me

that they support the burial hypothesis. If it was not a burial it would be the first time, to my knowledge, that fragments of almost all parts of a skeleton would have been found together in a Paleolithic site, outside of a burial context. But if we accept the burial hypothesis, another question arises: it is indeed really difficult to understand how to fit a complete body in so small a space. Therefore if we accept this hypothesis we should be led to consider another one: the possibility of a secondary burial.

To conclude, we have arguments to support human intervention but we cannot yet define the exact nature of this intervention.